Diversity and Pluralism in Islam

Diversity and Pluralism in Islam

Historical and Contemporary Discourses amongst Muslims

Edited by
ZULFIKAR HIRJI

I.B.Tauris *Publishers*
LONDON • NEW YORK
in association with
The Institute of Ismaili Studies
London, 2010

Published in 2010 by I.B.Tauris & Co. Ltd
6 Salem Road, London W2 4BU
175 Fifth Avenue, New York NY 10010
www.ibtauris.com

in association with The Institute of Ismaili Studies
210 Euston Road, London NW1 2DA
www.iis.ac.uk

Distributed in the United States and Canada Exclusively by Palgrave Macmillan,
175 Fifth Avenue, New York NY 10010

ISBN: 978 1 84885 302 7

A full CIP record for this book is available from the British Library
A full CIP record is available from the Library of Congress

Library of Congress Catalog Card Number: available

Designed and Typeset by 4word Ltd, Bristol, UK
Printed and bound in Great Britain by TJ International Ltd, Padstow, Cornwall

The Institute of Ismaili Studies

The Institute of Ismaili Studies was established in 1977 with the object of promoting scholarship and learning on Islam, in the historical as well as contemporary contexts, and a better understanding of its relationship with other societies and faiths.

The Institute's programmes encourage a perspective which is not confined to the theological and religious heritage of Islam, but seeks to explore the relationship of religious ideas to broader dimensions of society and culture. The programmes thus encourage an interdisciplinary approach to the materials of Islamic history and thought. Particular attention is also given to issues of modernity that arise as Muslims seek to relate their heritage to the contemporary situation.

Within the Islamic tradition, the Institute's programmes promote research on those areas which have, to date, received relatively little attention from scholars. These include the intellectual and literary expressions of Shi'ism in general, and Ismailism in particular.

In the context of Islamic societies, the Institute's programmes are informed by the full range and diversity of cultures in which Islam is practised today, from the Middle East, South and Central Asia, and Africa to the industrialized societies of the West, thus taking into consideration the variety of contexts which shape the ideals, beliefs and practices of the faith.

These objectives are realized through concrete programmes and activities organized and implemented by various departments of the Institute. The Institute also collaborates periodically, on a programme-specific basis, with other institutions of learning in the United Kingdom and abroad.

The Institute's academic publications fall into a number of inter-related categories:

1. Occasional papers or essays addressing broad themes of the relationship between religion and society, with special reference to Islam.
2. Monographs exploring specific aspects of Islamic faith and culture, or the contributions of individual Muslim thinkers or writers.
3. Editions or translations of significant primary or secondary texts.
4. Translations of poetic or literary texts which illustrate the rich heritage of spiritual, devotional and symbolic expressions in Muslim history.
5. Works on Ismaili history and thought, and the relationship of the Ismailis to other traditions, communities and schools of thought in Islam.
6. Proceedings of conferences and seminars sponsored by the Institute.
7. Bibliographical works and catalogues which document manuscripts, printed texts and other source materials.

This book falls into category two listed above.

In facilitating these and other publications, the Institute's sole aim is to encourage original research and analysis of relevant issues. While every effort is made to ensure that the publications are of a high academic standard, there is naturally bound to be a diversity of views, ideas and interpretations. As such, the opinions expressed in these publications must be understood as belonging to their authors alone.

Contents

Editor's Note   ix

About the Contributors   xi

List of Illustrations   xvii

1. Debating Islam from Within:
    Muslim Constructions of the Internal Other
        ZULFIKAR HIRJI   1

2. Pluralism and Islamic Traditions of Sectarian
    Divisions
        ROY P. MOTTAHEDEH   31

3. Being One and Many Among the Others:
    Muslim Diversity in the Context of South Asian
    Religious Pluralism
        DOMINIQUE-SILA KHAN   43

4. Religious Pluralism in the Light of American
    Muslim Identities
        PATRICE C. BRODEUR   61

5. Islamic Art and Doctrinal Pluralism:
    Seeking Out the Visual Boundaries
        JAMES W. ALLAN   83

6.   The Contestation and Resolution of Inter- and
     Intra-School Conflicts through Biography
          R. KEVIN JAQUES   107

7.   Traditions of Reform, Reformers of Tradition:
     Case Studies from Senegal and Zanzibar/Tanzania
          ROMAN LOIMEIER   135

8.   Justifying Islamic Pluralism: Reflections from
     Indonesia and France
          JOHN R. BOWEN   163

Notes   185

Glossary   221

Bibliography   223

Index   247

Editor's Note

This volume is the result of a series of seminars on 'Muslim Pluralism' hosted at The Institute of Ismaili Studies between 2002 and 2003. The seminar series and this volume were developed, in part, as a response to the events of September 11, 2001. Since that moment, words and images concerning Islam and the histories, beliefs and practices of Muslims have proliferated globally. Muslims and non-Muslims have regularly contributed to these debates. The articulations and representations of Islam presently in the public sphere hallmark common foundations and exhibit different and divergent views on issues both pedestrian and divine. This complex portrait of a kaleidoscopic and kaleido-phonic Islam is not solely a product of modern times but has a long history. It challenges the notions that Muslims everywhere are the same or should be the same. With this background in mind, the seminar series aimed not to present the social fact that Muslims are diverse, rather its aim was to examine how Muslims frame, address and attend to their own diversity over time and in different contexts. This subject remains the central concern of this volume.

The contributions of J.W. Allan, John R. Bowen, Patrice Brodeur, and Roy P. Mottahedeh were part of the seminar series. The contributions of R. Kevin Jaques, Roman Loimeier, Dominique-Sila Khan, and my own were subsequently developed to expand the historical scope and geographical scale of the inquiry and to further develop the volume's emerging themes. I should like here to record my sincerest appreciation to each of the authors for their efforts, patience, and scholarly insights. In addition, I should like to acknowledge the contributions of the scholars who participated in the seminar series.

I should like also to acknowledge that from the inception of the seminar series up to the volume's publication, this project has received the gracious support of the Institute's directors, faculty, staff members and students. The volume has greatly benefited from the support of Dr Farhad Daftary, the editorial expertise of Fayaz Alibhai and other members of the editorial team at the Institute, and the staff of I.B. Tauris, who have been instrumental in seeing this volume to press.

Finally, I owe a personal and deep debt of gratitude to Ruba Kana'an, whose advice and encouragement have remained constant over the long course of this project.

Z. Hirji

About the Contributors

James W. Allan is a recognized world authority on Islamic metalwork. He is currently Emeritus Fellow of St Cross College, University of Oxford. His research interests include Islamic metalwork, Islamic ceramics and Shi'i art. He has recently completed research on the history of the Persian steel industry up to 1900, and his book on Shi'i art, *The Art and Architecture of Twelver Shi'ism: Iraq, Iran and the Indian Sub-continent* is currently in press. His recent publications include: 'My Father is a Sun, and I am a Star. Fatimid Symbols in Ayyubid and Mamluk Metalwork' (2003); *Persian Steel: The Tanavoli Collection* (Oxford, 2000); 'Silver Door Facings of the Safavid Period' (1995); 'The Transmission of Decorated Ceilings in the Early Islamic World' (1994); *Metalwork of the Islamic World: The Aron Collection* (London, 1986); and *Islamic Metalwork: The Nuhad Es-Said Collection* (London, 1987).

John R. Bowen is the Dunbar-Van Cleve Professor in Arts & Sciences at Washington University in St Louis. He studies problems of pluralism, law and religion, and in particular, contemporary efforts to rethink Islamic norms and law in Asia, Europe and North America. His most recent book on Asia is *Islam, Law and Equality in Indonesia: An Anthropology of Public Reasoning* (Cambridge, 2003), and his *Why the French Don't Like Headscarves* (Princeton, 2007) concerns current debates in France on Islam and laïcité. *Can Islam be French?* appeared from Princeton in late 2009 and concerns Muslim debates and institutions in France, to be followed by *The New Anthropology of Islam* from

Cambridge in 2010. His three current research projects concern: (1) the interplay of civil law and religious norms on family in England, France and the United States; (2) comparing Islamic judicial practices across a global country sample; and (3) examining variation in operant models of ethnic and religious difference across Europe.

Patrice C. Brodeur is Associate Professor and Canada Research Chair on Islam, Pluralism and Globalization at the Faculty of Theology and the Science of Religions at the University of Montreal, Canada. His main academic interests include: contemporary Islam; pluralism and globalization; identity construction and power dynamics; perceptions of 'self' and the 'other'; and the relationship between the study of religion and applied religion, especially the role of inter-religious dialogue in promoting democracy, pluralism and peace-building.

He has co-edited two books: with Eboo Patel, *Building the Interfaith Youth Movement: From Dialogue to Action* (Oxford, 2006); and with Sondra Myers, *The Pluralist Paradigm: Democracy and Religion in the 21st Century* (Scranton, 2006). He has published many articles, including: 'From Postmodernism to "Glocalism": Towards an Integrated Theoretical Understanding of Contemporary Arab Muslim Constructions of Religious Others'; 'The Changing Nature of Islamic Studies and American Religious History'; 'Theory and Method in the Study of Women in Islam'; and 'Introduction to the Guidelines for an Inter-faith Celebration'. He is currently completing a book manuscript entitled *Contemporary Arab Muslim Perceptions of Religious Others*.

Zulfikar Hirji is Associate Professor of Anthropology at York University, Toronto. He was formerly a Research Associate at The Institute of Ismaili Studies (IIS) and Junior Research Fellow at Wolfson College, University of Oxford. His research focuses on the social and cultural expressions of Muslims in historical and contemporary contexts, and looks at the diverse ways in which Muslims express and articulate their deepest human concerns as well as matters of daily life. He has conducted fieldwork in East

Africa, Oman, UAE, Pakistan, Syria, Canada, and USA amongst
different Muslim communities. He has studied a range of issues
including family networks and migration, cultural workers and
social movements, the socio-legal formation of identity, and
violence in religiously plural societies. He has published a number
of articles and his current research concerns the sensory aspects of
Muslim culture. He is the co-author of *The Ismailis: An Illustrated
History* (London, 2008), and is currently co-editing an interdisciplinary volume on *Places of Worship and Devotion in Muslim
Societies* with Ruba Kana'an.

R. Kevin Jaques is Associate Professor, Department of Religious
Studies, and Director, Middle Eastern and Islamic Studies Program,
at Indiana University. His research interests are in Islamic legal history, Islam in Southeast Asia and Indian Ocean communities,
religious authority in times of social and cultural upheaval, and
methods and methodologies in the academic study of religion. He
has published numerous articles in leading journals. His first book,
*Authority, Conflict, and the Transmission of Diversity in Medieval
Islamic Law* (Leiden, 2006), explores Ibn Qadi Shuhbah's (d.
851/1448) presentation of Islamic legal history and the trends in
legal thinking indicated in the biographies of the legal authorities
mentioned in his text. His forthcoming book, *Ibn Hajar al-
'Asqalani*, examines the life and impact of al-'Asqalani
(d. 852/1448), the last of the great scholars of prophetic traditions
in the medieval period.

Dominique-Sila Khan was born in Paris in 1949. In 1981, she
obtained her first doctorate in literature at the Sorbonne University and completed a second PhD in anthropology in 1993. In
1987, she moved to Jaipur, India, where she works as an independent researcher. She specializes in Hindu-Muslim interactions
in South Asia and shifting religious identities. Her first book is
*Conversions and Shifting Identities: Ramdev Pir and the Isma'ilis
in Rajasthan* (New Delhi, 1997), and the second is *Crossing the
Threshold – Understanding Religious Identities in South Asia*
(London, 2004). Her third book, *Sacred Kerala* (New Delhi, 2009)

examines interactions between Hindus, Muslims and Christians in Kerala, India. She has also contributed a number of articles to various publications and volumes. She teaches occasional courses for American and European university programmes, and has given lectures at various seminars and conferences in India, France and England. She is a member of the Kerala Council for Historical Research and an Associate Fellow of the Institute of Rajasthan Studies.

Roman Loimeier is Associate Professor at the Institute of Social Anthropology (Ethnologie) at the University of Göttingen. He has taught at the Universities of Bayreuth, Leipzig, Bamberg, Göttingen and the University of Florida (Gainesville), and has been visiting professor at the L'Écoles des hautes études en sciences socials, Paris. Since the early 1980s, he has been working in Senegal, Nigeria and Tanzania, and has published extensively on both the history and the development of Muslim societies in sub-Saharan Africa. He is the author of numerous publications, including: *The Global Worlds of the Swahili: Interfaces of Islam, Identity and Space in 19th and 20th Century East Africa*, with R. Seesemann (Hamburg, 2006); and, most recently, *Between Social Skills and Marketable Skills: The Politics of Islamic Education in 20th century Zanzibar* (Leiden, 2009). His disciplinary focus has been shifting from Islamic studies to anthropology and history, and back again.

Roy P. Mottahedeh was born in New York in 1940 and graduated from Harvard University in 1960 with an AB in History. He spent the next year travelling in Europe and the Middle East as a Shaw Traveling Scholar of Harvard University. In 1967, he was elected for a three-year term to the Harvard Society of Fellows as a Junior Fellow, and he received his PhD in History from Harvard in 1970. Later that year, he was appointed an Assistant Professor at Princeton University, and he received tenure there in 1976. He has been awarded MacArthur and Guggenheim Fellowships. In 1986, he accepted an appointment as Professor of Islamic History in the Harvard History Department. He currently serves as Gurney

Professor of History and Director of the Prince Alwaleed Bin Talal
Islamic Studies Program at Harvard University. He is the author of
three books: *Loyalty and Leadership in an Early Islamic Society*;
The Mantle of the Prophet: Religion and Politics in Iran (London,
2001); and *Lessons in Islamic Jurisprudence* (Oxford, 2003). He
is also the author of numerous articles on topics ranging from
the Abbasids to the Shiʻis of contemporary Iraq. He is the co-
editor of a volume with Angeliki Laiou, entitled *The Crusades from
the Perspective of Byzantium and the Muslim World* (Washington,
DC, 2001).

Illustrations

1   Opening page of the *Monajat* of Hazrat 'Ali, Isfahan 1010/1601, Gulestan Palace Library no. 2251 (*Golestan Palace Library. A Portfolio of Miniature Paintings and Calligraphy*, Tehran 2000, p. 76)

2   Rug depicting Nur 'Ali Shah and Mushtaq 'Ali Shah, Kashan 1221/1806, Tanavoli Collection (P. Tanavoli, *Kings, Heroes and Lovers*, Scorpion Publishing, London 1994, no. 54)

3   Silver coin of Shah Tahmasp II (1135–45/1722–32), minted in Tabriz, including the words, '*'Ali wali allah*', and the names of the 12 imams, Ashmolean Museum (Photo: Ashmolean Museum)

4   Mosque of al-Aqmar façade (Photo: Creswell Archive, Ashmolean Museum, no. 1010)

5   Embroidered fragment decorated with the words '*ana qamr*', Fatimid period; Ashmolean Museum, Newberry Collection, accession number EA 1984.402 (Photo: Ashmolean Museum)

6   Candlestick in the name of Muhammad b. Sadr al-Din Yusuf b. Salah al-Din, copper alloy inlaid with silver and gold, early fourteenth century; Nuhad Es-Said Collection (Photo: Nuhad Es-Said Collection)

7   Mihrab, mausoleum of Umm Kulthum, Cairo 519/1125
     (Photo: Creswell Archive, Ashmolean Museum, no. 3883)

8   Incense-burner of Sultan al-Malik al-Nasir Muhammad
     Ibn Qala'un, brass inlaid with silver and gold, Cairo early
     fourteenth century; Nuhad Es-Said Collection (Photo: Nuhad
     Es-Said Collection)

9   Embroidered fragment decorated with a repeating '*al-'izz*',
     Cairo, *c.* third quarter of the thirteenth century; Ashmolean
     Museum, Newberry Collection, accession number EA
     1984.44 (Photo: Ashmolean Museum)

Debating Islam from Within: Muslim Constructions of the Internal Other

Zulfikar Hirji*

Foreignness does not start at the water's edge but at the skin's.
Clifford Geertz[1]

On the evening of 6 February 2006, the BBC's *Newsnight*, a daily television news programme broadcast from London, United Kingdom, held two debates concerning Islam and Muslims.[2] The first debate centred on the issue of freedom of expression and was a direct response to demonstrations held by some Muslims in London in front of the Danish embassy, protesting against cartoons lampooning the Prophet Muhammad that had been first printed in the Danish newspaper *Jyllands-Posten* on 30 September 2005. Whereas the cartoons raised an outcry from many Muslims around the world, some of the placards carried by the demonstrators in London, as well as their chants and behaviour, also raised an outcry from some non-Muslim and Muslim members of the British public. The second debate focused on the issue of 'Islam's compatibility with Western democracy' and made some overt references to Samuel Huntington's 'clash of civilizations' thesis.[3] Both debates were moderated by Jeremy Paxman, regarded as a leading news analyst and television presenter in the UK, and each debate involved a panel comprising Muslims and non-Muslims.[4]

It became evident, particularly in the course of the first debate, that each of the four Muslim panellists held differing views on the

* I should like to thank David Parkin and James Piscatori for their comments on an initial draft of this chapter.

issues being discussed. One of the panellists went so far as to
denounce two of his fellow Muslim panellists. He called them
'non-practising Muslims' and 'hypocrites' on the basis that one of
them (a female) was 'not wearing the *khimar* (headscarf) and the
jilbab (long gown)', and the other (a male) was 'not wearing a
beard'. In response to another Muslim panellist's references to
'British Islam', the same panellist also referred to statements made
by the Prophet, stating that 'there is only one Islam, the Prophet
never talked about British Islam or Saudi Islam'. Subsequently, two
other Muslim panellists began to refer to the Prophet's behaviour
and manner of speaking in order to support their arguments. One
of these panellists commented that 'the Prophet did not interrupt
someone when he was speaking' and another panellist commented that 'the Prophet never got emotional in the heat of
discussion'. The non-Muslims, including Paxman, also raised the
issue about who spoke for 'Islam' apart from those who held
'militant views', and why there were so few moderate Muslim
voices in the public sphere during this crisis. Indeed, one of the
non-Muslims, a member of the British Parliament outraged by the
comments of one of the Muslim participants, told him: 'I am far
more capable of representing my Muslims [than you]'.[5]

The engagements between the Muslim panellists, their modes
of expression and choice of references, as well as the questions and
statements articulated by the non-Muslim panellists, resonate
with the central concerns of this volume: the contexts and manner
in which Muslims debate amongst themselves and contend with
the differences between them, and the processes by which Muslims discursively construct each other, as well as the socio-cultural
tools they employ in so doing. This introductory chapter examines these concerns with reference to a number of contemporary
academic debates, and develops a thematic framework in which
to situate the case studies contained in the volume. It is in this
latter context that I will have occasion to return to aspects of the
Newsnight debate.

*   *   *

The present-day world population of Muslims comprises men and women who live in many different geographic locations and environments, speak many different languages, have different forms of social organization and modes of subsistence, and encompass a diverse range of cultural practices. In addition, despite sharing a creed affirming the absolute oneness of God, the historical person of Muhammad as His last Prophet, and the Qur'an as His final message to humankind, Muslims have for more than 1,400 years held many different and often conflicting views about Islam. This plurality of views has ranged from the interpretation of foundational texts, religious authority, ritual practice, political power, law and governance, and civic life, to the form and content of individual and communal expressions.

These facts should go without saying. Nevertheless, phrases such as 'Islam is…' or 'Islam is not…', and 'Muslims believe and think that…' or 'Muslims do not think that…', can be heard with increasing frequency in contemporary times. Such expressions have the effect of reducing 'Islam' to a dogma that is interpreted as being at odds with the modern world and regarded as potentially in conflict with the values of the West. By implication, Muslims are portrayed as an undifferentiated mass who are uncritical in their belief and thinking about matters both human and divine. By extension, statements that generalize about Islam negate the inherent diversity of Muslims and the differences between them.[6]

The events of 11 September 2001 and thereafter have increased the use of 'Islam is' and 'Muslims think' statements by non-Muslims and Muslims alike, thus reifying perceptions that Islam is a fundamentally revolutionary and violent religion, and that all Muslims are fixated on the destruction of those who do not share their worldview. Ironically, the militant actions and theological justification of violence by some Muslims have also made it plain that Muslims do vary in their interpretations of certain aspects of their religion. Indeed, such acts and discourses have precipitated many Muslims to either repudiate or support the actions and views of their co-religionists. Whatever postures Muslims have taken, the events of 9/11 and their effects have resulted in varying degrees of introspection.

But in seeking to make sense of the situation, Muslims and non-Muslims have propelled various terms and labels into the public sphere, including '*umma*', 'the Muslim Community', 'Sunni', 'Shia', 'Sufi', 'Salafi Islam', 'Wahhabi Islam', 'Quietist Islam', 'British Islam', 'French Islam', 'American Muslims', 'Fundamentalist Muslims', 'Liberal Muslims', 'Moderate Muslims', 'Radicalized Muslims' and 'Jihadis'. Used regularly by Muslim and non-Muslim commentators and analysts in often indiscriminate and newly mixed ways, some of the aforementioned terms signal distinctions between Muslims solely on the basis of doctrinal propensities. Other terms, despite having long, complex histories and broad semantic fields that cannot be fully explained in a media-driven, soundbite culture, have been used to explain or account for the actions and attitudes of whole groups or a few individuals.[7] Few terms, if any, reference identity in terms of other markers such as occupation, economic status, gender and language group, and a previous generation of ethnic identity markers, such as 'Arab', 'Persian' and 'Turk', seem to be increasingly (for better or for worse) absent from public discourses or are used as synonyms for Muslim, without qualification.

For Amartya Sen, the renowned economist, social thinker and Nobel laureate, it is the reduction of Muslims and other groups to the religious aspect of their identity that he finds highly problematic. For example, in describing himself, Sen states:

I can be, at the same time, an Asian, an Indian citizen, a Bengali with Bangladeshi ancestry, an American or British resident, an economist, a dabbler in philosophy, an author, a Sanskritist, a strong believer in secularism and democracy, a man, a feminist, a heterosexual, a defender of gay and lesbian rights, with a non-religious lifestyle, from a Hindu background, a non-Brahmin, and a non-believer in an afterlife (and also, in case the question is asked, a non-believer in a 'before-life' as well).[8]

Thus for Sen, the 'solitarist approach', by which a single identity marker such as religion is called upon to define, assess and classify an individual or a community, 'reflects a profound misunderstanding of the nature of human identity in its inescapable plurality', and disregards the anthropological fact that all human beings have multiple and polyvalent identities and plural affiliations.[9]

With reference to Islam in particular, Sen argues that solitarist approaches to identity underpin and support the illusion that Muslims everywhere deal with matters of existential concern only through the prism of religion and the view espoused by some Muslims that they *should* do so. For Sen, each of these perspectives has been crucial to the formulation of Samuel Huntington's 'clash of civilizations' thesis, as well as interpretations of Islam that espouse 'a *jihad* (here meant as "holy war") against the West'.[10]

Sen's proposition may be entirely accurate in accounting for the factors that make potent the agendas of those on both sides of the contemporary divide who forward paradigms that serve to vilify the other. However, for some Muslims and academicians of Islamic history, Sen's analysis may seem somewhat apologetic, if not ahistorical, because it can be shown that contemporary constructions of Muslim identity through the prism of religion alone, however distorted or narrow they may appear to commentators such as Sen, are not without precedent in the history of Muslims.

From the time of the Prophet, concerns about matters of doctrine, authority, ritual, governance, social behaviour and culture have been at the heart of cool-headed debates and outright hostilities between Muslims. It was through such engagements that Muslims came to define their place within the Abrahamic family of revealed religions, i.e. their relationship with Jews and Christians. Concomitantly, such engagements were the means by which Muslims shaped the contours of how they understood 'Islam' and determined who a 'Muslim' was, and took stock of the variety of communities of interpretation that grew up amongst them.

In this regard it should be noted that the Qur'an, the seminal textual authority of all Muslims, contains an extensive vocabulary on religious identity, communal identification, and modes and means of differentiation. For example, the Qur'an refers regularly to *mu'minun* (believers), with exclusive reference to those who adhere to the message of the Prophet Muhammad, i.e. Muslims.

But the term is also used to refer to individuals who adhered to messages sent down by God through prophets before Muhammad (Qur'an 2:62; 5:60–80; 28:52–54). *Mu'minun* is also used in opposition to *kafirun* (Qur'an 3:28; 4:139–141), a term referring (in a general sense) to those individuals who ignore or reject God's message(s). The Qur'an also uses other qualifying terms for groups with religious dispositions that are effectively antithetical to those who believe in Islam. These terms include *mushrikun* (idoloators) (Qur'an 2:170; 16:100; 30:31; 37:69–70), used in the sense of those who ascribe partners to God (sometimes in reference to pre-Islamic Arabs), the *Ahl al-Kitab* (People of the Book) (Qur'an 2:105; 2:109; 3:64–65, 3:69–72; 57:29), with reference to Jews and Christians, here because of their rejection of Muhammad's message despite his coming having been foretold in each of their scriptures, and *munafiqun* (hypocrites) (Qur'an 9:67–68; 33:73), referring to those who claim to be believers, but in their hearts remain uncommitted to Islam.[11]

Against this background of differences, the Qur'an also contains language that expresses different levels of relatedness between groups and individuals on the basis of religious ties.[12] For example, the category *Ahl al-Kitab* (People of the Book), while referring to Jews and Christians, also includes Muslims, communities for all of whom a 'messenger' and a 'book' are also central tenets of religious belief. Hence, the category of *Ahl al-Kitab* marks both difference as well as common ground between these religious groups. Another term used in the Qur'an to group together larger segments of society is *umma*, whose general meaning is 'community'. The Qur'an frequently uses the term *umma* with exclusive reference to Muslims (Qur'an 3:110), but also uses it with reference to humankind (Qur'an 2:213). Much of this Qur'anic terminology pertaining to distinctions and similarities has been crucial in Muslim efforts toward self-definition throughout history, both in relation to different groups of non-Muslims, and in relation to the differences and divisions between Muslims themselves. It should also be noted that Muslim interpretations of such Qur'anic vocabulary have in turn been varied and dependent on how the Qur'an is approached and understood.

In addition to the Qur'an, Muslims historically also drew upon the words and deeds of the Prophet and other founding members of the early community of believers to contend with the differences that regularly arose between themselves and other communities in their milieu. The different ways in which these references were interpreted, and then used by Muslims to forward claims about the ideal complexion of the community of believers, are discussed in detail in Roy Mottahedeh's case study on the *hadith al-tafriqa* (traditions on divisions) in this volume. Suffice it to say here that, in sociological terms, Muslims have always used religious criteria to define themselves in relation to external and internal others, and have done so with reference to their foundational texts, as well as the attitudes and actions of seminal personalities in the history of Islam.

Insofar as these precedents exist, it should come as no surprise that, for many Muslims today, religion is a critical marker of personhood and community, increasingly overriding other markers such as social status and ethnicity. However, the point often missed out in contemporary as well as historical representations of Muslims is that, even when religious identity is regarded as primarily influential in marking personhood and community, Muslims have differed quite widely in their understanding of many religious issues. Hence, Muslims who mark their identities in strictly religious terms are not all the same and do not have identical interpretations of their foundational texts. This is the type of intra-communal plurality with which this volume is concerned.

More specifically, the case studies presented in this volume are particularly concerned with the manner in which Muslims in different historical and geographic contexts have struggled with individuals and groups within their own religious community whose approaches to religious and worldly matters differ from their own. As such, these case studies afford an opportunity to listen in on intra-Muslim debates about matters of doctrine, jurisprudence, religious authority, ritual practice, governance and representation. When compared with each other, they indicate some of the ways in which Muslims construct, develop and delimit ideas of self and community amongst themselves.

By taking up the subjects of intra-communal difference and religious plurality amongst Muslims, this volume departs from examinations of Muslims that focus on how Muslims (*en bloc*) perceive the West, a subject around which many contemporary discussions coalesce, or how the West perceives Islam and its practitioners, a subject which has been given consistent attention in Western academia since Edward Said's publication of *Orientalism*.[13] Stepping away from these well-worn subjects requires treading on sensitive ground: how Muslims view other Muslims. As is evident in many of the contributions in this volume, however, this trope is not new. It arises from deep within the historical discourses that Muslims themselves have generated. But the trope has particular poignancy for Muslims today because, as mentioned above, many Muslims are engaged in defending or denouncing the actions and approaches of some of their co-religionists, particularly in the public sphere. Moreover, the advent of new technology and the mobility of contemporary times have increased the density of actual and potential interactions between Muslims from different backgrounds and with differing views. In some cases, such as Iraq, interfaces between Muslims with different doctrinal outlooks have resulted in serious conflict which, according to some analysts, is set to have a profound influence on the Middle East and the Muslim world.[14] In other instances, such as at the International Islamic Conference held in Amman, Jordan in June 2005, 175 Muslim scholars and intellectuals from different Muslim communities put aside their differences and affirmed their joint commitment to Islam's central tenets and community of believers.[15] Such events attest to the inherent diversity amongst Muslims, but at the same time speak to a spirit of toleration that exists between groups who historically have not always seen eye to eye. In sum, these differing responses to Muslim difference speak to the fact that Muslims are increasingly having to take stock of the 'other within'.

*   *   *

Socio-cultural constructions of the 'other' are not unique to Muslims. Discursive propositions which name and order differences between humans are ubiquitous in humanity's ethnographic record. From the perspective of the study of religions, Jonathan Z. Smith argues that 'propositions about difference are relative and not absolute'.[16] That is, 'otherness' is a reciprocal concept that necessarily implies the presence of the 'self'. Smith also notes that, amongst religious groups, the 'proximate "other"', i.e. the 'other that is most similar or closest to the self', or what in this volume is called the 'internal other', has a distinctive bearing on socio-cultural formulations of the self. Smith states that:

> ... the issue of problematic similarity or identity seems to be particularly prevalent in religious discourse and imagination. Thus the ancient Israelites created a myth of conquest, fabricating themselves as outsiders and therefore as different from their encompassing and synonymous group, the Canaanites, from whom they cannot be distinguished. Paul never writes against Jews or members of Greco-Roman religions, but always against fellow Christians from whom he insists on contradistinguishing himself and his teachings. John of Pian del Carpini and William of Ruysbroeck, thirteenth century missionaries to the Mongols, have no difficulty in recording scores of positive comparisons between the feared Tartars and their own Christian-European culture, even though they are at war; rather their deepest perceptions of problematic difference are focussed on the Nestorian Christians who remain largely unintelligible to them. From heresy to deviation to degenerations to syncretism, the notion of the different which claims to be the same, or, projected internally, the disguised difference within, has produced a rich vocabulary of denial and estrangement. For in each case, a theory of difference, when applied to the proximate 'other', is but another way of phrasing a theory of self.[17]

The presence of the self–other paradigm and the social construction of difference are age-old tropes in human narratives, and have often been the subject of philosophical investigations.[18] In Western European thought, it is with the rise of Post-Structuralism in the twentieth century, under the stewardship of the philosopher

Jacques Derrida and the social historian Michel Foucault, that there has been an increased concern with human constructions and expressions of difference.[19] These thinkers, and other scholars following them, have challenged the view that complete and unfettered identities simply exist, and that their essential aspects are expressed through culture. Rather, they argue that identity, be it nationalist, religious or gendered, is always relational and contextual; its articulation simply exposes what individuals or groups regard to be the fixed and bounded aspects of who they are. Moreover, self-identification is regarded as a process that brings into sharp focus what is 'other' than the self, even if this is not explicitly articulated. Hence, it is through differentiation that similarities are constructed and identities come to be fixed. In this regard, some scholars have argued that the process of self-identification is itself an act of power that has the potential to silence or absent the 'other'.[20] And, as such, discourses about identity are in essence discourses about relations of power between groups and between members of a group.

Some aspects of the theoretical discourses on difference and power, as articulated in the Western European intellectual tradition, have been applied to the study of Islam and Muslim societies. For example, with reference to the divisions that arose between Muslims throughout history, Mohammed Arkoun has asked: 'How is the legitimacy of power monopolized by a group over all other established groups?'[21] This volume approaches such questions by describing, examining and comparing the discourses of different groups of Muslims in different historical and geographical contexts about their internal differences, primarily based upon the intellectual traditions in which they were engaged. By virtue of this focus, the contents of this volume are relevant to the social and historical studies about Islam and Muslims, as well as the range of studies in the social sciences and the humanities concerned with the socio-cultural constructions of identity, difference, and the group. Moreover, this set of case studies provides a lens through which to view the various intellectual frameworks used by some Muslims, past and present, to articulate, conceptualize and reconcile difference.

Thus, it would also seem logical to link up the general theme of intra-communal difference to the issue of 'pluralism', the means by which acceptance and toleration of difference in various forms between bounded groups is encoded or expressed in socio-political or socio-religious systems. However, it should be noted that only a few case studies in this volume touch on Muslim attitudes concerning forms of 'political pluralism', the much-debated and variously configured political philosophy which at its core is con-cerned with uniting individuals and groups with different social and cultural backgrounds, lifestyles and associations, usually in the context of a state.[22] Similarly, the studies in this volume do not comprehensively address Muslim attitudes toward 'religious pluralism', a project which seeks to define 'Islam's position' on Judaism, Christianity and other religious systems, and Muslim co-existence with non-Muslims.[23]

The reasons for putting both these forms of 'pluralism' at a dis-tance stems from the irony that 'pluralism', in either its religious or political guise, frequently presumes that there exists a uniform, timeless, and authentic Islam, or an essential set of 'Islamic' ele-ments that can be applied to all aspects of life to which all Muslims subscribe, or that the diversity of Muslim voices and perspectives can be uniformly represented in the public sphere, either by a single authority (individual or group) or constructed through consensus. However, as the case studies in this volume show, the historical and contemporary record is unable to support such assumptions, and shows that often consensus is not an easy thing at which to arrive. Indeed, if the case studies in this volume are representative of intra-communal discourses had by some Muslims on differences between them, then it may be suggested that debates between Muslims on what constitutes Islam and what it means to be a Muslim may themselves be what perennially char-acterizes manifestations of Islam in all places and at all times. Put differently, when 'Islam' is examined through the discursive acts of Muslims and as a socio-historical phenomenon in all its diver-sity, it can be shown to be perennially in the making, unfolding, being understood and expressed in varying ways, even if some Muslims insist that all Muslims *should* understand and define

'Islam' in one uniform way, or that Muslims *should* return to a time past when it is alleged that all Muslims interpreted and expressed their understanding of Islam similarly.

*   *   *

Any scholarly study that takes seriously what social actors have to say about their life-worlds betrays an anthropological bias. In this volume, the bias stems partly from the editor's predilection. This factor aside, it is the case that, among the social sciences and humanities, documenting human diversity and tending to its theoretical consequences has been the remit of anthropology. For example, if works such as R. Weekes's *Muslim Peoples: A World Ethnographic Survey* even marginally remain a valid point of reference for an understanding of the various groups and communities that make up the world's Muslim population, then the social and cultural diversity amongst those who self-define as Muslims is indeed quite staggering.[24] Hence, it is no coincidence that for some time now anthropologists have recognized that Muslims everywhere are not the same and that Muslims express and unfold Islam in many varying ways. From the 'Islam is a blue print of the social order' thesis of Ernst Gellner[25] and the comparative, symbolic and performative approaches of Clifford Geertz,[26] to Abdul Hamid El-Zein's[27] many 'Islams', and Michael Gilsenan's[28] more provocative idea that 'Islam is everywhere what Muslims say it is', anthropologists have regularly questioned the manner and usefulness by which Islam could be taken up as a heuristic category. More recently, the recognition that Muslims are not everywhere the same has been coupled with anthropology's disposition towards 'reflexivity' (i.e. the analysis of one's own pre-conceptions and pre-occupations) and against reification. This has further prompted anthropologists to question what it means to study Islam and Muslims.[29]

Daniel Varisco's cogent summary and critical analysis of the relevant studies concerning anthropology's engagement with Muslims and Islam concludes that it is what Muslims say and do that should be anthropology's remit, rather than attempts to formulate an anthropological definition of Islam.[30] As with Amartya Sen above, Varisco fears that attempts to undertake the latter project simply conflate with contemporary efforts that seek to define Islam in order to make it 'a homogenous target, a straw religion easily denounced and demonized'.[31] For Varisco, the 'real issue [anthropologists need to address] is how Islam, however defined, is represented in native or indigenous views and by outsiders'.[32]

Like many other contemporary anthropologists who study Muslims in society and through culture, Varisco takes his cue from Talal Asad's highly influential proposition that Islam must be studied as a 'discursive tradition'.[33] Briefly stated, Asad argues that studies of Islam must first and foremost be conducted from the perspective that Muslims understand Islam, i.e. 'from the concept of a discursive tradition that includes and relates itself to the founding texts of the Qur'an and the Hadith', and that such understandings must be analysed within a particular socio-historical context, taking into account factors such as power and agency. Asad's research programme for an anthropological analysis of Islam and prescribed method of analysis have not been without its critics. For example, Leila Abu Lughod has raised questions about how orality and gender figure in such a project: a preponderant focus on 'texts', if read too narrowly, can stifle the voices of many Muslims who use non-textual means to articulate themselves; and the very 'texts' that Asad speaks of as foundational have often been denied to women or are read in ways that deny women access to them.[34] A criticism stemming from the latter observation may legitimately be levelled at this volume: the very salient issue of gender, perhaps one of the most enduring ways in which difference is constructed in Muslim contexts, remains unattended to here.[35]

Another problematic feature of Asad's project is its call for a deeply contextualized mode of analysis that implies a move away from comparison and, particularly, frameworks that aim to identify Islam's 'essential features'. But while Asad's analytical apparatus mirrors anthropology's move away from generalizing through comparison for the purposes of essentializing and hypotheses testing, it does not denounce comparison for the purposes of showing cultural variation and specificity.[36] Indeed, Asad has elsewhere stated that 'modern anthropology is charged with comparing embedded concepts (representations) between societies differently located in time or space'.[37] This type of comparison is congruous with the approach taken in this volume. Here, multiple instances of discourses on intra-Muslim difference are presented in order to identify the recurring tropes, strategies and 'overlapping perspectives' on plurality held by those who self-identify as Muslim.[38] In short, there is no intent to arrive at a list of features through which we can identify an Islam or a Muslim.

The present volume is, therefore, similar in approach to the studies of Dale Eickelman and James Piscatori,[39] which looks at pilgrimage of various types carried out by Muslims in different historical and contemporary contexts; Barbara Metcalf,[40] which examines spatial manifestations of Muslim identity in North America and Europe; Leif Manger,[41] which looks at multiple manifestations of Islam in different societies in order to examine the trope of local/global; Stephen Headley and David Parkin,[42] which examines the various manifestations of prayer amongst Muslims in the Indian Ocean region; and Amyn B. Sajoo,[43] who explores the engagements that Muslims in different contemporary contexts have with 'civil society'. Each of these volumes presents a series of finely grained case studies that provide an opportunity to tease apart some of the overlapping themes and points of convergence about a concept or idea that is regularly debated by Muslims.

The case studies in this volume yield three cross-cutting themes on 'difference', as they are manifested in Muslim discourses across space and through time: 1) the paradigmatic *umma*; 2) the social construction of the internal other; and 3) the discourses and counter-discourses of debating Muslims. In the following section, each of these themes is examined in turn, with reference to the case studies appearing in this volume.

* * *

The paradigmatic *umma*

Soon after the death of the Prophet in 632, Muslims quarrelled over the question of leadership of the *umma* (community of believers). This was a central issue in the first civil war between Muslims (656–661). The war forged and solidified the initial main cleavages amongst the believers, and framed the identities of groups who came to be referred to as 'Sunnis', 'Shi'is' and 'Kharijis': 'attitudes to the first civil war enter into the self-definition of all the major Muslim sects', states the historian Patricia Crone.[44]

Some 200 years later, intra-Muslim divisions appear as a distinctive issue in the *hadith* (i.e. collected reports of the utterances and actions of the Prophet and other early Muslims) and form a distinctive genre known as the *hadith al-tafriqa* (*hadith* concerning divisions). According to Roy Mottahedeh's case study, the *hadith* on difference most frequently occur in the form: 'The Jews divided into seventy-one sects (*firqa*), the Christians into seventy-two sects, and my community will divide into seventy-three sects'. If such *hadith* are taken to be accurate transmissions of the Prophet's utterances, then the divisions that arose between Muslims during the first civil war, for example, were part of prophesy. By contrast, some historians who dispute the authenticity of many *hadith* would argue that the *hadith* on divisions, like other *hadith*, are a reflection of the diversity or the increasing divisions amongst Muslims, witnessed by those who compiled or reported the *hadith* in their own historical contexts. Whatever the reading might be, intra-communal divisions were an established feature of the Muslim religious landscape by the time the *hadith* were collected, compiled and put down in writing. They subsequently became a topic of theological reflection.

In Mottahedeh's estimation, intra-communal division seems to have been cause for consternation amongst early Muslims in the sense that it gave succour to a chilling fatalism: 'the ever-lengthening time between the revelation of Islam and the end of time' would necessarily witness the corruption of God's message and the fragmentation of the *umma*; increased division within the community of believers was a sign marking the approach of the

Day of Judgement. It is not surprising then to read in Mottahedeh's study that such *hadith* fuelled theological discourses in
which particular groups (i.e. Sunnis and Shi'is) present themselves to be the only group amongst the seventy-three that would
be saved by God. Conversely, scholars such as the jurist and theologian Abu Hamid al-Ghazali (d. 1111) argued that the *hadith* on
the one and seventy-three sects meant that only one amongst the
seventy-three would suffer 'hellfire', and that all the others would
go to paradise. Other scholars went to great lengths to classify and
categorize groups so as to account for all 'seventy-three' sects.[45]
These formulations, be they forms of soteriology or heresiography, interpreted difference amongst the community of believers as
the setting in of socio-religious decrepitude.

However, as Mottahedeh shows, the poets Hafiz (d. 1389–1390)
and Rumi (d. 1273) provided some alternative perspectives on the
issue of sectarianism and intra-communal division. In Hafiz's
work, for example, preoccupation with sectarian differences ('the
two and seventy jangling creeds') is seen to be a distraction from
true knowledge gained on the mystical path. Similar sentiments
can be found in Rumi's writing, wherein there is a call for the individual to strive beyond sectarian difference towards a higher
consciousness. In Rumi, difference is also subverted to the individual's innate multiple inclinations or compulsions. 'In you are all
the seventy-two sects', he writes. Rumi also regards division in the
umma as part of God's master plan, stating that: '[All happens] so
that these seventy-two sects should remain in the world till the
Day of Resurrection' – this perhaps being Rumi's meditation on
the Qur'an 42:8, which states: 'And if God wished, He would have
made them into a single religious community (*umma*).'

Two propositions emerge from Mottahedeh's study. The first is
that if plurality within the community, and particularly differences arising from variant understandings of doctrine, is seen as
antithetical or corrosive to the well-being of the community itself,
then the doctrinally undifferentiated *umma* is given the status of
the ideal type of Muslim community. Moreover, if the trope of
'decay over time' is added to this narrative, then it can be argued
(albeit retrospectively) that this archetypal community existed

during the Prophet's lifetime, and is therefore possible to recreate. The second proposition is that, in Rumi's meditations on difference, the concepts of unity and plurality are regarded as entirely compatible. For Rumi, differences within the *umma* are preordained by God, and the *umma* is a no less viable proposition because people within it do not agree with each other. Indeed, as Mottahedeh states, the variant of the *hadith* on divisions that is most often regarded as authoritative by scholars is the version in which only one of the seventy-three sects would go into hellfire. Such a view can thus be understood as a *de facto* endorsement of intra-communal plurality. In sum, Mottahedeh's study on the *hadith al-tafriqa* draws out the fact that notions of the *umma* in historical Muslim discourses oscillated between an ideal social type that equated unity with uniformity, and an ideal social type that saw no conflict between unity and diversity.

From the earliest periods of Islam, it is evident that Muslims have had competing understandings of the *umma* and variant interpretations of the impact of intra-Muslim differences on the community of believers. The case studies of Dominique-Sila Khan and Patrice Brodeur in this volume, which raise questions about Muslim formulations of the *umma* amongst Muslims in India and America respectively, indicate that such multiple conceptions of the *umma* remain part of Muslim discourse and self-understanding up to the present day. As such, they serve as evidence for Ahmad Dallal's point that, despite having undergone transformation over time, the *umma* remains a 'source of social identity' for Muslims in diverse contexts.[46]

Khan's study looks at the interface between competing representations of 'Islam and Muslims by Muslims' in pre- and post-independence India. In so doing, Khan indicates how in the subcontinent, the *umma*, rendered as '*ummat*' in Urdu/Hindi, was dependent on the formulation of a singular, uniform definition of Islam. This imagined Islam was jointly constructed by British lawmakers during colonial times for the purposes of governance and by some local Muslim reformers, who were politically competing with groups who espoused an equally imagined Hinduism. For both colonial officials and Muslim reformers, this Islam was synonymous with a highly legalistic understanding of the Sunni interpretation of Islam. It belied the extant, multi-layered and diverse character of religious practices and beliefs displayed by the people who came to be classified as Muslims under colonial law. As Khan explains, sustaining such a narrow understanding of Islam meant 'abolishing beliefs and practices (i.e. what is often referred to collectively as "popular Islam") that were characteristic of a good part of the local population'. This was achieved by reformers who declared various religious practices as '*shirk* (heresy) and *bidat* (innovation)', which was then reinforced in the context of the colonial courts that categorized different versions of Muslim practice as 'orthodox' and 'heterodox' in order to govern local populations. From Khan's perspective, both forces then had a hand in attempting to clear the ground of Muslim practices and interpretations that did not fit an imagined orthodoxy, and producing a normative definition of Islam. This was the Islam that was eventually adopted into the socio-legal apparatus of India when it became a nation-state.

According to Khan, the colonial imagination which conceived of religious communities as bounded and internally homogenous entities, and was carried over into the Indian nation-state, has had a profoundly disturbing impact on contemporary understandings of religions in modern-day India. She states:

> For many non-Muslim Indians today the word 'Muslim' has a restricted meaning: it refers most often exclusively to Sunnis. The same can be said of the term 'Hindu', which is generally restricted to Brahmins and members of the upper castes.
>
> The diversity amongst Muslims, when expressed, is often spoken about in terms of simple dichotomies, such as Sunni/Shi'i, exoteric (legalistic)/esoteric (Sufi), *ba-shar/be-shar* (orthodox/ heterodox), tolerant Chishtis/intolerant Naqshbandis, etc.

But what Khan's study also points to is that, while there has been a successive impact of state categorizations on formulations of 'self' and 'other' amongst Muslims in India, the contemporary religious landscapes on the Indian subcontinent continue to betray a plurality amongst Muslims which needs to be investigated and theorized. In this regard, Khan cites contemporary instances in which 'Sunnis' and 'Shi'is' share *pir*s (preacher-saints), and 'Muslims' share *dargah*s (shrines) with 'Hindus'. She argues that these types of interfaces between individuals and groups not only put to the test conventional categorizations of 'Islam' and challenge the paradigmatic *ummat* as formulated during the colonial period, but also show how religious behaviour is not easily contained or subsumed by the apparatus of the state. Hence, Khan's study raises the question as to how some social actors and groups are able to enact their beliefs outside official categorizations, and thereby resist the state as well as those who claim absolute religious authority. Stated differently, how does the 'internal other' manage to retain its agency and distinctiveness in hegemonic contexts?[47]

Brodeur's case study of Muslims living in post-9/11 America provides a somewhat contrasting picture to Khan's study. In the American context, Muslim constructions and references to the *umma* have as much to do with the global community of Muslims and their different relationships to the 'West' as they have to do with intra-Muslim plurality within America. In Brodeur's view, the most prevalent theories of pluralism have as yet to take full account of the role of transnational forces in the formation of Muslim identity at the levels of the state or local community. Hence, in American Muslim evocations of identity, in which notions of the *umma* jostle with the notion of 'America', both '*umma*' and 'America' act as ideal types: the former often infers a paradigmatic united (and perhaps even uniform) community of Muslims, whereas the latter stands for the 'secular West'. Nevertheless, as Brodeur indicates, dual identification, often phrased as, ' "We are both Americans and Muslims", betrays an ambiguity as to how these two identities relate to one another in practice'; it is an ambiguity that requires analysis. Brodeur shows that Muslims in America have adopted different approaches to the problem of being American *and* Muslim, and that for some Muslims in America this has meant unravelling the category of the *umma*.

Certainly, since 9/11 there has been a clearer recognition that what has hitherto passed uncritically in discursive formulations as the '*umma*' is more complex, both in terms of the myriad of groups and organizations it contains in America and globally, and in the sense that the *umma* has voices within it that Muslims and non-Muslims may consider undesirable, but are nevertheless the voices of co-religionists.

Ironically, it may be that, while Muslims in America attempt to reconcile the presence of competing interpretations of Islam in their geographical midst or on the world stage, and thereby reconstitute their ideas of the '*umma*', the American state, which may be feeling increasingly under threat in recent times, may not be equipped to contend with intra-communal differences amongst Muslims. That is, the state's unyielding desire to construct and delineate its citizenry through mechanisms such as censuses and surveys may immediately construct 'an Islam' and 'a Muslim' according to a set of narrowly conceived and bounded categories, undifferentiated and uniform, not unlike the paradigmatic '*umma*'. This is partially proven to be the case in terms of the surveys of Muslims cited by Brodeur, many of which begin with indicators such as 'mosque attendance', to measure the extent of a Muslim presence in American towns and cities. Hence, at the level of the state, the manner in which Muslims are represented to the state and by the state may well undermine whole groups of Muslims who do not conform to the 'Islam' defined by those who have been seen by the state as having the authority to define Islam, and concurrently have power and influence over the state. Such practices do not and would not promote intra-communal plurality, nor do they promote multiple ways of being a Muslim in America or elsewhere. This observation raises the issue of how a state can recognize and attend to the inter-communal difference and the presence of the internal other amongst religious groups such as Muslims that the state imagines to be bounded and internally homogenous with a clearly designated authority.

Marking out the 'self' and the 'internal other'

Whereas the studies of Mottahedeh, Khan and Brodeur are indicative of how constructions of the *umma* are formulated in response to intra-communal differences and divisions, the studies of James Allan, Kevin Jaques and Roman Loimeier examine in greater detail how divisions between Muslims are generated and maintained through the use of socio-cultural tools, and how these efforts result in the marking of the 'self' and the 'internal other'. Before turning to the cases, it should be noted that studies of this type constantly work in response to received categories, definitions and scholarly positions in which intra-Muslim differences, by and large, have been reified, taken for granted or remain virtually unexamined. Thus, Allan's case study on doctrinal pluralism in Islamic art states from the outset that, in the almost century-long discourse of Western European scholarship on 'Islamic Art', virtually no scholarly study has looked at how the artistic products of Muslims can be distinguished on the basis of doctrinal difference. Jaques, on the other hand, works through the complex architecture of biographical literature generated by Muslim historians in order to determine how it was that Shafi'i and Hanafi *madhab*s (schools of jurisprudence) came to distinguish themselves from each other in the process of their early formation. The discursive tradition of prosopography that produced these texts and the images of the paradigmatic *madhab*s do not seem to be of great concern to Muslims who follow particular schools of jurisprudence, nor have the fissures and re-formulations of self and other amongst the *madhab*s been fully investigated by scholars of Islamic jurisprudence. Likewise, Loimeier's study, which charts the flux and flow of traditions of reform amongst a range of Muslim groups in Senegal and East Africa from the nineteenth to the twentieth centuries, challenges boundaries and definitions of 'Sufi' and 'Islamist' which are conventionally used by Western scholars in their analyses of Islam and Muslim groups in sub-Saharan Africa. All of this is to say that categories initially used as heuristic devices to separate out, order and analyse particular aspects of Islam or Muslim life have often become social facts. It is a process that serves to reify and take for granted particular notions of self and other, rather than examine claims and counter-claims about self and other as part of a discursive landscape that is in constant flux and flow.

Returning to the theme of how Muslims mark out the internal other and the self, Allan concedes from the outset of his study that distinguishing between the artistic products of 'Sunnis', 'Shi'is' and 'Sufis' means 'sorting out elements which are actually due to doctrine as opposed to variations resulting from geography, history, or ethnic and cultural differences'. This observation raises questions about the extent to which religious beliefs can be articulated or manifested independently of society, culture or history, and conversely, the extent to which varying interpretations of doctrine or practice within a religious community arise from or are determined by extant social, cultural and historical differences. The scope of Allan's study does not allow him to tackle these issues directly. However, Allan puts forward the case that a number of artistic products produced by Muslims have hallmarks that suggest that they were produced for or by a person or group with a distinctive doctrinal position, and on this basis they may, at least, be compared and contrasted.

In his survey of architecture, texts and objects, Allan finds that it is often through textual inscriptions and the use of symbols through which the doctrinal provenance of an artistic product might often be readily determined. Thus 'Shi'i' artistic products may be identified through their inscribed references to the Imam/Caliph 'Ali, a lineage of Shi'i Imams, particular prayer formulae known to be regularly associated with Shi'i forms of piety, or decorative programmes that make use of symbols that have been regularly associated with Shi'ism. But Allan cautions that such identification is not always straightforward. In particular, he points to the fact that the Imam/Caliph 'Ali and the *Ahl al-Bayt* are significant for Muslims of different doctrinal persuasions, and, therefore, artistic products bearing references to them do not always point to a specifically Shi'i provenance.

In addition to inscriptions and symbols, Muslim groups also produced artistic products for use in rituals. These can be seen to have been developed on the basis of distinctive readings of doctrine. For example, some Shiʻi groups produced ʻ*alam*s (staffs) for use in Muharram processions and utilized *imamzada*s (mausolea for the members/descendants of the *Ahl al-Bayt*) to bury their dead, and some Sufi groups produced *kashkul*s (begging bowls) and built *khanaqa*s (dervish lodges); both products were related to Sufi asceticism. Here again, however, ambiguities arise in equating particular artistic products with particular groups. That is, Sunni communities also used mausolea to bury their elite, and Sufi groups have been both pro-Sunni and pro-Shiʻi. Similarly, for Allan, Qurʾan manuscripts are some of the most difficult to ascribe doctrinal provenance. He states that: ʻAfter all, the Qurʾan is the Qurʾan, and the text is regarded as immutable, whichever Muslim group one may adhere toʾ. Thus, attempts to identify the provenance of such manuscripts have to focus on material additional to the text such as style, decoration, patronage and dedication inscriptions.

Despite the complexities associated with assigning a particular doctrinal identification to Muslim artistic products, Allan cites a number of instances in the Muslim historical record where Muslim groups marked their presence or ascendancy over other Muslim groups by developing a distinctive religio-artistic vocabulary for their artistic products, or by subverting an extant vocabulary in order to signify a break from the views of such groups and mark out their own distinctive doctrinal position. Allan's key examples come from the art and architecture of the Fatimid Ismaili Shiʻis (in Egypt) (r. 909–1171), and the Sunni dynasties such as the Ayyubids (r. 1171–1250/1260) and Mamluks that succeeded them (r. 1250–1517).

It is generally acknowledged that the Fatimids developed an artistic vocabulary which drew particular attention to the distinctive Shiʻi Ismaili esoteric interpretation of Islamic doctrine, which accords a significant role to the imamate and the family and descendants of ʻAli. This was achieved in a number of ways, but particularly through the use of Qurʾanic inscriptions, symbolism and decorative motifs associated with light. The Mamluk dynasty, which came to power in Egypt a century after the fall of the Fatimids, appears to have co-opted and subverted Fatimid

symbols and artistic conventions. For example, when comparing
Arabic calligraphic inscriptions on Fatimid and Mamluk objects
such as metalwork and coins, Allan finds that, in Fatimid-period
products, inscriptions around circular shapes are regularly related
to ʿAli and the Shiʿi Ismaili Imams and, more significantly, are
read anticlockwise or 'on the inside'. By comparison, in Mamluk
material culture, such inscriptions tend to be exclusively associated with the Sultan and his power, and appear to have been
purposefully reversed so as to be read clockwise or 'on the outside'.
For Allan, such processes may be interpreted as a form of
co-option and subversion of the long-established Shiʿi Ismaili
artistic vocabulary, and as a means by which Mamluk patrons
visually signalled a break with the past and symbolically marked
the state's 'return to Sunnism'.

What Allan describes for Muslim artists is comparable to the
literary techniques used by Muslim historians of the thirteenth
century to define and delineate between *madhhab*s (legal
schools), whose writings are examined in Jaques's case study.
Jaques details the mechanics of how Muslim historians used the
prosopographical genre of biography and its conventional literary
devices of cross-referencing, rhetorical flourish, narrative embel-
lishment, and gloss, to construct and dismantle the identities of
and relations between two founding figures of the Shafiʿi and
Hanafi *madhhab*s, Abu Ibrahim Ismaʿil b. Yahya al-Muzani (d.
878) and Abu Jaʿfar Ahmad b. Muhammad al-Tahawi (d. 933).
The case study shows how marking out the internal other has
been historically carried out between groups who adhere to the
same doctrinal position – in this case, between adherents of two
Sunni *madhhab*s.

Amongst the many examples Jaques cites of strategic differentiation by literary means amongst *madhhab*s and between their
members is the use of a historical gloss and a dream sequence in
the Shafiʿi-leaning historian Ibn Yunus's (d. 958) biography of al-
Tahawi. According to Jaques, Ibn Yunus's life history of al-Tahawi
provides a highly truncated account of al-Tahawi's relationship
with al-Muzani, his former teacher, and suggests that al-Tahawi's
conversion from the Shafiʿi to the Hanafi *madhhab* was, in part,

the result of a dream in which al-Muzani appears to al-Tahawi, calling out 'I break with you'. Jaques argues that Ibn Yunus's omission of many of the historical details concerning al-Tahawi's association with al-Muzani is common in Muslim biographical literature. The purposes of such glosses were pragmatic insofar as they saved the author space. But they were also strategic insofar as they allowed the author to 'create new impressions about the individual under review'. Jaques also shows how Ibn Yunus used the literary device of the dream sequence and phrases such as 'I break with you' as a means of presenting al-Tahawi 'as a social climber', who had little doctrinal conviction and whose ambition was to saddle up to a prominent local Hanafi *qadi* (judge) in order to gain prominence himself. In sum, Jaques's excavations provide an opportunity to witness the literary apparatus that Muslim scholars used to make plain the differences that arose between them. Such activities make clear that Muslim historians, biographers and other literati developed sophisticated mechanisms to prop up their associates and/or defame their opponents – what in contemporary times may be termed 'spin'.

Both Jaques's and Allan's studies also indicate that Muslim groups define themselves by means of marking their proximity with or distance from persons, groups or interpretative programmes contemporary to them, and from the immediate as well as distant historical past. Hence, strategies marking out differences are not only employed against internal others who live within temporal proximity, but also between those who live at a temporal distance. Such processes are fully evident in Loimeier's case study of 'traditions of reform' in Senegal and Zanzibar/ Tanzania from the nineteenth century up to the present day. Here, 'trans-generational disputation' serves as a primary discursive strategy in marking distinctions between the self and the internal other for present-day social actors.

In the case of Senegal, for example, Loimeier shows that contemporary disputes amongst members of the Tijaniyya and Muridiyya *tariqa*s (Sufi orders), and between them, are rife with negative or positive references to the past practices of individuals and groups. Discourses about the past serve to legitimize or delegitimize the views and actions of rival groups and individuals in the present by re-imagining and re-presenting the socio-historical roles and intellectual legacies of groups and individuals from that historical past. When examined over the *longue durée*, such discourse and the strategies used in its formulation are shown by Loimeier to be a self-perpetuating framework in which all groups fall in and out of favour and gain and lose their legitimacy. Hence, in such cases, religious opponents can be seen to cast each other as the 'internal other' within the same discursive space and through time.

Loimeier discusses comparable examples of such processes of trans-generational disputation in East Africa, particularly in the region of present-day Tanzania, among and between members of the Qadiriyya, Alawiyya and Shadhiliyya *tariqa*s. Here, disputes within and between *tariqa*s often coalesce around ritual practices such as particular types of *dhikr* (meditative prayer) and activities associated with *mawlid al-nabi* (celebrations of the Prophet's birthday). Insofar as communal rituals are a public means of expressing beliefs, it is not surprising that they readily become markers of group identity and thus provide ready-made ground for contestation between Muslim groups. From an anthropological perspective, contemporary and historical debates between Muslims on matters such as ritual practice provide 'ethnographic windows' through which to view the landscape of competing definitions amongst Muslims about what Islam is and what being a Muslim means.[48] Again, for Loimeier, these 'contexts of dispute' include the immediate space–time framework and the multi-generational past. That is, when legitimacy is accorded to a particular practice in the present generation by the leaders of a particular group, it should be read as a form of conversation taking place between present-day opponents and proponents, as well as groups or individuals from the past. If understood in this more complex fashion, then one generation's 'Sufi quietism' may be interpreted by the next generation as 'radical reformation', and so on.

Thus, for Loimier, treating intra-communal Muslim disputations as 'trans-local, trans-historical, trans-traditional or trans-generational' phenomena provides a more comprehensive way of understanding Muslim practices and locally generated definitions of Islam, and ultimately allows us to dispense with essentialized understandings and reified terminology and categorizations. As such, Loimeier's study suggests that the 'internal other' is constantly being re-cast in relation to changing understandings of the 'self'. The self–other paradigm is both a relational and a contextual construct: each component of the paradigm anticipates and responds to its opposite within a multi-dimensional space–time context.

Each of the cases in the volume discussed thus far makes evident that the 'other within' is crucial to the definition of 'the self' for a range of Muslim groups. But this is achieved in different ways. For some Muslims, the internal other is re-conceptualized over time so as to facilitate a *rapprochement* with newly formulated understandings of the self. The works and deeds of the ancestors are re-considered, as it were, often using the lens of contemporary concerns and issues. In some cases, debates about self and internal others are altogether forgotten, boundaries are taken for granted, and the relations of power that generated differences remain only as literary fragments to be excavated and unearthed by later generations of curious historians. In other cases still, negating the presence of the internal other or stating ascendancy over them is achieved by means of subversion or co-option of an extant representational corpus. However, what is important to note is that all groups, even when they are cast out discursively, claim to be practising Islam. That is, no group would readily identify itself as the 'other', or would label their interpretation of Islam as 'heterodox' or 'heretical'. In this regard, an example from my own fieldwork in Zanzibar comes to mind, in which a group who were accused of formulating '*bid'a*' (innovation) returned the insult to their accusers, publicly naming (and at the same time shaming) them as '*watu wa bid'a*' (the people who 'wax on' about innovations).[49] Such strategies, and those reflected in the case studies discussed so far, reflect the vibrant and discursive character of Muslim societies both in the past and in the present. This view cuts against the rather well-worn portrait of Muslim societies as static and fossilized spaces, in which those in authority simply issue edicts from the pulpit without challenge or contestation.

Discourses, counter-discourses and the rules of engagement

By now, it is evident that Muslims have regularly debated amongst themselves on a range of matters concerning Islam and continue to do so. The discourses that Muslims generate amongst themselves provide the discursive contexts in which definitions of the 'self' emerge. In many of these discourses, it is evident that the 'self' is not exclusively and straightforwardly constructed in response to the 'external other' (i.e. the West), even if this 'other' is invoked in the course of such discourses. Rather, it is the 'internal other' that plays a crucial role in Muslim self-articulations and understandings. Further evidence of this comes from the case study presented by John Bowen on the justification and coexistence of competing norms in Islam amongst leading Muslim public intellectuals in Indonesia and France. This case also exemplifies the discourses, counter-discourses and rules of engagement that pervade debates amongst Muslim groups around the world.

Bowen undertakes his study of Muslim discourses of 'pluralism amongst Muslims' in Europe and South-East Asia amongst Muslim public intellectuals on the basis that: 'Many are asking whether Muslims should base their actions on the traditions of jurisprudence or whether they should rethink Islam in terms of its broader principles and, if so, what those principles should be.' Bowen delineates three contending options. One is 'intra-cultural pluralism', which has emerged as a possibility amongst Muslims in Indonesia. Leading scholars such as Professor Hazairin of the University of Indonesia Law School have argued that, because the legal schools that arose in classical Muslim times and the principles of law that legal scholars generated were developed for an 'Arab society', it is worthwhile considering whether these classical principles are relevant in non-Arab contexts. Another option regards the position of Muslims in non-Muslim lands (*dar al-harb*)[50] as being essentially exempt from normative legal precepts that would apply to Muslims living in Muslim lands (*dar al-Islam*). This division of the world into different realms wherein different rules apply is advocated by some Muslims living in

Europe and North America. A third option, advocated by some Muslim intellectuals in Europe, opts for a 'focus on the broad principles of Islam and discard[ing] much of the legal tradition' via an examination of the convergences between the socio-legal principles shared by Muslims and their host society (i.e. Europe), or by invoking the general principles (*maqasid*) that underlie the Muslim legal tradition as a means of generating new rules of social engagement. This range of options represents the depth and breadth of the Muslim discursive landscape on the issue of pluralism. As Bowen succinctly states, they take into account 'current social settings and draw on long-standing forms of argumentation from within the Islamic traditions of jurisprudence and learning'.

This, then, is the common ground between Bowen's study and those of a number of other authors in this volume: they indicate that Muslims in different contexts are engaged with contemporary issues such as the structures of governance and the nature of authority, but the manner in which such issues are addressed is with reference to a set of authoritative references and distinctive modes of articulation that draw upon both the foundational texts of Islam and the discursive traditions of Muslims, as well as the texts and traditions of non-Muslims. What is also evident is that amongst Muslims there exist varying degrees of tolerance for intra-communal difference on matters of existential concern. For some Muslims, such as Hazairin in Indonesia, differences are seen as necessary, on the basis that Islam has grown up in different historical and cultural contexts, whereas for others there can be no fundamental differences between 'French Islam' and 'Indonesian Islam'. It would not be out of place here to recall the comments made by one of the Muslims in the BBC television debate described at the outset of this chapter, who appeared to recoil at his co-religionist's suggestion that there was a 'British Islam'. For him, like some of the intellectuals mentioned by Bowen, Islam is both indivisible and immutable.

The range of views expressed by the panellists on the BBC news programme and the case studies in this volume also suggests that, while Muslims in different contexts may debate amongst themselves about various issues, they share common points of reference in their debates, such as the Qur'an and the Prophet, if only to legitimize their particular points of view or to delegitimize the points of view of their co-religionists. This underscores the point that Muslims may be united in the primacy they accord to particular sources of religious authority, but engage with, interpret and apply these sources differently in different contexts. The application of this perspective on Islam and Muslims cannot sustain statements that 'Islam is ...' or 'Islam is not ...' and 'Muslims believe and think that ...' or 'Muslims do not think that ...'. Rather, it makes evident the diverse and variant ways in which Muslims debate between themselves, contend with difference, ultimately unfolding Islam from within. In re-viewing Islam in this manner, we come face to face with Muslims, the variously configured 'communities of discourse'[51] that are attempting to make sense of their deeply felt religious convictions and their existential realities. Making sense of this diversity requires both a critical assessment of our home-grown assumptions and questions about Islam, and also contends with the fact of difference amongst Muslims. Above all, it requires us to address what the late anthropologist Clifford Geertz identified as the central challenge of pluralism – 'learning to grasp that which we do not necessarily embrace'.[52]

2

Pluralism and Islamic Traditions of Sectarian Divisions

Roy P. Mottahedeh

The central organizing system for sectarian division among Muslims is a scheme that divides Muslims into seventy-two or seventy-three sects.[1] This scheme is not totally unfamiliar to readers of English literature. In the 1888 edition of Edward Fitzgerald's creative re-imagining of Omar Khayyam's *Rubaiyat*, the forty-third quatrain reads:

> *The Grape that can with Logic absolute*
> *The Two-and-Seventy Sects confute:*
> *The subtle Alchemist that in a Trice*
> *Life's leaden Metal into Gold transmute.*

This essay is not written to celebrate the power of wine to dissolve sectarian differences, although such an essay might be a more challenging task. But I think we should pause for a moment at the name of Omar Khayyam, the Iranian Muslim mathematician and astronomer who died in the early twelfth century. Omar Khayyam's scepticism was as thrilling to his medieval contemporaries as it was to our Victorian forefathers who first made him a figure of interest in the West. Matthew Arnold, for example, was scandalized to find out how much he resonated with Omar Khayyam's scepticism.

In fact, it is both one of the virtues and great shortcomings of modern sensibilities to believe in a thorough-going and homogenized system of thought. An apocryphal story is told of the Mughal emperor Akbar, who in 1581 founded his own religion, the celebrated Din-i Ilahi or 'Divine Religion', which he and his vizier Abu al-Fazl formulated to accommodate the multiple truths of existing religions. When Akbar, who had already purchased four hooves of the donkey that bore Jesus into Jerusalem, agreed to buy a fifth hoof, the vizier said: 'But, Your Majesty, no donkey has five hooves.' To this the emperor replied: 'Who knows? One of them might be genuine.' This hopeful, but not absolutely committed, form of belief helps us to understand the culture in which a text of hedonism, like that of Omar Khayyam, can exist alongside the most rigorous texts on the ascetic and self-denying life written by contemporaries of Omar Khayyam. Incidentally, Akbar's interesting religious experiment did not survive the emperor's death.

Before turning to the question as to how sectarian division need not be an obstacle among people of true faith, I would like to turn to a discussion of the meaning of the traditional division into seventy-odd sects. For many Muslim authors, this division seemed firmly anchored in sayings ascribed to the Prophet Muhammad, the *hadith* or 'traditions' which, if seen to be scrupulously transmitted, have a near scriptural authority for most Muslims. In one form or another, this *hadith* is quoted by almost every author on religious differences among Muslims and often gives structure to the books written on the subject.

Often called the *hadith al-tafriqa*, or 'tradition concerning division', it occurs in one of its most frequent forms as: 'The Jews divided into seventy-one sects (*firqa*), the Christians into seventy-two sects, and my community will divide into seventy-three sects.' This form of the *hadith* is found in Ibn Majah (d. 887), Abu Da'ud al-Sijistani (d. 889), al-Tirmidhi (d. 892) and al-Nisa'i (d. 915), four of the six so-called 'canonical' Sunni collections of *hadith*. The *hadith* also occurs frequently in a different version: 'There will befall my nation what befell the children of Israel. The children of Israel divided into seventy-two religious groups (*milla*) and my community will divide into seventy-three religious groups (*milla*), one more than they. All of them are in hellfire except one religious group.'[2]

The addition about hellfire is sometimes followed by the account of a question addressed to the Prophet as to who are the saved sect (*firqa*) or religious group (*milla*) not in hellfire, to which the Prophet answers: 'That group/sect which I and my Companions believe in.'[3] A variant of this *hadith* explicitly identifies the sacred sect as the *ahl al-sunna wa'l jama'a*, i.e. the Sunnis. The *hadith* also exists in Twelver Shi'i texts – however, without the coda identifying the saved sect and with the understanding that the saved sect is the Imami (Twelver) Shi'is.[4] The Zaydi Shi'is likewise use a variant of this *hadith*.[5]

An important variant of the tradition says that, 'The children of Israel divided into seventy-one sects (*firqa*) and my community will divide into seventy-two, all of them in hellfire except one. It is the [majority Muslim] community (*jama'a*)', presumably the Sunnis.[6] The very learned (and covertly Ismaili) heresiographer al-Shahrastani (d. 1153) supports the view that the Zoroastrians divided into seventy sects, the Jews into seventy-one, the Christians into seventy-two, and the Muslims into seventy-three.[7] The principle of progression in numbers is preserved here. Not the least curious thing about this family of traditions is the claim that Islam should be superior in number of sectarian divisions (whereas to be superior in number of people of piety, or antecedent prophets, would seem a more reassuring feature of a religious tradition). Perhaps the corruption wrought by time, a frequent theme in traditions, a corruption made more severe by the ever-lengthening time between the revelation of Islam and the end of time, might argue for the greater number of sectarian divisions among Muslims.

The tenth-century geographer al-Muqaddasi says that seventy-two sects are in heaven and one in hell, according to what he considers a more sound line of transmission (*isnad*).[8] Similarly, the great theologian al-Ghazali (d. 1111) supports a reading that 'all are in heaven except the *zindiqs*' (Manichaeans, outrageous heretics).[9] The opinion that all but one of the sects was saved was not widely held and was not followed by pre-modern Muslim writers of heresiographies. Al-Ghazali gives a different view of the sectarian divisions of his time in one of his Persian letters. After quoting the *hadith* in the form, 'My community (*umma*) will divide into seventy-odd (*nayyif*) sects, one of which will be saved', al-Ghazali says:

> The cause of this diversity is that the community consists of three groups: the best, the worst and the middling. The best of the community are the Sufis, who have devoted all of their own personal will and desire to the will of God. The worst are the morally vicious, and those people who exercise oppression, drink wine, and commit fornication, and give free reign to the desire for whatever they want and are able to do. They deceive themselves in thinking that Almighty God is generous and merciful, and they depend upon this (mercy). In the middle are the people among the masses of mankind who possess moral soundness (*salah*). So every one of these divisions has twenty-four parts, and together they make seventy-two parts (*fariq*).[10]

Such scholars of Muslim heresies almost invariably quote the tradition of seventy-odd sects in their books on heresies. A large number of them work to fit the heresies into a scheme of seventy-odd. An example is the learned heresiographer 'Abd al-Qahir b. Tahir al-Baghdadi (d. 1037), who in his *Farq bayn al-firaq* claims that there are twenty sects of Shi'is and twenty sects of Kharijis, but is unable to give any detail about them.[11] This kind of effort forced heresiographers to multiply heresies and to combine them, as each category might be a single heresy or a category of heretics.

Over a century ago, Ignaz Goldziher noticed that a few later writers found the seventy-two or seventy-three-fold division of sects to be an ill-fitting suit of clothes. He quotes the great scholar Fakhr al-Din al-Razi (d. 1209), who, in his commentary on the Qur'an, writes: 'Some have attacked the authenticity of this tradition. They say that if by seventy-two they mean the fundamentals of religious beliefs (*usul al-adyan*) then they do not reach this number; and if they mean the practices (*furu'*), then the number passes this number by several multiples.'[12] Goldziher also suggested that the family of division traditions owed their inspiration to another, possibly older, very well-attested tradition: 'Faith has seventy-odd branches and modesty (*al-haya'*) is one of them.'[13] The learned contemporary scholar Mahdavi-Damghani has pointed out that this is an independent sentiment with its own line of transmitters.[14] Indeed, as Goldziher observed, here the 'seventy-odd' are all praiseworthy 'branches', and this tradition gave rise to an independent genre of literature called *shu'ab al-iman*, or 'branches of faith'.[15] It is interesting to notice that, unlike the traditions based on 'sect/religious group' distinctions, this 'branches of faith' tradition is found in both Bukhari and Muslim, who are considered by many Sunnis to be more authoritative sources.[16]

The interest in the number 'seventy-odd', however, is a consistent theme and deserves independent attention. As Annemarie Schimmel has noted in her book on number significance, the Islamic tradition follows the Bible in its fascination with heptads, from which the interest in ten times seven springs. The seventy nations, the seventy judges of the Sanhedrin and the seventy years of Babylonian exile are only a small number of the many Biblical 'seventies'. According to Islamic tradition, the Prophet recited the Qur'an seventy times during his journey to the Divine Presence and also asked for forgiveness seventy times a day.[17]

Just as important as seventy was seventy-two, because it has links with three, six, eight, nine and twelve. Already in late antiquity, its numerological significance – as, for example, the number of degrees in an arc divided by the sacred pentagram equals seventy-two – was added to the significance of seventy-two in the Bible. According to the New Testament, seventy-two disciples were sent to preach the gospel in seventy-two languages of the world. The Bible was translated into Greek by seventy, or seventy-two, scholars, each isolated from all others, and miraculously the seventy or seventy-two translations matched;[18] hence, of course, the Septuagint.

In the Islamic tradition, seventy-odds are very frequent. Seventy-two were killed at the martyrdom of the Prophet's grandson, al-Husayn, at Karbala. In a tradition (of modest authority but in a respected collection) the Prophet asks: '"Do you know the distance between heaven and earth?" They said: "We do not know". He said: "The distance between the two is seventy-one or seventy-two or seventy-three years and the sky extends for the same distance ...".' The distance to hell was not dissimilar; a tradition relates: 'We were with the Messenger of God and heard the sound of something falling ... The Messenger of God said, "That was a stone that was thrown into Hell seventy years ago and it was still falling into Hell until it reached its bottom".'[19]

Interestingly, a Shiʿi source says that God's 'Greatest Name' has seventy-three letters, of which Imam Muhammad al-Baqir knew seventy-two letters. The medieval Jewish Cabbalists held that Yahweh's name consisted of seventy-two letters, or that Yahweh had seventy-two names.[20] Both the Muslim and the Jewish esoteric traditions believed that God saves those who call on Him using his 'Greatest Name'.

That seventy meant 'a sizeable number' and seventy-odd meant 'a sizeable number and then some' is fairly clear. In many (and perhaps most) cases, the expressions are meant to be pictorial numbers and not exact 'head counts'. In the *Surat al-Tawbah*, the Qur'an addresses Muhammad and says (9:80): 'Whether [O Muhammad] you ask forgiveness – or do not ask forgiveness – for them [the Hypocrites] seventy times, God will not forgive them because they did not believe ....' Here, clearly, 'seventy' is a pictorial number, and current English usage would be as well served if one were to say 'whether you asked forgiveness a hundred times ...', since there is no exact number of times and the number is only rhetorically significant. The commentators I have consulted are in no doubt about the pictorial meaning of the number here. The specialist in rhetoric, al-Zamakhshari (d. 1144), for example, writes on this verse in his Qur'an commentary : 'Seventy assumed the role of a metaphor for numerousness in their speech.'[21]

One of the many traditions that uses seventy-odd to signify numerousness is the following: 'The Messenger of God said: "He who helps a [Muslim] believer [in his difficulty], God – Almighty and Glorious – will remove him from seventy-three afflictions, one of which is this world; and seventy-two afflictions at the time of the Great Affliction, when people will be occupied with their souls in the hereafter".'[22]

A deeper theological insight into the question of sectarian division, however, comes from the Sufi mystical tradition. Hafiz (d. 1389–1390) epitomizes this tradition when he says:

> *Heaven was too weak to bear the burden of responsibility – they gave it to my poor crazy self.*
> *Forgive the war of the seventy-two warring religions; Since they did not see the truth they have struck out on the road of fancy.*

Or, to give this last line in the more poetic translation of Gertrude Bell:

> *Though the soft breath of Truth readies my ears,*
> *For two-and-seventy jangling creeds he hears,*
> *And loud-voiced Fable calls him ceaselessly.*

In the two Hafiz translations, 'religions' in the former and 'creeds' in the latter are *millat*; 'fancy' in the former and 'Fable' in the latter are *afsanah* (tales).[23] For Hafiz, sectarian divisions are the fancy or fable that preoccupy those who have not struck out on the mystical path.

The highest and the most developed reflection of the Sufi tradition is in the *Masnavi* of Jalal al-Din, known in the West as Rumi (d. 1273). Rumi depicts the confrontation between a partisan of predestination or divine 'compulsion' (*jabr*), and a partisan of free will:

> *In just this way there is a dispute [bahth] between the partisans of compulsion and those [partisans of] free will till the resurrection of mankind.*
> *If the disputant had been able to refute his adversary, their schools of thought [madhahib] would have fallen out of sight.*
> *Since [presented with unquestionable truth] these [disputants] would not be able to escape [admitting the truth] in reply, they would recoil from that road to perdition.*
> *Yet, in so much as their continuation on that course was divinely ordained, [God] feeds them with arguments,*

> *So that [one disputant] not be compelled by the difficulties posed by*
> *[another] disputant, and [each] may be prevented from seeing his*
> *opponent's success.*
> *[All happens] so that these seventy-two sects should remain in the*
> *world till the day of resurrection.*
> *Since this is the world of darkness and that which is hidden, the*
> *earth [and its uncertainties] is necessary for [this] shadow [to*
> *exist].*
> *Until the resurrection the seventy-two sects will remain, and the talk*
> *of those who introduced ideas without religious foundation will*
> *not fail.*
> *The high value of a treasure is [shown by the circumstance] that*
> *there are so many locks upon it ...*[24]

As Nicholson, the great commentator on the *Masnavi* rightly
remarks, the argument of the passage is 'that religious heresies
are necessary and [even] providential'.[25] The whole passage can be
seen as a commentary on the first part of the well-known
Qur'anic verse: 'And if God wished, He would have made them
into a single religious community (*umma*) ...' (42:8). God has not
given certainty to mankind. On this earth, man must puzzle out
the correct meaning in the shadow – and not in plain sight – of
certain truth. God even nourishes the opposing sides of disputes.
As earthly creatures, we see only the high value and not the
real nature of truth because it is locked away and thus difficult
to access.

Rumi has a somewhat different approach to the seventy-two
varieties of Muslims in a passage on doubt and faith:

> *Take care, O believers, for that [vein of philosophical] doubt is*
> *within you; within you is many an infinite world.*
> *In you are all the seventy-two sects; woe [to you] should [that*
> *philosophical] doubt extend its hand from within.*[26]

Without question, this passage urges the believer to master his or
her doubts in the name of belief. And yet it regards the internal
world or internal forum as a place where inevitably there are

encounters of all sorts of belief, here symbolized by the seventy-two sects. That such an internal forum exists is a consequence of the many infinite worlds inside each human being.

In yet another passage, Rumi addresses sectarian difference within a mystical vision of the universal – if not fully conscious – worshipfulness of all creation:

> *Each glorifies [Thee] in a different fashion, and that one is*
> *unaware of the state of this one. Man disbelieves in the*
> *glorification uttered by inanimate objects, but these inanimate*
> *objects are masters [in performing] worship.*
>
> *Nay, the two-and-seventy sects, every one, are unaware of [the real*
> *states of] each other and in a [great] doubt.*
>
> *Since two speakers have no knowledge of each other's state how will*
> *[it] be [with] wall and door?*
>
> *Since I am heedless of the glorification uttered by one who speaks,*
> *how should my heart know the glorification performed by that*
> *which is mute?*
>
> *The Sunni is unaware of the [Predestinarian's] [mode of]*
> *glorification.*
>
> *The Sunni has a particular [mode of] glorification; the*
> *Predestinarian has the opposite thereof in [taking] refuge*
> *[with God].*[27]

Nicholson well summarizes the passage as saying that everything glorifies God by displaying some of His attributes in a special way known to God alone, who has the infinite knowledge necessary to understand all the particulars of the world. This glorification is an act of worship, and, willing or not, every object, animate or inanimate, glorifies God. Both the Sunni (and Rumi was a Sunni) and his opponent, the Predestinarian, glorify God – even though one may be right and one may be wrong about a specific article of belief – insofar as the beliefs of both express diverse aspects of Divine self-manifestation.[28]

Finally, Rumi explodes the two and seventy 'sects' as mere epiphenomena of lesser religious consciousness. In an ecstatic passage on Love of the Divine and the Divine as Love, Rumi writes:

> *Love is a stranger to the two worlds; in it are two-and-seventy*
> *madnesses.*
> *It is exceedingly hidden, and [only] its bewilderment is manifest: the*
> *soul of the spiritual sultans is pining for it.*
> *Its religion is other than [that of] the two-and-seventy sects: beside*
> *it the throne of kings is [but] a split-bandage ...*
> *Then what is Love? The Sea of Not-being: here the foot of the*
> *intellect is shattered [when it tries to swim] ...*
> *Would that Being had a Tongue, that it might remove the veils from*
> *existent Beings!*
> *O breath of [phenomenal] existence, whatsoever thou mayest utter,*
> *know that thereby thou hast bound another veil upon it [the*
> *mystery].*[29]

While the intellect may be destined to speculate, the religion of love passes beyond sectarian difference. Love manifests itself in great variety, called here seventy-two madnesses, and ultimately takes the lover beyond the phenomenal world. Ultimately, beyond the babble of sectarian differences, the soul seeks a mystery which language cannot express.

Rumi has brought us to the end of our quest. The scheme of seventy-odd sects may be inspired by an earlier tradition about sixty-odd or seventy-odd branches of faith. Seventy-odd is very likely meant to convey the idea of considerable number. Whether one agrees with the usual interpretation that only one sect is saved, or the minority interpretation that only one is lost, the only punishment for right or wrong belief mentioned in these traditions is otherworldly, i.e. heaven or hell.

The Sufi tradition goes beyond these commonsensical understandings of religious pluralism among Muslims. Arguments for pluralism often depart from the suppositions that there are good impulses in all humans, or that most forms of belief are refractions of the vision of God. Rumi would accept both suppositions and transcend them. For him, it is a logical necessity that people dispute about religion, even among Muslims. God put the arguments inside us, each of whom continues a wide variety of opinions, symbolized by the seventy-two sects, in our internal forum. This plurality arises from flaws, created by the intellect, yet each opinion is in its way an attempt to worship God. The deeper religion is the trans-religious mystery of love of God which the intellect can never really understand. This love manifests itself in many (i.e. seventy-two) madnesses and takes the soul beyond the world of being. Ultimately, we not only accept pluralism among Muslims, but among all the mysterious paths of the love of God.

Rumi, whose *Masnavi* may be the greatest spiritual epic of the Islamic tradition, proves to be above categorization as a 'pre-modern' or 'modern' sensibility. He believes that there are right and wrong opinions about Islam (and, indeed, about religion in general). But he leaves such judgement to God, since we live in the world of 'shadow', where conflict is inevitable. He urges upon us the ultimate pluralism: to respect the other's quest as springing from the same impulse as our own, without giving up faith in our own spiritual belief.

The Islamic tradition offers more than one path to pluralism. I think a strong argument for pluralism can be made on the basis of some thinkers' view of innate human nature, *fitra*. In any case, Rumi's path seems to me spiritually and intellectually powerful. But it also tells us something about the uses of tradition. Hundreds of millions of Muslims have lived over the past fourteen centuries since the life of the Prophet, and there are many voices and approaches in this vast and varied tradition.

Given the sociological realities of the religious world in which we live, Muslims must and can find in their tradition authentic voices that speak for an acceptance of pluralism. The wanton killing of Iraqis in an attempt to ignite a civil war between Sunnis and Shi'is warns us of the need to establish a strong ethical basis for pluralism among Muslims. And the fates of Muslim minorities – in the case of India, the second largest Muslim community in the world – show that, if one urges Muslims to embrace pluralism, one should also urge their non-Muslim neighbours to embrace

difference. Here I address a criticism to the stubborn secular religion of France. Surely a Muslim woman should be free to wear a
headscarf to school, as a Jewish man should be free to wear a yar-
mulke and a Catholic nun to wear a habit.

The message of Rumi is not some mealy-mouthed multiculturalism. Rumi is a devout believer. Yet he recognizes that others are
not only free to disagree with him, but that God supplies the arguments of disagreements. Certainty is structurally impossible in
the mundane realm and, as the Sufi theologian al-Ghazali had
said, instead of 'true religion' we have human knowledge of religion. Yet we all see the high value of truth and right belief and
would surrender to it if it were self-evident. Correct belief may be
one path, but all imaginable forms of belief live inside us and their
presence is not to be denied. The seventy-two sects are not even
fully aware of each other's existence, although the members of
these sects – like every inanimate object – knowingly or unknow-
ingly worship God.

And let no one say Rumi is impossibly far from the Qur'an, the
pivotal text which for so many Muslims remains central to their
belief. In the fifth *sura* of the Qur'an, *Surat al-Ma'ida*, verse 48
reads:

> To you We sent the scripture with truth, confirming the scripture
> that came before it, and guarding it in safety; so judge between
> them by what God has revealed, and follow not their vain desires,
> diverging from the truth that has come to you. To each among you
> have We prescribed a law and a clear way. If God had so willed, He
> would have made you a single people, but [God's plan] is to test you
> in what He has given you; so vie with each other in good works.
> The goal of all is [to hasten] toward God; for it is [God] who will
> show you the truth of the matters in which you differ.

For the Qur'an, too, diversity of belief is divinely initiated, and the
common goal, known or unknown, is God. God urges all communities of belief to strive with each other, as in a race in all
virtues. We can see this passage as a direct inspiration to Rumi.

3

Being One and Many Among the Others: Muslim Diversity in the Context of South Asian Religious Pluralism

Dominique-Sila Khan

Having one of the largest Muslim populations in the world, India is, according to its Constitution, a 'secular state' where people are free to practise the religion of their choice or to abstain from professing any particular faith. The official census conducted every ten years has long ceased to ask citizens about their caste (*jati*). However, it continues to register their religious affiliation, as did the British census during the colonial period. Although figures may be misleading, they certainly reflect some aspects of the reality: about 12 per cent of the people register themselves as followers of Islam – and it is often asserted that, if the partition between India and Pakistan had not taken place, Muslims would presently have made up more than a quarter of the total population. At this juncture, two important questions arise: What actual choice do the citizens have (in terms of categories in censuses) when asked about their religion? And what motivates a secular state such as India to register a person's religious affiliation?

Let me examine the first question. Theoretically, in a secular democratic state, citizens may reply to such questions as they wish, regardless of official classifications. They may declare that they have no religion or propose their own, even invented, denomination. However, in India, since its independence, the majority of answers given by citizens responding to the question of religious affiliation in censuses have fallen into the officially recognized categories of Hindu, Muslim, Christian, Buddhist, Sikh, Jain, Jew and Parsi. There are very few respondents who place themselves outside these categories and state, for example, that they have no religion, are 'atheists', 'animists' or 'Mohammedan Hindus'.[1]

The current situation has its roots partly in the British colonial period when some of these categories were introduced. Such categories, the juridical process by which they were enforced, and the manner in which they were adopted by locals and the state, triggered a complex process which resulted in a limited number of options from amongst which people are practically obliged to choose when responding to an official census.[2]

The second question, concerning the state's motivation, can be understood in terms of law and, particularly, of personal law. Categories such as 'Hindu' and 'Muslim' derive from a model of governance established by the British in colonial Bengal in 1857, after the assumption of direct rule by the Crown, and later adopted, by and large, throughout the Raj. This model was essentialist and binary: one could be classified as 'Hindu' or 'Muslim'. Such a process was achieved after having considerably simplified the former colonial legal formulations that were much more complex, such as the one applied until a certain period in the Bombay Presidency.[3] The Raj's formula of communal governance was subsequently adopted by secular India, with the similar purpose of applying different personal laws to distinct communities.

Hence, the creation of a law defined as 'Hindu personal law' or 'Muslim personal law' demanded that the categories of Hindu and Muslim should also be properly defined in the Constitution, so that laws could be applied without difficulty. As has often been remarked, this resulted in a rather paradoxical situation. That is to say, the classification, which has been established by a secular state in order to ensure the freedom of its citizens, has consequences that affect the very ideal of secularism espoused in the Indian Constitution. While the legal structure inherited from the colonial period is preserved, plurality is transformed into a simplistic binary division, and pluralism tends to be replaced by dualism. No room seems to be left for those who stand 'on the threshold'.[4] Does this reflect what one can observe in contemporary India?

This paper is an attempt to examine the self-expressions of individuals and communities about their personal and communal identity as a form of counterpoint to those same expressions, as they are re-presented in official documents such as a constitution or a census.[5] It also attempts to provide some means of understanding how plurality may be understood in South Asia. My discussion is based on examples from fieldwork conducted in North India, mainly Rajasthan and Gujarat, during the last twelve years.

Being One: The construction of Islam as a uniform religion in South Asia

When asked which community they belong to (the word 'community' in Hindustani is generally expressed as *jati* – which means 'caste'), most Indian Muslims simply reply '*musulman*'. Whereas, were the same persons to answer this very question asked by their co-religionists, they might define themselves more specifically by mentioning their *jati*, which, among the Ajlafs,[6] generally correspond to a traditional occupation such as *lohar* (blacksmith), *kasai* (butcher), *manihar* (bangleseller), or, among the Ashrafs, the *Sayyids* (descendants of the Prophet's family), the *Mughals* (descendants of the Mughals rulers) or others. All this shows that, in the South Asian context, Islam appears as one uniform religion only when confronted with the 'other'.

Muslims as Muslims

Three years ago, during a trip to Kutch, in Gujarat, I visited the well-known tomb of the sixteenth-century Nizari Ismaili Muslim missionary Pir Dadu, located in Bhuj (the Nizari Ismailis are a branch of Shi'i Muslims). The *sajjada-nishin* (spiritual successor of the Pir) was not there, but there was a caretaker (*mujavar*) and I asked him about his community – curious to see if he would be aware of Pir Dadu's Ismaili-Shi'i connections. The *mujavar* (a modest title he claimed for himself) initially responded to my questions concerning religious affiliation by stating: 'Well, I am a Muslim, of course ….' Dissatisfied with this too brief answer, I said: 'Yes, indeed, I know, but what kind of Muslim are you?' He looked puzzled and did not reply. Eventually, because I insisted, he repeated: 'Isn't it clear? I said I was a Muslim ... a Muslim is a Muslim ....' 'Sunni or Shi'a?' I asked. He answered: 'I am a Sunni.' 'And what about Pir Dadu?', I added. 'He was also a Sunni, of course', replied the *mujavar*.

The idea of a single Islam

The above example refers to the contemporary Indian context. I would argue that it reflects a phenomenon that emerged about one century ago, out of the British colonial context. From the colonial operations of classification and communal governance resulted perceptions and articulations about religion which were wholly different from those articulated prior to colonization. The dominant framework which colonial officials worked with was that there was 'one form of Hinduism' and that there was 'one form of Islam'. Indeed, it has been argued that the term 'Hinduism' did not exist until the eighteenth–nineteenth century, and that there had not been, in the past, one single Indic faith that could be named as such. Hinduism, as it is now understood, is partially the consequence of colonial imagination. But it was also adopted and used by local revivalist organizations such as the Sanatan Dharm Movement and by philosophers like Vivekananda. Thus, while the British conceived of Hinduism on the model of the world's 'great religions', along with Christianity and Islam, reformists spared no effort to prove – and eventually create – the timeless existence of one single indigenous Hindu creed, the '*sanatan dharm*' – the eternal religion.[7]

As for Islam, the issue is more complex. The apparently simple way of distinguishing between 'one faith' and a mere jumble of beliefs and practices, by determining the historical existence of one founder and the authority of one scripture, may be misleading. The fact of having a common origin and heritage does not necessarily result in the formation of a religion that can be unambiguously perceived as one. The bitter controversies and the bloody wars that have been fought between Catholics and Protestants, or Sunnis and Shi'is, at various times in history provide ample evidence for this.

In the field of Islamic studies, emphasis on the extraordinary diversity of past and present Muslim traditions is a relatively new trend. Aziz Esmail has suggested that it is only in the modern period that a new self-consciousness emerged, that was partly a product of Muslim reaction to Western imperial power. One of the results of this process was an idea of Islam which gave birth to a new obsession: 'separating the "Islamic" from the "non-Islamic".'[8] Indeed, Esmail states:

> what many text-books on Islam assume to be the standard definition of Islam is by and large an uncritical assumption. It assumes an orthodoxy when, in fact, the orthodox definition was the outcome of a long historical process. This process was a struggle in which many intellectual actors who had once been prominent on the stage were treated as marginal.[9]

I should like to briefly recall the different factors that contributed to the construction of a uniform Islam and the notion of a single Muslim community in India between the end of the nineteenth and the beginning of the twentieth century. In his book entitled *The Origins and Development of the Tablighi Jama'at (1920–2000)*,[10] Yoginder Sikand provides a survey of the various Muslim movements that influenced India before and after independence. It shows how the formation of this *ummat* could occur only by reforming or abolishing beliefs and practices (i.e. what is often referred to collectively as 'popular Islam') that were characteristic of a good part of the local population. Such beliefs and practices were condemned as *shirk* (heresy) and *bidat* (innovation). These reformers used a powerful 'language of shared symbols serving an abstract concept of community'.[11]

The climate of these religious reforms was highly political, in which social status along with other means of accessing power was at stake. Thus, like their Hindu counterparts, members of the Muslim elite 'felt the need for numbers'[12] – in order to maintain or improve their position in a country where the 'others' were the majority. This 'race for numbers' resulted in the gradual construction of a Muslim community and of one Islam which, ultimately, were placed in opposition to one imagined Hindu community[13] and a uniform Hinduism. At this juncture, it would be interesting to examine the extent to which such ideas are expressed in contemporary India.

Uniformity as solidarity: A minority's concern

The issue connected with the formation of a new Muslim *ummat* in post-independence India deserves to be briefly discussed here. It cannot be separated from the various attempts that were made at shaping one single Hindu identity. Paradoxically, if Pakistan has not yet achieved the process that should transform it into a 'fully fledged' Muslim state, secular India, with its majority of people referred to as Hindus, may well be on its way to creating a Hindu nation, albeit unwittingly. In order to become a reality, the 'inferiority complex of the majority', as Jaffrelot has it, supposes a number of conscious calculations that ultimately appears as a 'game of numbers'.[14] That is, the alleged threat posed by Muslims in India to Hindus, and their supposedly aggressive missions of conversions, has its counterpart in the invention of a Hindu 'resistance movement'. This perceived threat, in turn, appears to trigger reactions among Muslims.[15]

As such, within the contemporary Indian context, the unity of Islam (among Muslims) may be regarded as imagined, insofar as it may be perceived as a temporary wave of religious solidarity. In the same way that sectarian quarrels within a religious community are downplayed when threatened by a common 'external other' but resurface in times of peace, present-day uniform presentations of Muslims in India and elsewhere are likely to be shattered in the future. In some cases, the unity between one's co-religionists is not a positive construction but a negative one. Ironically, it may result in the imagined uniformity of the religion of the adversary.

Among the factors that contribute to the idea that there are, indeed, monoliths such as Hinduism, Judaism and Christianity are the various discourses in which a certain number of characteristics continue to be seen as 'typical of one religion'. Some of these stereotypes are reinforced when there are fears or responses to real or imaginary threats, naïve testimonies of recognition or even blind fascination. Some of these stereotypes are, indeed, so enduring that they continue to be repeated without any consideration for the facts on the ground.

Take, for instance, the issue of violence versus non-violence. The colonial imagination in India saw and re-presented Islam (and perhaps, by extension, all Muslims themselves) as basically and intrinsically violent: not only its history, but its very roots were supposed to account for this phenomenon. Non-violence (Sanskrit, *ahimsa*), on the other hand, is often believed to be a creation of 'Hindu' and related indigenous religious movements, such as Buddhism and Jainism. Let me provide one example from 'Hindu' popular history which suggests an alternative reading of this widespread assumption.

A local legend, nowadays told mostly by Muslims, seeks to legitimate the present form of the goddess cult of Shila Devi, an aspect of Kali, whose image was brought from Bengal in the sixteenth century and is enshrined in the royal temple of Amber, the former capital of Jaipur State. According to an oral tradition, human sacrifices to Shila Devi were regularly performed until, in the sixteenth century, a Sufi saint appeared and taught the goddess a lesson, forcing her to renounce this custom and be content with animal sacrifices. Gebi Pir, as the mysterious mystic is referred to, still has a shrine at Amber, where he is equally worshipped by Muslims and Hindus.

In the legend, non-violence appears as a characteristic of Islam rather than of Hinduism. Here, the dichotomy between the tenets of Islam and the 'barbarian' custom of human sacrifices, portrayed as typical of the Hindu warrior-princes, is played up.

Tradition has it that Man Singh, the very ruler who installed the sacred image and once allowed the cruel ceremony to be performed, became a devotee of the Muslim saint. It may not be out of place to add that Raja Man Singh I was also Akbar's commander-in-chief, and that his campaign in Bengal, from where he brought the idol, was fought on behalf of the Mughal emperor.

Similarly, Mahatma Gandhi's ideal and 'strategy' of non-violence has often been misinterpreted. Many scholars have argued that this ideal originated from Gandhi's native region, Gujarat, where Jainism was still influential. Indeed, the Jains are known for their reluctance to kill the smallest creature – a trait that has become one of the most worn-out clichés repeated by Westerners but also by Indians, including the Jains themselves. Similarly, Gandhi's highly praised tolerance for different systems of belief is regularly perceived as a characteristic of a 'tolerant' and 'universal' Hinduism. Actually, an often forgotten chapter of his life concerns his association with the Pranami movement, whose seventeenth-century founders espoused and practised tolerance and passive resistance. The grand and encompassing vision of the religious leaders of the Pranami, tradition declared their religion to be the fulfilment of all other previous, albeit incomplete, religions. What is crucial is that Gandhi's early associations with the movement have been considerably underplayed, if not consciously obliterated, in numerous biographies on him, as well as in his autobiography.[16]

In his autobiography, Gandhi admits, *en passant*, that his mother, Putli Bai, was a Pranami and that he himself, in his childhood, followed his mother who introduced him to this religion: he went to their shrine in Porbandhar and, as is still the custom for the contemporary followers of the movement, read from the Gita as well as from the Qur'an.[17] What Gandhi omits is the fact that the holy scripture of the sect, the Qulzam Sharif, explicitly defines the Pranami religion as 'Islam' or '*din-e-islam*', as does the seventeenth-century biography of its founders, the *Bitak* of Laldas – never calling it Pranami or Nijanandi, as it is currently done. Indeed, the Pranami movement is often portrayed by non-Pranamis (when not by Pranamis themselves) as one of the numerous Hindu 'orthodox' Vaishnava sects that flourished in India.

In a central episode of the hagiography of Mahamati Prannath, one of the founders and the main sacred figure of the Pranamis, there is an encounter between Prannath's twelve disciples and the Mughal emperor Aurangzeb, one of the 'selected souls' or '*ummat-i-khass*', whom the master strives to awaken. However, failing to recognize his real self, Aurangzeb sends his soldiers to put the faithful into jail. It is at this juncture that Prannath's disciples consciously resort to 'passive resistance' – a strategy that is said to originate in the ideal of non-violence.[18]

In sum, Gandhi's early association with the Pranami tradition may suggest (contrary to the present declarations) that the 'father of the nation' was not a 'fully fledged' Hindu: he was, at least, during the first years of his life, more of a crypto-Muslim. As he readily admits when alluding to the Pranamis (although these words are seldom quoted): '… many people thought they were secretly Muslim …'.[19]

However, the point I wish to make here is not so much about origins as about the politics of religious representation: how would we categorize the Pranamis? How do contemporary categorizations account for the historical development of such groups and their multi-stranded and sophisticated discourses and practices? The case of the Pranamis exemplifies the limits of labels such as 'Islam' and 'Hinduism'.

Being Many: Plurality and pluralism

For many non-Muslim Indians today, the word 'Muslim' has a restricted meaning: it refers most often exclusively to Sunnis. The same can be said of the term 'Hindu', which is generally restricted to Brahmins and members of the upper castes.[20]

The diversity amongst Muslims, when expressed, is often spoken about in terms of simple dichotomies, such as Sunni/Shi'i, exoteric (legalistic)/esoteric (Sufi), *ba-shar/be-shar* (orthodox/heterodox), tolerant Chishtis/intolerant Naqshbandis, etc.[21]

Such dichotomies do not correspond to the situation on the ground (both in the past and in the present) and appear full of contradictions and exceptions. For example, the Shi'is also consider themselves to be 'orthodox' Muslims, and some Sufis have been fierce guardians of Sunnism. The point of the matter is that the types of Muslims mentioned above live in contemporary India in various configurations and guises.

Not only do all these classes of Muslims exist in modern India, but many more types can be found. Actually, new complexities emerge at every stage of field inquiry. Apart from the fact that these traditional divisions do not cover the whole range of Islamic traditions, they are often expressed with multiple caveats. Confronted with reality, the factual and 'passive' plurality of Islam gives way to a dynamic pluralism that plays an important role at the social and economic levels. Traditional divisions become mere clichés that hardly coincide with the facts.

I will illustrate the phenomenon of pluralism with a scene I once saw. Seated under the stone canopy of a small *chilla* (cenotaph), four Muslims who came to worship the same *pir* each exemplified a particular version of Islam: the first one, who was a royal musician, wore the traditional red turban (*pagri*) typical of the Maharaja's servants; the second wore a white skullcap, a fashion conventionally associated with Sunni Muslims; the third person donned a tall cap, usually associated with Sufis (Muslim mystics); and the fourth devotee wore the white and red headgear often associated with Arabs.

Let me propose here another typology that completes, but also challenges, the conventional divisions that have been mentioned above. This three-fold classification emerged from long fieldwork conducted mainly in Rajasthan and Gujarat. I will first introduce and describe these categories, before trying to analyse their meaning for the concept of pluralism.

Multi-Islamic Islam: Many Muslims in the mind of one Muslim

The weight of traditions, the impact of reforms, ambition and fear, shame and pride are factors which combine within a single person: he or she wishes to remain faithful to sacred traditions and, at the same time, to be perceived as 'civilized' and 'modern'. Let me describe the case of Abdul Sattar, the caretaker of a tiny *chilla* located in Jaipur and dedicated to a mysterious Sufi saint popularly known as 'Sarpvale Baba' (lit. the Snake Pir), who simultaneously appears as a *be-shar qalandar* (wandering Sufi mystic) and as an 'orthodox' Sunni. Abdul Sattar's personal story accounts for the phenomenon that endows him, like many of his co-religionists in India, with a kind of multiple personality. This Ajlaf, born into a poor family, became the disciple of an Aghori yogi[22] (Hindu ascetic), before being accepted as the main *murid* of a Muslim wandering dervish who once attended the *chilla* of Sarapvala Baba. After his *pir*'s death, Abdul Sattar became the new caretaker of the shrine. Although he may be conventionally classi-fied as a 'Sunni', like many traditional *qalandar*s, Abdul Sattar did not initially follow the *shari'a*. A few years ago, he was approached by a learned Muslim, who may have been a member of the Tablighi Jama'at or of a similar reforming organization. This per-son attempted to correct what he regarded as Abdul Sattar's ignorance. Be this as it may, the man taught Abdul Sattar (among others) how to perform the five daily prayers and how to read the Qur'an. Abdul Sattar accepted his teaching and declared that he would abide by the Sunni *shari'a*. However, he never thought of relinquishing his position at the shrine of Sarpvale Baba, whose cult is strongly condemned by some Sunnis, owing to the ambiguous status of the shrine's eponymous founder.[23] In fact, Abdul Sattar effectively superimposed onto his former beliefs and practices the elements that were taught to him by the member of the reforming organization. This character embodies in Abdul Sattar different and seemingly contradictory aspects of Islam, but it is worthwhile not-ing that these contradictions do not seem to concern him.

Crypto-Islam: Imamshahi and Ismaili Guptis

This category is partly the consequence of precautionary dissimu-lation or *taqiyya*, as practised during different periods of history by numerous Shi'i communities in South Asia. The case of the Nizari Ismaili communities in South Asia is illustrative of this practice: the Nizaris survived in the guise of Sunni Sufis or Hindus of various denominations, being later, for this reason, referred to, in some instances, as Guptis or 'the secret ones'.[24] The various and far-reaching consequences of this practice of precautionary dissimulation have not been sufficiently studied.[25] Here, I am concerned with more recent politics of dissimulation among certain Gupti groups as a response to emergent Hindu fundamentalism. Before analysing this aspect, I should like to recall a central episode in the early modern history of the Ismailis in India.

In the late 1800s and early 1900s, Sultan Muhammad Shah, Aga Khan III, attempted to gather around himself members of the Nizari community of South Asia, many of whom had for generations lived in concealment. Aga Khan III convinced many of his followers, who were outwardly living as Hindus, to come out of concealment and profess openly their faith, as a branch of Shi'i Islam.[26] During this time, there were some members of the community who adopted Sunnism, Twelver Shi'ism or became 'fully fledged' Hindus. Others still chose to remain Guptis.

Among the latter communities, there were those who accepted the Aga Khan as their imam, joining the wider Nizari Ismaili community, albeit forming a separate *jama'at* referred to as the 'Gupti *jama'at*'. But there were also those, such as the Imamshahi Guptis, who did not join with the Aga Khan and maintained their former affiliation to the Imamshahi Satpanth.[27]

For these Imamshahi Guptis, whose centuries-old practice of *taqiyya* had been used to assume a complex and fluctuating set of identities, there has remained the necessity of continuing *taqiyya* due to the recent threats posed by emerging Hindu right-wing organizations in Gujarat and throughout India. In particular, the *dharm paravartan* (conversion) campaign of the VHP (Vishva Hindu Parishad or 'Pan-Hindu' Committee), which started in the late 1980s, forced the Patidars (members of an agricultural caste representing about 75 per cent of the Imamshahis) who wished to follow the traditional Imamshahi Satpanth to remain Guptis.[28]

The story (which was related to me by a number of informants) goes as follows. In the 1980s, the *mujavar* of the Pirana shrine, Kaka Karsan Das, assuming the Hindu title of *Acharya*, and claiming to be the true spiritual leader of the community, started a series of reforms aimed at 'Hinduizing' the movement, in order to make it acceptable to the ideology of the Sangh Parivar (a group of Hindu right-wing organizations and political parties). Such Hinduizing efforts included certain modifications in the rituals and in the sacred literature of the Imamshahi Satpanth. At this time, those who followed Kaka Karsan Das gave up all pretence of being Muslims and strove to prove their 'original Hindu faith' by means of confession and practice. Others among the community preferred to resort to *taqiyya* and continued to secretly perform the traditional ceremonies of the Imamshahi Guptis under the guidance of a Sayyid, who claimed descent from Imam Shah, and of a few 'rebellious' Patidars.[29] The case of two Satpanthi women living at Pirana and belonging to the Kachia Patel community (a caste of vegetable sellers) is illustrative of such actions.[30] These two women claimed to be staunch devotees of the Satpanth and they refused to acknowledge the Kaka's reforms, but, for fear of persecution, outwardly accepted the new, Hinduized, version of Satpanth. While attending some of the reformed Satpanthi rituals organized by Karsan Das, they continued to perform secretly the 'original' version of the Imamshahi ceremonies in Ahmedabad, under the guidance of the person whom they regarded as their true *murshid,* the Sayyid who claimed to be the spiritual heir of Imam Shah and the *gaddi-nishin* (hereditary head) of the main shrine.

They also recited in front of me the traditional version of the Satpanthi *du'a'* (prayers). These prayers begin with the *shahada*, the Muslim profession of faith. Therefore, it is logical to conclude that these devotees are true followers of Islam, although outwardly they behave as members of the reformed community led by Kaka Karsan Das. Hence, unlike the case of Abdul Sattar described above, who knowingly oscillates between two modes of being Muslim, the two women outwardly suppress their Muslim identity in response to the pressures of an internal other, but maintain their beliefs in private.

Islam as practised by Hindus: The case of Prem Mali

The third category I should like to examine is that of 'Islam as practised by Hindus'. This may sound like a conundrum, but it deserves some serious consideration. The fact that many Hindus visit Muslim shrines, where they make offerings and vows, is generally analysed and understood in two ways by the authors, who have studied this interesting, although quite common, phenomenon in South Asia. Some scholars view the sharing of sacred spaces, times and figures of differing religious traditions as the consequence of common belief in the divine power of deities and saints.[31] The reverence for a specific sacred figure has nothing to do with one's particular creed, but rather transcends religious boundaries. Others interpret phenomena such as the worship of Muslim *pir*s by devout Hindus as a reflection of the intrinsically eclectic nature of Hinduism. Some devotees themselves insist that going to Muslim shrines and participating in Muslim festivals does not prevent them from remaining 'fully fledged' Hindus. Some Muslims, instead, think that the Hindus who worship the *pir*s do not in any way come closer to Islam, as their perception of a Sufi shrine remains 'typically Hindu' and does not encourage them to change their usual beliefs and rituals. Before giving my interpretation of this phenomena, let me provide an example of such practices, which I observed during my fieldwork in Jaipur.

The shrine of Mama-Bhanje, located near Jaipur, is one of the many Muslim *dargah*s scattered in the capital of Rajasthan and around it. Although the majority of devotees, Muslims and Hindus alike, belong to the lower caste groups, mainly artisans' communities such as nilgars and chhipas (respectively Muslim and Hindu dyers), the lohars (ironsmiths of both communities), kasais and katiks (Muslim and Hindu butchers) and malis (Hindu gardeners), a relatively recent transformation encourages the Muslim caretakers to re-align the shrine, as well as their religious practices along more 'normative' forms of Islam, or rather along Sufi Ashraf[32] (noble families) and *ba-shar* (orthodox) patterns.

The most interesting fact about this shrine is the regular presence of a Hindu priest, Prem Mali, a middle-class government servant who generally visits the *dargah* (Muslim shrine) once a week.[33] Prem Mali claims to be possessed by the *shahid* (saintly martyr), allegedly buried in the sacred compound. The mysterious *shahid*, whose name seems to be unknown to caretakers and devotees alike, but is referred to as 'Mama' (maternal uncle), is believed to have miraculous healing powers that Prem Mali acquires during his trance. His *bhanja* (maternal nephew), buried near him, is instead endowed with more limited powers. Nearly every Sunday, Prem comes to the shrine and attends to a crowd of devotees, although he never accepts money nor even sits for the traditional *langar* (common meal) in which Hindus and Muslims, both of high and low castes, participate.

What follows is an account of my observation of Prem Mali at the shrine in April 2002. The Hindu priest climbed into the enclosure of the main tomb where offerings of flowers, incense and *itr* (perfume) had just been made. After a short time, he came into a trance and started to mutter a few words that were actually the beginning of the *shahada*. He went on speaking in Urdu and raised his hands in the gesture of a *du'a'*. Then the devotees, both Hindus and Muslims, came near him one by one and he asked them what they wanted. In turn, he answered their questions and proposed solutions to those who explained their problems. I noted that as long as Prem Mali was possessed by the *shahid*, he uttered certain Arabic and Urdu words, but when the possession/ healing session was over, he resumed his former personality and apparently became an 'ordinary' North Indian, Hindi-speaking Hindu.

Now, a few days later, when I paid Prem Mali a visit at his home in Jaipur, I observed that he kept images of gods and goddesses in a manner commonly practised by Hindus. Hence, those who did not visit the *dargah* of Mama-Bhanje would never suspect that he was in any way connected with Islam or Muslim practices. However, even if such an accusation were brought forth about his Muslim activities at the shrine, he could probably state in defence that it is not him who recites the *shahada*, but rather the saint who was buried there. The fact that Prem Mali assumes a different (Hindu) name when he is at the Muslim shrine (Prem is not his real name) would also be brought forth as further evidence that it is not he who acts out Muslim practices.

What is striking in many cases is that individuals alleged to be possessed display a remarkable knowledge of Muslim traditions.[34]

How do such persons figure within the categories of Hindu and Muslim? If we admit, for example, that the *shahada* is a real profession of faith, any person who recites it without being constrained by force must *a priori* be deemed a Muslim.

Can one be described or categorized as a Hindu and a Muslim at the same time? Again, this question makes sense only if we think in terms of separate and clear-cut categories; it is obvious that they do not at all disturb the devotees for whom they constitute a common phenomenon, albeit divine and supernatural in its orientation.

Redefining Islam in the South Asian context: A preliminary conclusion

The evolution of the multiple Muslims communities mentioned above, having their roots in South Asia and the Islamic religious tradition (as developed in that region of the world in opposition to an 'other', i.e. Hindu traditions), provide examples of the diverse ways in which religious plurality is addressed.

The dominant tendency which one can observe nowadays in the activities of various Muslim reforming organizations is to adopt a sharply marked and bounded understanding of Islam in opposition to a clearly defined Hinduism. In this way, different groups, such as the Imamshahi Guptis or the Sikh Muslims, as the descendants of the musician Mardana (Guru Nanak's Muslim disciple),[35] but even the Pranamis in the context of contemporary India, increasingly find themselves in the position of having to make a choice about their religious affiliation. Much less frequent seems to be the opposite tendency, which characterizes, for instance, some Pranami religious leaders: to accept Islam and other traditions, by espousing a universal religion which encompasses, albeit transcends, all other faiths. Similarly, in the twentieth century, the movement inspired by the Chishti Sufi Inayat Khan around 1910 started as a form of 'encompassing Islam' – a tradition deep-rooted in philosophical Sufism and in 'popular', devotional Islam, which still finds living expression all over South Asia in the worship of *pir*s and *shahid*s in *dargah*s that function as ecumenical shared spaces. Later, Inayat Khan's move-ment was to evolve into a religion called 'Universal Sufism' that eventually renounced even being defined as Islam.[36]

At this stage, we should find a response to the following ques-tion: should we continue to perceive these movements as 'syncretistic'? In a similar way, the apparently strange cases of Abdul Sattar and Prem Mali, discussed above, are far from having become rare; similar practices can be observed in everyday reli-gious life. These tendencies have been hastily perceived as 'marginal', if not 'abnormal', forms of religious 'syncretism'.

As I have explained elsewhere,[37] the term 'syncretism', which has been used indiscriminately to account for all religious move-ments or communities that cannot be easily defined as 'Hindu' or 'Muslim', is rather misleading. By oversimplifying a number of complex and distinct phenomena, this term ultimately conceals more than it reveals. 'Syncretism' is a concept that could, instead, be applied to all world cultures and religions, if one accepts the fact that these have never been 'pure' or 'fixed' entities, and that, everywhere and at each stage, civilizations are necessarily 'syn-cretistic', and that is the reason why the ideal models of one encompassing and universal Hinduism or Islam must necessarily be 'syncretistic' if they do not want to shrink to the size of mere sectarian movements that are readily accepted by a minority and forcibly imposed upon the masses as 'orthodoxy'.

The three-fold model described in this article has been sug-gested in order to challenge the taken-for-granted categories that continue to be used in most discussions about religion. Religion, at the individual level, appears as a multi-layered social and men-tal phenomenon that can be analysed with the help of sociological but also psychoanalytical categories. By examining cases of cross-religious possession (a Hindu possessed by a Muslim *pir* and a Muslim possessed by a Hindu deity), Shail Mayaram comes to the conclusion that the usual discourse about 'self' and 'other' needs to be reframed in the religious field as well. Characteristically, one of her informants ends up declaring, 'We believe in both Hinduism and Islam', which logically leads her to think that these ideas 'translated from an individual to a macro-cultural level suggest a far more negotiable and fluid terrain of collective identities'.[38]

While religion is a complex social phenomenon, faith will certainly always remain a strictly personal matter that no material power can ultimately manipulate. And the very fact that communities are constituted by individuals may well continue to ensure enough fluidity to check the tide of religious extremism that has been continuously growing in our times.

To conclude in the same challenging way, let me mention the interesting way in which the contemporary Pranami mainstream, defining itself as 'basically' Hindu, solves the practically insuperable obstacle which stands in their path to a 'fully fledged' Hinduization: the fact is, their religion is constantly referred to as 'Islam' – and never as *Hindu dharm* or even Pranami – in their holy books. The sacred character of the scriptures, and the frequency with which the word is mentioned, precludes any possibility of changing the texts. A solution, however, has been found. In the modern Pranami glossaries, the denomination 'Islam' is defined in the following way: 'The meaning of Islam is peace, faith, devotion on the path to God.'[39]

The 'true spirit' of religion, if any, has certainly inspired this definition which, modern and ecumenical as it is, reaches far back in the past, to the times when Islam emerged as the 'Surrender to God', not so much a new religion as the culmination of previous faiths. As Aziz Esmail has it: 'ultimately even "religion" is a territory with indistinct borders'.[40]

4

Religious Pluralism in the Light of American Muslim Identities*

Patrice C. Brodeur

Introduction

The unprecedented events of 11 September 2001 galvanized American Muslims to examine themselves introspectively, as well as to take account externally of their collective role in the American public square. Internally, a serious process of introspection emerged in light of the Muslim identity of the terrorists, exacerbating an already tense intra-communal tension between a wide range of American Muslim identities. From the outside, the new intensity of the post-9/11 public pressures linked to older patterns of Islamophobia[1] reinforced this self and collective soul-searching, raising many questions anew: How have American Muslims managed their identities as Muslims *and* Americans? How have they negotiated these identities with the rest of the Muslim community worldwide (*umma*)? How are American Muslim identities being articulated and received by non-Muslim Americans at various levels of society? To what extent are processes that have to do with identity, (re)construction and (re)articulation giving way to a critical engagement with public notions of religious pluralism that have grown out of the American soil? This chapter examines these questions, starting with a survey of selected theories on pluralism, followed by a case study of contemporary American Muslims.

* I would like to thank Connecticut College for helping me carry out the initial research for this article, as well as the Rockefeller Foundation and the Joan B. Kroc Institute for International Peace Studies at the University of Notre Dame for the time and space to complete it.

Theories on pluralism

The concept of 'pluralism' was first coined over 200 years ago by Enlightenment philosophers Christian Wolff and Emmanuel Kant.[2] Subsequent theories about pluralism spread from European philosophy in the nineteenth century to a wide range of Western academic disciplines in the twentieth. In the early twenty-first century, the word 'pluralism' has now reached the broader educated public, resulting in countless explicit and implicit definitions that invite academic clarification.

The recent *Routledge Encyclopedia of Philosophy* offers four entries under 'pluralism'. Under the general entry, Edward Craig defines 'pluralism' as:

> a broad term, applicable to any doctrine which maintains that there are ultimately many things, or many kinds of thing; in both these senses it is opposed to 'monism'. Its commonest use in late twentieth-century philosophy is to describe views which recognize many sets of equally correct beliefs or evaluative standards; and in this sense it is akin to 'relativism'.[3]

This broad definition sets the stage for more specific ones, as presented in the other three entries: cognitive, moral and religious pluralism.

Stephen Stich divides cognitive pluralism into three interrelated types: descriptive, normative and evaluative cognitive pluralism. Of the first type, he states that:

> [descriptive cognitive pluralism] has been much debated in anthropology, comparative psychology and the history of science. [It] maintains that different people go about the business of cognition – the forming and revising of beliefs and other cognitive states – in significantly different ways.[4]

Some examples include the cognitive differences between pre-literate versus modern, men versus women, artists versus scientists, well-educated versus poorly-educated, etc.

The second type, normative cognitive pluralism, is not so much concerned with describing different cognitive systems. Rather, it seeks to assess the usefulness of each system. That is, should we or should we not use cognitive system A, B or C? Normative cognitive pluralism lies at one end of a continuum, the other end of which belongs to normative cognitive monism. Thus, while normative cognitive pluralism 'asserts that there is no unique system of cognitive processes that people should use, because various systems that are very different from each other may all be equally good',[5] normative cognitive monism claims that 'all normatively sanctioned systems of cognitive processing are minor variations of one another'.[6] According to Stich, what is important to realize is:

> Among [Western] philosophers, both historical and contemporary, normative cognitive pluralism is a minority view. The dominant philosophical view is that there is only one good way to go about the business of reasoning, or at most a small cluster of similar ways.[7]

In other words, more Western philosophers are clustered towards the normative cognitive monism end of the spectrum than they are towards the normative cognitive pluralism end.

The third type, evaluative cognitive pluralism, despite its name, is more akin to a descriptive rather than a normative thesis. Stich states:

> [Evaluative cognitive pluralism] maintains that people's intuitive concepts of cognitive evaluation, concepts like those that we express with terms like 'justified' or 'rational', vary significantly from culture to culture.[8]

In other words, evaluative cognitive pluralism is not about simply describing a variety of cognitive systems or of assessing how valuable each one is *sui generis*, i.e. assessing its own normativity. Rather, it compares the different rationalities or justification schemes involved in each cognitive system, which 'poses a serious challenge to the tradition of analytic epistemology'.[9] That is, this type of evaluative cognitive pluralism evaluates the diversity of human systems on the basis of Western philosophical categories of rationality that often go unexamined, or are not examined enough.

By contrast to the conventional types of pluralism mentioned thus far, the contemporary philosopher Michael Lynch examines pluralism from the point of view of the central Western philosophical concept of 'truth'.[10] He highlights three theories. First, he discusses the theory of Hilary Putnam, who argues that 'there is a plurality of ways for propositions to relate to reality. The word "true"', Putnam suggests, 'has different uses, depending on whether we are talking about morality, mathematics, physical reality, and so on.[...]'. 'If so', Lynch argues back, 'how can we explain the fact that we can make generalizations about truth?'[11] Second, Lynch cites the theory of Crispin Wright, who 'presents a case for pluralism about truth by arguing for what he calls a minimalist view of the concept [of truth]', while still adhering to taking 'truth as a robust *property* of propositions'.[12] The many different basic principles about truth form a family of principles that are realized by different underlying properties in different discourses. Yet, this family of principles serves 'to single out a single concept of truth'.[13] Wright's approach therefore recognizes the plurality of truth claims linked to different properties, while still claiming that a single concept of truth is possible. Finally, Lynch himself argues for a third type, a functionalist theory of truth. He states:

> A functionalist theory of truth, therefore, takes the concept of truth in every context as the concept of a higher-order functional property of propositions. But that property, by its very nature, can be realized differently in different contexts ... [Therefore, t]he functional role of truth is defined in terms of the place it occupies in a certain network of principles.[14]

Lynch concludes that:

> [pluralist theories of truth] account for the fact that every traditional theory of truth seems plausible in some domains but not in

others. But they also raise serious concerns. For one thing, they seem to imply a pluralism not just about truth but about every philosophical concept related to truth. Thus pluralist theories, no matter what their details, must give us a way to understand what makes one type of 'discourse' differ from another.[15]

But where do the sources of those differences in discourse about 'truth', and therefore 'pluralism', reside? Edward Craig tries to clarify this point by arguing that:

[defining pluralism] is no purely theoretical exercise, for there are also social and political influences favouring certain types of pluralism. Many societies are now culturally and religiously diverse; and 'postcolonial' attitudes make for a far more egalitarian and less judgmental approach to other peoples' practices and beliefs. Sustaining such an attitude, where different cultures find themselves in close contact with each other, indeed for many purposes intermingled, is not without its problems; and it is not clear how far religious believers can sincerely regard other religions in so tolerant a way without in effect giving up their own.[16]

While Craig calls for a contextual reading of the implicit definitions attached to 'pluralism', his last sentence above implies a dichotomous notion of truth, at least as supposedly understood by religious believers. In contrast, Lynch's functionalist theory of truth makes the concept of 'truth' contextual rather than that of 'pluralism', never really defining the word 'pluralism' itself. On the basis of these brief quotes, both philosophers fail to explain the exact relationship between the concepts of 'truth' and 'pluralism'.

The case of American Muslims developed in the third part of this chapter will help clarify this ambiguous relationship. How do the limits of religious 'truth' in highly plural societies translate into practice, such as in the case of American Muslims who live within a highly diverse American religious landscape? How do American Muslims live an authentic Muslim identity when facing so many competing truth claims? According to my understanding of Craig's argument, the more American Muslims increase their tolerance and respect for other religions, the more diluted their own religious identity should become. Craig's perspective implies mutually exclusive truth claims on the part of religious believers, an assumption scholars of religion have dismissed, given the various ways religious believers position themselves relative to others. It is not only that truth claims often imply significant differences in how the concept of truth is understood; it is also that various religious traditions have truth claims which both include and exclude religious others, depending on their degree of closeness to key religious truths. For example, most evangelical Christians hold a notion of truth which separates dichotomously between saved Christians and everyone else. In contrast, most Muslims include Jews and Christians as People of the Book worthy of their tolerance and even respect, while still excluding most other religious and non-religious worldviews.

Therefore, Craig's contextual argument about pluralism is only valid insofar as it raises the important notion that 'pluralism' is understood differently depending on the context of its users. But it fails to understand how different notions of 'truth' among religious believers can coexist at once and possibly change over time, depending on the context. The problem with Lynch's functionalist argument is almost the reverse: while it does provide a strong corrective to Craig's weak understanding of various notions of 'truth', Lynch's argument would benefit from Craig's contextual reading of the variety of definitions for the concept of 'pluralism'. In addition, Lynch does not provide a clear distinction between 'pluralism', as it relates to the variety of individual notions of 'truth' and that of collective behaviour when facing such diversity of truth claims within one pluralistic nation-state.

In different ways, both Lynch's and Craig's respective arguments would suggest that an individual cannot simultaneously serve two masters at once, despite the diversity of understanding regarding both 'truth' and 'pluralism'. Indeed, for decades already, American Muslims, as all other religious Americans, have faced a variety of choices, and all major religious communities reflect a broad spectrum of truth claims and positions on pluralism. However, since 11 September 2001, strong outward social pressure linked to Islamophobia and a narrow nationalistic patriotism has often reduced this broad spectrum of choices to a narrow dichotomy: American Muslims must either serve America or serve Islam. Yet, the evidence I will present in the third part of this chapter about American Muslims demonstrates that it seems possible to serve both, at least in part. To understand this complex relationship between notions of 'truth' and 'pluralism' among American Muslims requires the examination of other theories of pluralism.

Another philosophical current concerning pluralism is termed 'moral pluralism'. Here, what is challenged is not the allegiance to a particular worldview with its specific notion of 'truth' and subsequent implications for understanding 'pluralism'; what is challenged is the very basis of the general argument that claims that human life should adhere to one single foundational system. The philosopher Daniel Weinstock states that:

> [moral pluralism is] the view that moral values, norms, ideals, duties, and virtues cannot be reduced to any one foundational consideration, but that they are irreducibly diverse … [This is so because] morality has developed to protect and promote basic interests related to human wellbeing and flourishing, but that since there is no unique form that human wellbeing must take, there can consequently not be a theory of morality unified around one supreme value.[17]

Weinstock gives a proviso that, unlike the idea of relativism where anything goes, 'moral pluralism holds that there are rational constraints on what can count as a moral value'.[18] The debate as to what those rational constraints are continues in no small measure because the analytical process itself is influenced by subjective contextual constraints. However, one thing is certain: moral pluralism is not politically neutral. It tends to justify 'a liberal view that particular conceptions of the good life ought not to be invoked in the formulation of public policy'.[19] This liberal position, when translated into political discourse, allows for what has come to be known in the West as the separation between church and state. This is an uneasy separation. For example, in the United States, there are individuals and groups, both religious and non-religious, who argue that the notion of moral pluralism is what underlies the need for separation between church and state. They claim that, to respect various moral points of view, the state should not intervene in promoting one moral claim over another; it should act as an arbiter between competing views and protect the right of minority perspectives. This position allows for various moral positions to co-exist within one society, especially in terms of an individual's social life, in particular with regard to norms of pleasure such as those related to drugs and sexual mores, to give but two hotly debated contemporary examples. This *de facto* moral pluralism on the social ground of the American landscape can nevertheless remain subordinate to a higher and singular truth claim, as in the case of collective responsibilities in the name of national security. This example proves the relative nature of the rational constraints behind the moral claims affecting notions of 'truth' and 'pluralism'.

Now there are 'some philosophers [who] have argued that the diversity of our moral concepts is a distinctive feature of modernity'.[20] Yet, for Alasdair MacIntyre, to take only one well-known example, this diversity of conflicting moralities is 'a sign of cultural decay'.[21] Many religious people would agree wholeheartedly with him. To my mind, the challenge of modern and post-modern forms of moral pluralism is the sheer number of available alternatives in comparison to prior historical periods.

These multiple moralities co-exist within what Mark Taylor defines as the moment of complexity in our emerging network culture.[22] Such a moment poses particular challenges for religious people, many of whom claim that their religion provides a coherent system of its own, with the ultimate rationality, morality and finality. Many American religious believers, especially among Christians but also among Muslims, believe that their worldview is therefore not only the best for them; it is the best for everyone else too. They subscribe to an exclusivist worldview that does not seek to co-exist side by side with other moralities and truth claims; they seek to overtake it through various conversion strategies. The resulting religious competition mirrors that of the economic market place. The public realm of politics is no longer perceived as the arbiter of those differences in world-views; it has become a terrain to be conquered, with the same lobbying mentality normally associated with competing business interests. These exclusivist religious perspectives resist the emerging network culture because they might lose many of their institutional and, in the Christian case in particular, theological privileges.

This resistance on the part of those who are popularly known as 'fundamentalists'[23] represents one end of a spectrum on the question of what to do in the face of a society full of various truth claims. At the other end are those who advocate religious pluralism and welcome the emerging network culture. The various reactions to the events of 11 September 2001 have exacerbated the great tug-of-war between the two ends of this spectrum. Certainly, these events shattered the liberal hope (in the West) that there would be a steady progressive flow towards the religious pluralism end of this spectrum. As for historians of religion and philosophy, it has forced many of us to re-examine critically the manner in which American notions of religious pluralism resulting from a particular Western genealogy are currently being exported through the promotion of often narrow definitions of democracy and freedom worldwide. Their underlying assumptions have emerged out of a particular history worth examining briefly.

Philip Quinn argues that, over the last two centuries, three factors have contributed to the development of religious pluralism in the predominantly Christian West: first, the aftermath analysis of traumatizing political events; second, the academic study of religion; and third, inter-religious dialogue. The first factor concerning trauma occurred in two stages. The first stage was one in which 'Christian denominations learned tolerance for one another in the aftermath of the Wars of Religion.'[24] These encounters were then followed by a gradual yet traumatic loss of power for Christian institutions that nevertheless resulted, in the nineteenth and twentieth centuries, in greater tolerance of the growing

numbers of secularists and, more recently, of other religious
worldviews, especially newer immigrant religious communities.
With regard to the second factor, Quinn states:

> When one can read the important texts of other religious traditions
> in good translations with helpful commentaries, one can experi-
> ence for oneself their power, nobility and allure. When one learns
> that the beliefs of other religious traditions are supported by
> experiences and arguments similar to those that support the belief
> of one's own tradition, one is apt to acknowledge the epistemic
> rationality of the participants in other traditions.[25]

'The third and most important factor is the increasing frequency
of intense and cooperative personal interaction among participants in diverse religious traditions. Exclusivists attitudes are
under pressure in such contexts.'[26] Indeed, the most powerful tool
for deep transformation remains face-to-face dialogue, especially
if conducted under clearly agreed upon aims and communication
guidelines.[27] The third section below will briefly consider the
extent to which various American Muslims are engaged in the
academic study of religion as well as in inter-religious dialogue,
and the impact these encounters have on their individual worldviews regarding pluralism in particular.

Diana Eck's definition of pluralism provides an appropriate
finale to this discussion of various theories on pluralism, because
it integrates Quinn's three factors and provides some direction for
further discussion, particularly with respect to the American
landscape. Eck states:

> Pluralism is not an ideology, not a leftist scheme, and not a free-form
> relativism ... [It] is not just another word for diversity. It goes beyond
> mere plurality or diversity to active engagement with that plurality
> ... Pluralism is the dynamic process through which we engage with
> one another in and through our very deepest differences ... It does
> not displace or eliminate deep religious commitments or secular
> commitments for that matter. It is, rather, the encounter of commit-
> ments ... Such dialogue is aimed not at achieving agreement, but at

achieving relationship … Finally, the process of pluralism is never complete but is the ongoing work of each generation.[28]

Eck's definition clarifies the role of human agency in the process of pluralism. Her definition provides a powerful framework for both academic analysis and policy making. However, it does not consider the power dynamics that influence whether or not, and to what extent, achieving 'relationship' is possible, since human agency is subject to human power. The case study which follows aims to demonstrate this point by way of analysing how Muslims in America are going about choosing their definitions of pluralism, especially religious pluralism, given their unique context as a growing religious minority in the most powerful nation-state in the world today.

Comparing Western and Islamic histories on the question of pluralism

In the first section above, I compared several theories on pluralism that have emerged in the West, recognizing that in this unique historical context lie the elements that help explain the diverse yet subjective definitions of religious pluralism being debated today. This Western story is internally diverse because each nation-state developed its own brand of secularism, with very different degrees of separation between church and state, as demonstrated by an extreme separation in France, a close relationship in England, and a middle path in the United States of America.[29] I believe it is therefore inappropriate to seek to impose on emerging democracies worldwide any one Western interpretation of pluralism in general, and religious pluralism in particular, for two reasons. First, this diversity of Western interpretations and realities on the ground calls for a recognition that no one version is the perfect model anywhere, whether in the West or elsewhere around the world. Second, because this internal Western diversity emerged naturally within its own historical trajectory, it cannot be imposed from outside on other societies. What is required at this point of advanced Western influence on nation-building discourses worldwide is an examination of whether these values of respect for religious diversity have existed in other societies, at different times and to what degree. The urgent tasks of contemporary thinkers is to retrieve those histories unique to different areas and peoples around the world, and use them as the local foundations from which becomes possible a healthy integration of the unavoidable dominant Western discourse on democracy, with its corollary notions of religious pluralism.

As a prelude to our case study on competing American Muslim identities in a post-9/11 world, it is useful to consider this question in terms of Islamic history. Were there historical stages and political developments that led to the emergence of Islamic forms of religious pluralism, which can be compared to those that gradually emerged in the Christian, and later secular, West between the sixteenth and twentieth centuries? The case of the famous medieval Andalusian *convivencia* between Jews, Christians and Muslims comes to mind.[30] Such historical comparisons can be perilous if conducted anachronistically and without due attention to historical context. For example, it is often unknown that tolerance for religious diversity in al-Andalus, the Arabic name for this Iberian region, presupposed two important boundaries. The first of these was theological: only Jews and Christians, as the 'People of the Book' mentioned in the Qur'an, reaped the fruits of this tolerance. Other kinds of non-Muslims or fringe Muslim groups did not. The second boundary was political: as long as an Islamic state was in power and controlled the hegemonic Islamic value system, this limited religious pluralism was possible. Hence, unlike the case of early and late modern Western history, the limited religious pluralism that existed during the medieval period of Andalusian *convivencia* did not emerge from an internal Islamic struggle about Muslim diversity that would have resulted in tolerance for intra-Muslim diversity, with positive repercussions for the treatment of non-Muslims at large. Moreover, the concept of the 'People of the Book', as a certain prescriptive tolerance towards others, was already extant in the Qur'an. This concept shaped the theological category that influenced the political discourse.

Any comparative historical analysis that seeks to uncover possible parallels in the development of values promoting religious pluralism requires a careful analytical and interpretive balance between two tasks. First, as done briefly above for the case of Andalusian *convivencia*, each historical focus needs to be analysed within its unique historical horizon in order to uncover the specific rational constraints that led to the internal emergence of these values, akin to what we would call religious pluralism in the West today. Second, a responsible retrieval of these older values is then necessary for the promotion of religious tolerance today, with an effort to retain or adapt the older language and symbols for contemporary political purposes. This balanced approach also needs to avoid two opposite dangers. On the one hand, unexamined generalizations can be manipulated as part of a paternalistic hegemonic discourse of assimilation, which often happens in the West regarding Muslims in particular. On the other hand, unexamined generalizations of an opposite nature can be equally manipulated as part of a contemporary apologetics of resistance against the dominant Western discourse on democracy and pluralism, which often takes place in both majority Muslim countries and within Muslim minorities in many Western countries, including the United States of America.

This comparison of Western and Islamic histories on the question of pluralism is important because many contemporary Muslims and Westerners retrieve it for various political purposes, with a broad spectrum of responses as mentioned above. The following section demonstrates how such retrieval patterns exemplify one of several strategies that emerge in the process of using the past to either promote greater exclusivism or greater religious pluralism, and many positions in between. Deconstructing the case of competing American Muslim identities in a post-9/11 world clearly reveals the complexity of truth claims and diversity of moralities, all of which are shaped by very different rational constraints. Through this case study, it becomes possible to criticize certain aspects of current Western theories on pluralism, while still using them to shed some light on the growing challenges of managing religious pluralism today.

Competing American Muslim identities in a post-9/11 world

It is difficult to make generalizations about American Muslims, especially when it comes to their numbers. In the last five years, population estimates have fluctuated between two and ten million, and turned 'a typically scholarly pursuit into a politically charged one'.[31] Both American Jewish and Muslim communities know the impact these numbers have on political perceptions, whether domestic or foreign. Absence of demographic clarity in terms of religious identity in the United States stems from the fact that relying on the national census to answer questions about religious identity is almost impossible, because questions about religion are purposely excluded following the secular principle of the division between church and state. There is, therefore, no other way to study American Muslims without relying on these recent surveys. Fortunately, the purposes for most of these surveys are broader than simply tallying how many American Muslims exist. Moreover, since the question of number is not central to my argument, their use for my own purposes remains invaluable; an article written ten years ago on the changing nature of American Muslim identities in the context of religious pluralism would have been impressionistic at best. Today, my analysis can rely on the findings of four surveys: 'The Mosque in America: A National Portrait',[32] 'The American Muslim Poll' (2001 and 2004),[33] and 'Islam and Muslims: A Poll of American Public Opinion'.[34] Their respective statistical information provides different vignettes into American Muslim understanding of themselves in relation to each other, and their perceptions of their religious community in relation to the broader non-Muslim American society, as well as to the *umma* worldwide.

How these individual and collective responses relate to one another has been studied in general by the Danish sociologist of religion, Ole Riis. In a way that is reminiscent of Weinstock's position stated in the first section above, Riis argues that 'there is a variety of modes of religious pluralism. Rather than different approaches to a common ideal, these modes of pluralism are political responses to different historical challenges.'[35] In the United States, the political response to diversity of religious practices and worldviews was to promote a form of religious pluralism that narrows religion to the private sphere, because religious beliefs, practices and membership in religious organizations become a personal voluntary decision. A particular set of values to manage this religious diversity has emerged in the course of US history. Riis writes:

> In the American case, these values include freedom, toleration, justice, equality, achievement-orientation, and responsibility. The value system simultaneously stresses individual values, such as freedom and achievement, and collective values which safeguard freedom. According to Parsons, the strength of the American system lies in its ability to absorb particularistic moral movements in the greater, pluralistic system through value generalization. In Europe, a similar tendency is fettered by the nation states.[36]

Prior to 9/11, many American Muslim leaders demonstrated their commitment to these values inherent in the normative American understanding of religious pluralism, through an informal and free integrative process. Two examples of this process on a collective level are the decision by many local mosques to register as not-for-profit organizations (called by its legal number in the USA: 501c3) in order to make donations tax deductible, and the unavoidable process of going through local zoning boards to renovate or construct any building towards mosque congregational needs.[37] One example on an individual level is the choice by many American Muslims to participate in a variety of activities that parallel or overlap with other American religious activities, especially in the political realm.[38] The increase in Muslim participation in inter-faith activities after 9/11 is another more recent phenomenon.[39] In many of these events, American Muslims express eloquently their support for diversity by quoting the following Qur'anic verse: 'We have created you male and female, and have made you nations and tribes that you may know one another' (49:13). By contrast, other American Muslims implicitly downplay this verse by choosing not to participate in any inter-religious activities.[40]

These individual and collective kinds of examples demonstrate how most American Muslims have been absorbed into the American system through a value generation process, which developed internally within the local American Muslim communities as they were finding their place within the diverse American religious landscape. In 1990–1991, this natural process was suddenly jolted by the rise in anti-Arab racism and Islamophobia related to the Gulf War, resulting in an unprecedented growth in national Muslim organizations and implantation of local mosques throughout the 1990s.[41] But in the wake of 9/11, another jolt of much greater magnitude affected the whole American Muslim community.[42] With the widespread and loud display of American patriotism, most American Muslims felt individually pressured to declare their allegiance to the American nation in one form or another. Collectively, national American Muslim organizations immediately responded with declarations condemning these acts of terrorism.[43] They were framed not in exclusive terms of either/or (i.e. being an American or being a Muslim), but rather in inclusive terms: we are both Americans and Muslims. This inclusive expression can be interpreted as a judicious response for strategic political expediency, given the volatile situation immediately following 9/11. It can also be interpreted as a true expression of a vast majority of American Muslims, who suddenly saw their religious identity being hijacked by extremist voices within the complex transnational 'ummatic' community.[44]

A closer examination of this inclusive expression, 'We are both Americans and Muslims', betrays an ambiguity as to how these two identities relate to one another in practice. How is each identity understood by American Muslims and how do these two identities actually relate to one another? Depending on their implicit definitions, the assumptions associated with what 'American' and 'Muslim' mean carry different degrees of contradiction in terms of identity commitment. Let us examine two opposing cases.

On the one hand, an American Muslim using this statement may believe there is a universal and normative Islam that is a total way of life, which includes an understanding of politics that may differ, to varying degrees, from the politics practised in the United States at this point in time. This belief betrays a tension that requires this American Muslim to question seriously how far he or she can combine both his or her dual American and Muslim identities, especially when called to serve in the US army in a war against a majority Muslim nation. This problem first emerged publicly during the 1991 Gulf War. The recent military interventions in Afghanistan and Iraq have increased the immediacy of this difficult problem. In this first case, when the two identities collide, the Muslim identity takes first place over the American one.

On the other hand, another American Muslim using this same statement may believe that his or her identity as a Muslim minority requires him or her to respect the majority law of the land because there are provisions in Islamic law for such flexibility, especially on a short-term basis.[45] This radically different interpretation suggests a hermeneutical process that seeks to integrate Muslim values within an American political framework. This particularistic kind of Islam, however, reflects an implicit understanding of its functional limits (i.e. it gives up claims of making Islam a total way of life, particularly with respect to national politics). In this scenario, Muslims accept and uphold the political values upon which the USA is founded, especially those values related to religious pluralism. When the two identities enter into direct conflict, the American identity must take first place over the Muslim one.

To elucidate this more recent dualistic tension in American Muslim identity discourse, I build on a three-part schema set out by Riis in his analysis of religious pluralism. He states:

> Religious pluralism can be analysed at three consecutive social levels: At the macro-level, religious pluralism implies that the societal authorities recognize and accept a plurality within the religious field. At the meso-level, pluralism implies the acceptance of a multitude of religious organizations which function as competitive units. And, finally, at the micro-level, pluralism implies an individual freedom to choose and develop one's own private beliefs. These

modes of pluralism correspond with *religious toleration, denomi- nalisation and religious freedom.*[46]

On a macro level, the most prominent example is the White House's invitation to Muslims on the occasion of *'Id al-Fitr*, a tradition started by President Bill Clinton and continued by President George W. Bush. There are also many annual inter- faith breakfasts held by city and town mayors. These two examples point to how political authorities at various levels of government recognize American Muslims as part of the fabric of the new religious diversity in the United States. Conversely, by participating in these exchanges, a majority of American Muslim leaders have demonstrated, at least symbolically, that they sub- scribe to an American mode of pluralism which espouses religious toleration.

On a meso level, the proliferation of Muslim organizations, both in terms of community organizations (i.e. mosques) and interest groups of various kinds (i.e. charity, professional, aca- demic, advocacy, etc.), is proof that they are accepted as part of a multitude of religious organizations within a religiously competi- tive civic arena. Since 1965, when a new immigration law came into effect, thus bringing immigrants from around the world in much greater numbers than ever before, there has not only been an exponential growth in the number of Muslims in the USA; other religious communities have also increased rapidly, espe- cially of Buddhism and Hinduism.[47] All new immigrants have been free to choose how they want to relate to the American reli- gious pluralism system. For the vast majority, integration has been the preferred option. In this way, Muslims and many other reli- gious people have had to negotiate what values are their own, which ones overlap with American values related to religious plu- ralism, and what to do about the conflicting areas. In this process, religious communities have been the primary vehicle for the inte- gration of many new immigrants. They have provided spaces for community-based value generalization. Together with the formal educational system, religious communities have effectively edu- cated many new American citizens about the values of their adopted nation-state, including religious pluralism. They have greatly facilitated the construction of law-abiding citizens within their respective religious communities, at least for those who chose to remain affiliated with them. The implication of this unique American process of integration is that American Muslims function *de jure* as one religious group within a religiously plural nation-state. From the perspective of the state, Islam is therefore not viewed as a universalistic religion many Muslims believe it to be; Islam is de *facto* particularistic, in full equality with many other religions.

Finally, on a micro level, the proliferation of Muslim organizations, from Islamist communities to mystically oriented orders, some even claiming a Sufi identity above a Muslim one by not making the first pillar of Islamic doctrine (*shahada*) a requirement, demonstrates how pluralism implies not only an individual freedom to choose and develop one's own private beliefs, but also results in a *de facto* state-induced privatization process that is new in Islamic history. Indeed, the vast majority of American Muslims live their individual religious freedom on a daily basis, 'religious freedom' being understood in the limited contexts of their individual ritual requirements, which includes an individual right to gather collectively with like-minded individuals for the purpose of religious worship. Yet the way Islamic polities have, for the most part up to the colonial period, constantly relied on political leadership that made use of a variety of Islamic discourses to legitimate their own right to political power only shows how recent and utterly new the concept of religious pluralism within a secular state really is for American Muslims.

The adaptation that American Muslims are going through at all three levels – macro, meso and micro – requires not only their subservient integration into the legal, social and moral realities of the United States. It also calls for rethinking the very foundation of what an Islamic religious pluralism can mean in the global dynamics of an 'international community', whose norms are still secular and Western. In this new global reality, American Muslims have a powerful role to play,[48] as their theological and jurisprudential adjustments to make sense of the integration process within American religious pluralism are bound to affect the rest of the *umma*. Indeed, contemporary Muslims across the whole *umma* are formulating anew their personal and collective understanding of religious pluralism, whether they live in the United States or are part of the vast majority of Muslims who live within majority Muslim countries under the dominance of the West, in a so-called 'Pax Americana new world order'.

But these patterns of change are not only one way: the norms of the 'international community' are also being challenged by new transnational movements that cover the whole spectrum, from terrorism to non-violence. These new transnational patterns also affect how researchers need to analyse changing realities on the ground. For example, a traditional approach that would only study the phenomenon of American Muslim identity formation through a comparative national framework, i.e. where citizens of clearly identified nation-states are influenced by and influenced in turn by those of other countries, simply misses the greater complexity of competing identities, both within national discourses as well as beyond them, through transnational forms of identity and institution-building worldwide.

Conclusion

As American Muslims struggle to articulate the tension between the American and Muslim dimensions of their multiple identities, they confront more than the 'threat of double consciousness', defined by Sherman Jackson as the basic challenges of self-definition and self-determination for American Muslims.[49] They deal with three interrelated concerns: 1) their self and communal representations, greatly enhanced by the new phenomenon of surveys about themselves; 2) their place within the national discourse on religious pluralism and its impact on the ground, with all that this entails for self-determination; and 3) their influence on and by different understandings of what Islamic religious pluralism means today, in both various other national contexts throughout the 'ummatic' community and newer forms of transnational Muslim organizations, from al-Qaeda to mystical orders.

These three focuses are not fully co-extensive with Riis's layered (macro-meso-micro) analysis of religious pluralism for two reasons. The first focus relates to both his micro and meso levels, while the second focus relates to his macro level. So what about the third focus? Riis's analysis lacks a supra-national level to address how questions of religious pluralism are addressed in and by the 'international community'. Moreover, Riis's descriptive dualism, which distinguishes between universalistic and particularistic religions, and thus relates directly to the binary tension between American and Muslim identities, does not take account of the fact that the unresolved integration of both identities within the American Muslim community implies an ongoing global struggle as to where the sources of value generalization lie today. Do they rest in nation-states, or do they rest in increasingly powerful transnational organizations, many of which are religious in nature?

None of the theories on pluralism in general, and religious pluralism in particular, presented in this chapter provides a solid explanation for the intersecting levels of a complex web of human interaction today, from local to global. While the theories developed by Weinstock and Riis are extremely useful for their clarification of the plurality, respectively moral and social, of contexts within which identities function, they lack a transnational or meta dimension of analysis. Eck's relational definition of pluralism anchors the role of individuals in the dynamic process of pluralism as: 'we engage one another in and through our very deepest differences'.[50] Yet, her explanation overlooks the complex power dynamics of supra-individual dimensions that affect our thoughts and emotions, from the media and advertising to the myriad governmental and economic institutions that shape our daily lives. Even the new-style political philosophy recently suggested by Veit Bader, to take pluralism seriously by developing an evaluative framework based on the human condition as revealed in the social sciences, also fails to integrate substantively the complex dimensions of identity construction.[51]

The central modern concept of an independent human agency in search of an authentic self, that is to live freely within democratic nation-states, has been undermined by a revival of transnational terrorism and various forms of religious fervour that are greatly affecting world politics today. For American Muslims, and for that matter any human being, struggling to disentangle their competing identities in the face of intertwined local, national and transnational forces, the challenge of understanding how to manage our multiple individual and collective identities becomes more urgent than ever. The present case study on competing American Muslim identities proves that the concept of 'pluralism' requires more serious and immediate scholarly attention, a prerequisite for any substantial changes in political philosophy without which national policies are unlikely to change on the ground.

5

Islamic Art and Doctrinal Pluralism: Seeking Out the Visual Boundaries*

James W. Allan

Surprisingly little has been written about Islamic art from the perspective of its doctrinal plurality. Although Thomas Arnold, in his book *Painting in Islam* (1928), includes a chapter on religious art in Islam, his interest was focused on the religious people or religious stories which were painted by Muslim artists, not on what that represented in terms of the different doctrinal streams within Islam (e.g. Shi'i, Sunni, Ibadi or Sufi). More relevant examples are Sarwat Okasha's book, *The Muslim Painter and the Divine* (1981), which is subtitled 'The Persian Impact on Islamic Religious Painting', and Maria Vittoria Fontana's '*Iconografia dell'Ahl al-Bayt*' (1994), which is a study of Persian images from the twelfth to the twentieth century. However, both these studies are limited in their scope and put their emphasis firmly on painting and on Iran.

More recently, Stephen Vernoit published a short section on Shi'ism and the visual arts in the Khalili collection volume on *Occidentalism* (1997), while Patricia L. Baker produced a book on

---

* This article was written when the author was first involved with inter-faith issues in his previous job at the Ashmolean Museum. In 2007, he gave the Yarshater lectures at the School of Oriental and African Studies, the University of London, on 'Shi'ism, Architecture and Art: Iraq, Iran and India', and since then has completed a book on the subject. There was no time or opportunity to update the present article, and the reader is, therefore, referred to the future book for a further spectrum of ideas. Parts of this chapter are also published in J. Allan, 'My Father is a Sun, and I am a Star: Fatimid Symbols in Ayyubid and Mamluk Metalwork', *Journal of the David Collection* 1 (2003), pp. 25–48.

Islam and the Religious Arts (2003). However, the latter has no
chapter or section specifically dedicated to any of the doctrinal
streams listed above. Some articles, like those by Caroline
Williams and others on the Fatimid Ismaili Shiʿi buildings in
Cairo, are more specific, and look at the possible doctrinal significance of architectural form or decoration.[1] However, others, like
one by this author on the mosques of the Jabal Nefusa in Libya, are
not able to come to any real conclusion on a building's religious
identity, i.e. in this case, whether particular buildings were 'Sunni'
or 'Ibadi'.[2]

One of the problems of identifying doctrinal pluralism in
Islamic art is sorting out elements which are actually due to
doctrine, as opposed to variations resulting from geography, history, or ethnic and cultural differences. Thus, the 'four-*iwan*
mosque' is typical of Safavid Iran, and the 'centralised domed
mosque' is typical of Ottoman Turkey. But that does not mean that
one type of mosque is identifiably Shiʿi and the other is identifiably Sunni. Rather, it could be argued that each mosque type is
part of a different historical, geographical and cultural tradition
which has nothing to do with doctrinal differences. These examples raise a question about the extent to which doctrinal
expressions can exist independently of socio-cultural contexts.

Another source of confusion is the *madrasa*, which in its early
history was a Sunni reaction to the Ismaili Shiʿi *dar al-ʿilm*, and
hence might be seen as a distinct Sunni institution. However, the
madrasa became widespread in Ithnaʿashari Shiʿi Iran, where it followed the same architectural tradition as its Sunni forebears.
Similarly, one might expect Shiʿi shrines to have a distinctive form
and be visually different from shrines built by Sunnis. But that is
only the case for the great Imami shrines of Iraq, which by the time
of the Mongol invasions had developed into complexes with a
domed mausoleum, one or more porticoes, halls, *iwan*s and
minarets, and a surrounding wall. Elsewhere, the local Shiʿi shrine
building tradition focuses on an *imamzadeh*, or tomb tower of
some sort. Similar tomb towers can be found throughout the Near
East. That is, despite the disapproval of Sunni religious authorities,
the Sunni dead of Egypt, Syria and Turkey were regularly buried in

such types of mausoleums. In addition, local Shi'i shrines themselves were not all constructed in an identical manner. Hence, differences within the artistic output among particular doctrinal groups adds to the complexity of marking out visual boundaries in Islamic art.

These problems notwithstanding, the aims of this chapter are to survey a range of examples in different artistic media (architecture, texts and objects) through which doctrinal 'difference' can be discerned, and to examine one historical case in which these differences were particularly highlighted.

Survey

Architecture: Form, decoration and inscriptions

Beginning with architecture, Shi'ism gave rise to some unique building types such as the *takiya*, the arena or theatre used for performances of *ta'ziya*, plays re-enacting the martyrdom of the Prophet's grandson al-Husayn, around the day of 'Ashura'.[3] These performances seem to have begun in the 1840s and lasted just about a century, being ultimately forbidden by Reza Shah Pahlavi (r. 1925–1941) in 1935. However, the form of such buildings was far from standardized. Elements that were common to many *takiya*s were a central platform for the main action, a narrow space around it, and smaller secondary stages. The most famous, the Takiya Dawlat, was inspired by the Royal Albert Hall, where Nasir al-Din Shah (r. 1848–1896) attended a concert during his visit to London in 1873. It was constructed after his return to Tehran, and was demolished in 1946. A famous *takiya* which is still standing is that of Ma'avin al-Mulk in Kirmanshah, which was constructed around 1898 by a local family. It is a complex which contains three buildings: a 'Husayniyya', a 'Zaynabiyya' and an "Abbasiyya". These commemorate members of the Prophet's household, particularly al-Husayn b. 'Ali, Zainab bt. 'Ali, and are used as venues for Muharram ceremonies and to accommodate their participants. Other well-known Husayniyyas are the Husayniyya-yi Mushir in Shiraz and the Husayniyya-yi Amini in Qazvin.[4] Much smaller are the local *takiya*s in Gilani villages, known as *buq'a*s. The individual buildings within some *takiya* complexes, like the Husayniyyas, which incidentally occur more commonly alone, are also specific to Ithna'ashari Shi'ism. However, these are more often defined by the images of 'Ali and al-Husayn which they contain than by their architectural form.

Like Shi'ism, the Sufi or mystical tradition in Islam (drawing its adherents from both Sunnism and Shi'ism) also gave rise to a distinctive building type, the *khanaqa*, where Sufis met and lived, and where they carried out their devotions. These *khanaqa*s are found in their largest numbers during the fourteenth and fifteenth centuries in Cairo, and were usually built under royal patronage. The only architectural requirement is a range of individual cells and a prayer hall. The fact that many *khanaqa*s were part of larger complexes, which included a *madrasa*, mosque or mausoleum, means that they rarely have a single identifiable form. For example, the shrine at Mahan, which is the focus of the Ni'matallahi Sufi order, has breathtaking architectural components in its great halls and courtyards, but does not link in any identifiable way with any other Sufi complexes.

Occasionally, decoration on buildings plays a role in evoking doctrinal affiliation. Thus, for example, Watson, describing the Masjid-i 'Ali in Quhrud, notes that, in twelfth- to thirteenth-century Iran, lustre tiles are found almost exclusively in Shi'i religious buildings.[5] The reason for this is unclear, although it could presumably be the result of the tiles being made in a major Shi'i centre, Kashan, and hence local Sunni antipathy to their use.

Another way in which Shi'i religious buildings can sometimes be distinguished from their Sunni counterparts is by the inscriptions on them. In addition to the inscriptions on Fatimid Ismaili Shi'i buildings in Egypt, which I shall discuss in greater detail below, there are also many buildings with specifically Shi'i (probably Ithna'ashari) inscriptions in Iran. Two examples give some idea of the range. First, a lustre-painted diptych is the foundation plaque of an oratory which has long since disappeared but was built in Kashan, allegedly as a result of a *sayyid*'s (saint's) dream in February 1312: in the dream, the *sayyid* saw 'Ali, who ordered him to build an oratory in the Bagh-e Amir, near Kashan's city walls, an order which he recorded on the foundation tile. Second, a different testimony is provided by a tile-work inscription on the Shiʻi shrine of Harun-e Velayat, which was built in 1512 at Isfahan during the reign of Shah Ismaʻil I (r. 1501–1524).[6] The inscription over the eastern entrance is in tile mosaic, a technique which consists of tiny pieces of variously coloured tile, each one cut to shape to make up a complete design. Here, the doctrinal identity of the building is demonstrated by the saying of the Prophet, 'I am the city of knowledge and ʻAli is its gate', and the names of God, Muhammad and ʻAli, which are set at the apex of the arch. The foundation inscription does much to emphasize the importance of the building's founder, Shah Ismaʻil I, which in turn again emphasises the Shiʻi nature of the shrine.

Being able to identify Shiʻi buildings in this way raises the question of whether one can also positively identify Sunni buildings on a similar basis. In a sense, Sunni Islam is only identifiable in the negative. That is, as it developed, Sunnis did not make the types of specific references to the family of the Prophet in their artistic products in the same manner and to the same extent as did Shiʻis. It may be thought that it is only through the use of the names of the four 'Rightly Guided Caliphs' that Sunni Islam can testify to itself and its opposition to Shiʻism, with its overwhelming emphasis on ʻAli. Even so, the names of the first four caliphs are rarely highlighted in Sunni mosques, for example, but they do occur. Most notable are many of the mosques constructed by the Ottomans, where large wooden discs bearing the relevant names often decorate the interiors of the building.[7] However, the Ottoman evidence is itself confusing, since from time to time these discs also include the names of al-Hasan and al-Husayn, evidencing the general veneration for the *Ahl al-Bayt* (family of the Prophet), in the Islamic tradition.

The Qurʼan and religious texts

Moving from religious buildings to the Qurʼan, we find a rather similar situation. A Sunni Qurʼan is not noticeably different from a Shi'i one. After all, the Qur'an is the Qur'an, and the text is regarded as immutable, whichever Muslim group one may adhere to. Nevertheless, some interesting distinguishing features can occasionally be found in Qur'an manuscripts. Thus, the last page of an Iranian Qur'an dated 1817, now in the Ghassan I. Shaker collection, contains the words: 'the Prophet, peace be upon him and his family...', suggesting that the calligrapher may have been a Shi'i. Another Qur'an in the Ghassan I. Shaker collection, copied by a scribe from Mashhad in 1659–1660, has an opening page bearing a roundel, in which is inscribed: 'The Prophet, God bless him and his family, and grant them salvation, said, "If all the people agreed to love 'Ali, God would not have had to create hell."' Hence, these may have been ways of making clear the Shi'i beliefs of the scribe, patron or owner of a Qur'an. And this raises a very interesting point. Why are so few Ismaili Shi'i Qur'ans from the Fatimid period in Cairo known? For example, although the 1998–1999 exhibition of Fatimid art at the Kunsthistorisches Museum in Vienna included pages from two different manuscripts of the Qur'an, both of these probably originated in Fatimid Tunisia (i.e. before the conquest of Egypt and the establishment of Cairo).[8] No leaves which can confidently be ascribed to the Fatimids at Cairo have ever, to my knowledge, been published. Is it because we have simply been unable to identify them? Or were they indistinguishable from Sunni Qur'ans of the time? Or is it because almost none were produced? Or is it because they have not survived? And if the latter, is it because they were identifiably Ismaili Shi'i, indeed so outspokenly that they were deliberately destroyed by the Sunni dynasties that succeeded the Fatimids?

Apart from the Qur'an, there are particular texts or book types which do enable us to see attempts at defining intra-religious difference. A type of manuscript about which relatively little has been published is the prayer book. Under the Ottomans, there was an extensive production of these, as the recent catalogue of the Ghassan I. Shaker collection shows.[9] One of the most famous was the *Dala'il al-khayrat* of the Berber Shaykh al-Jazuli (d. c. 1465), of which the Ghassan I. Shaker collection contains three Ottoman examples (nos. 52–54): one is undated, but probably late eighteenth century, two others dated 1801 and 1821, and a nineteenth-century Moroccan example (no. 71). The collection also contains a devotional miscellany copied in 1877 (no. 69), which demonstrates the wider variety of prayer books produced for the faithful. Their Sunni character is particularly clear from the illustrations, where the artist includes roundels giving the names of the first four caliphs, without marking out any significance to 'Ali and his progeny. A Shi'i counterpart, the *Monajat* ('Whispered Conversations'), the text of which is attributed to 'Ali, was produced in Safavid Iran. It is usually found with a Persian translation, in verse or prose, alongside. The versified Persian rendition is attributed to the poet Hafiz (c. 1320–1389); the prose version is anonymous. As an example of the *Monajat*, one might cite the manuscript, calligraphed by Mir Imad Sayfi Hasani Qazvini and dated 1601, in the Golestan Palace library.[10]

Another text relating to 'Ali is the *Sad kalimeh* ('Hundred Words'), sayings and aphorisms that are attributed to 'Ali. It was compiled by al-Jahiz (d. 868), and later translated into Persian by Rashid al-Din Vatvat (d. 1177), who also added a commentary, and re-titled the work *Matlub-i kull-i talib* ('The object sought by every seeker'). The Persian poet Jami (d. 1492) made a verse translation of this text. An example calligraphed by Abdul Jabbar Isfahani and dated 1789 is in the Golestan Palace library.[11]

Another distinctively Shi'i text which was carefully copied and illuminated was the *Sahifa-ye sajjadiyyeh*, a collection of prayers and devotions attributed to the fourth Shi'i Imam, Zayn al-'Abidin (d. 714), the grandson of 'Ali through his son al-Husayn. An example calligraphed by Muhammad Shafii Arsinjani in 1892 is in the Golestan Palace Library.[12]

Naturally, none of the former three texts lent themselves easily to illustration, since they are sayings, prayers and devotions. A text which was often illustrated, however, is the *Ahsan al-kibar fi ma'rifat al-a'imma al-athar* ('The lives of the Holy Prophet and the Immaculate Imams'), compiled in 1433 by Ibn 'Arabshah Muhammad Varamini. An illustrated manuscript of the text dating from 1588 is in the Golestan Palace Library. Among its seventeen illustrations is one showing the episode of the assembly at

Ghadir Khumm, the occasion at which the Prophet is believed to have named 'Ali as his successor.[13]

Other illustrated Shi'i texts include the *Rawdat al-safa* ('Garden of Purity') of Mirkhwand (d. 1498). This comprises the history of the prophets, kings, caliphs and Shi'i imams, and a general history of Iran and the Muslim world to the end of the fifteenth century. The earliest surviving illustrated manuscript dating from 1595, in the Chester Beatty Library, is incomplete, but includes a picture of Muhammad investing 'Ali at Ghadir Khumm.[14] Another text worth mentioning in this context is the *Khavaran-nama*, a poem on the heroic deeds of 'Ali and his companions, composed in 1426 by Ibn Husam. A Punjabi manuscript written in 1686 contains no less than 157 illustrations.[15]

Again, as with Shi'ism, there is a strong tradition of Sufi illustrated manuscripts. Outstanding amongst these are the *Golestan* ('Rose Garden') of the poet Sa'di (d. 1290), of which there is an exemplary illustrated manuscript produced for Baysunghur (i.e. the grandson of Timur) in the Chester Beatty Library,[16] the *Haft awrang* ('Seven Thrones') of Jami, of which there is a superb illustrated copy produced for the governor of Mashhad, Ibrahim Mirza, between 1556 and 1565, in New York,[17] and Attar's (d. 1193) *Mantiq al-tayr* ('Conference of the Birds'), the finest surviving illustrated manuscript being that produced for the Sultan Husayn Bayqara (d. 1506), also in New York.[18] These examples raise the question as to why the texts of Jalal al-Din Rumi (d. 1273), one of the most famous Sufis, were so rarely illustrated.

Objects made of metal, ceramic and wood

Many of the objects which we can associate with Sufism come from Iran. There we have objects associated with dervishes: *kashkul*s (dervish begging bowls), dervish staffs, with their heads often in the form of 'Ali, and axes,[19] dervish caps and the woollen cloaks from which the name 'Sufi' comes. These, together with a dervish trumpet, can be seen on a rug from Kashan dated 1806, bearing images of two famous late eighteenth-century Ni'matallahi dervishes, Nur 'Ali Shah and Mushtaq 'Ali Shah.[20] Nur 'Ali

Shah was something of a folk hero in Iran, and was regularly portrayed in different media. One particular group of inlaid metal objects from fourteenth-century Iran also portrays dervishes and their shaykhs, often handing a bowl round between them.[21] The specific function of these objects is unclear, as they have unfortunately never been the focus of the research they deserve.

Shi'ism too was the creative force behind specific types of objects produced in Iran. One group of diverse pieces, made from metal and ceramic, bear the information that they were made in the month of Muharram of a particular year. An inlaid bronze *hammam* (bath) pail was ordered by 'Abd al-Rahman b. 'Abdallah al-Rashidi for the merchant Rashid al-Din 'Azizi b. Abu'l-Husayn al-Zanjani in Muharram 559 AH (1163 CE).[22] An inlaid cast bronze zebu and calf aquamanile in the Hermitage Museum bears an inscription saying that it was made by one Ruzba b. Afridun b. Barzin for his brother, Shah Barzin, in the month of Muharram 603 AH (1206 CE).[23] The inscriptions on these objects show that they were both commissioned as gifts, and they may have been designed to celebrate the day of 'Ashura'. From the same period come a group of *minai* (polychrome overglaze-painted) bowls made in Muharram 582 AH and 583 AH (1186 CE and 1187 CE), two of them by the famous potter, Abu Zayd Kashani.[24] Decorated with *ta'ziya* scenes, they were presumably designed to commemorate the death of al-Husayn at Karbala.

Other objects have an obvious and continuing use, the *'alams* (standards) so commonly used in religious processions in the month of Muharram. In the Iranian context, these owe their origin to the military standards used in Timurid and Safavid times, and had become part of Shi'i processions in Iran by the early seventeenth century, if not well before that. By the nineteenth century, they had become symbols of the different quarters of Iranian cities. From Iran, they spread with Shi'ism to the Deccan, in India, where they are first depicted in a Bodleian Library manuscript of 1610.[25] Numerous examples, including particularly fine ones dating from the eighteenth century, are now housed in the royal Ashur Khanah in Hyderabad.[26]

Another industry which thrived on Shi'ism was the locksmith industry of Iran.[27] Fine padlocks were used to lock the doors of the brass, silver or steel cages which surrounded the cenotaphs of saints in *imamzada*s. Smaller padlocks were also attached by pilgrims to such cages, and other grilles in *imamzada*s, perhaps as a symbol of a pilgrim's oath, or an agreement made between a pilgrim and a saint. There was also the business of making *ziyarat-nama*,[28] the steel plaques which provided pilgrims with the prayers to be recited in shrines, like those at Karbala and Mashhad. In addition, there was also the making of small tablets of clay from Karbala or Mashhad, on which the pious could place their foreheads during prayer.

As well as being the source of particular types of objects, Shi'ism also shows its distinctive face through the decoration applied to objects: not always through geometry or the arabesque, but certainly through the words that are calligraphed in Persian or Arabic. A particular example is the use of a prayer to 'Ali on so many Persian objects made of steel or of a copper alloy:

> *Call to 'Ali who causes wonders to appear*
> *You will find him your help in distress*
> *Every care, every grief will be dispelled*
> *Through your trusteeship. Oh 'Ali. Oh 'Ali. Oh 'Ali.*

Also typical of Shi'i metalwork is the prayer calling down God's blessing on the *chaharda ma'sum* ('Fourteen Sinless Ones', i.e. the twelve Ithna'ashari imams, the Prophet and Fatima) on large numbers of copper items, made in Iran or the Deccan.[29] They also occur on some *'alam*s, as well as on a group of small, portable, wooden *mihrab*s (prayer niches) of the Fatimid period.[30]

The use of Shi'i inscriptions brings us to the realm of coins. Here we find strong evidence of plurality in the coinage of various Shi'i rulers and dynasties. The Alawis, the Idrisids, the Fatimids, the Buyids, the Ilkhanids, the Sarbadarids, the Safavids, the Zaydis of Yemen – these and other Muslim rulers minted coins which made clear their beliefs to their followers and subjects. Thus, for example, in the ninth century the Idrisids sometimes used the

words: "Ali is the best of men after the Prophet, he despises whoever he despises, and approves whoever he approves."[31] The Zaydis
of the Caspian region used Qur'an 33:33: 'People of the House,
God only desires to put away from you abomination and to
cleanse you.'[32] The Fatimid Caliph al-Mu'izz (d. 975) issued coins
bearing the statement: "Ali ibn Abi Talib is the Nominee of the
Prophet and the Preferred Deputy and the Husband of the Radi-
ant Chaste One, the Revivifier of the Sunna of Muhammad, the
Pre-eminent among Messengers and the Inheritor of the Glory of
the Rightly Guided Imams."[33] The Safavids introduced the phrase
"*Ali wali Allah*' ("Ali is the deputy of God'), after the *shahada*
on the obverse of their coins, and surrounded this statement of
faith with the name and attributes of the twelve imams of the
Ithna'ashari Shi'is. Occasional Shi'i distiches also appear, and the
phrase '*bandeh-ye shah-e velayat*' ('slave of the ruler of deputy-
ship'), i.e. 'Ali, is commonly used as an epithet of the Safavid
monarch in whose name a coin is issued; other epithets include
'*ghulam-e imam-e mahdi*' ('slave of the twelfth imam'), '*ghulam-e
'Ali ibn Abi Talib*' ('slave of 'Ali b. Abi Talib'), and '*kalb-e astan-e
'Ali*' ('dog of the threshold of 'Ali').[34]

The Fatimid Ismailis

Amongst the various Muslim dynasties that developed a distinctive visual language, in which doctrinal concerns appear to figure
prominently, was that of the Fatimid Ismailis (909–1171). From
their base at al-Mahdiyya, in modern-day Tunisia, the Fatimids
conquered Egypt in 969. They established their Egyptian capital at
a new city called al-Qahira (Cairo), and established a caliphate
which rivalled that of the Abbasids based at Baghdad in wealth
and power. More importantly, the Fatimids opposed the Abbasids
in theological terms. The Fatimids were Ismaili Shi'is, whose leaders, imams, claimed direct descent from 'Ali. In this manner, the
Fatimid imams claimed legitimacy and religious authority over
the Abbasids. The role and significance of the Fatimid imams
were articulated and expounded upon by notable Ismaili thinkers,
and were reflected in Fatimid social institutions and artistic

output. More particularly, during the eleventh and twelfth centuries, the Fatimids decorated their buildings at Cairo with motifs and inscriptions to symbolize or make clear their doctrinal views. The same approach was taken with their design on coinage. Indeed, so distinctive was their use of particular motifs that, in one case, the design was deliberately reversed by the succeeding Sunni dynasties (i.e. the Mamluks and Ayyubids). The following sections will describe and analyse a range of examples from Fatimid architecture, coinage and art, which appear to have been used to convey their theological views.

Architectural inscriptions

The Fatimids used architectural inscriptions and motifs to speak out their message. Thus, the façade of the Mosque of al-Hakim (built between 990 and 1013)[35] originally had a marble inscription of Qur'an 28:4: 'Yet we desired to be gracious to those that were abased in the land, and to make them leaders (*a'imma*), and to make them the inheritors.'[36] In the Qur'an, this verse is the story of Moses and Pharoah, and takes place in Egypt; God's words could be directed as much to the Fatimid imam as to Moses; the word *a'imma* (plural of *imam*) would have ensured that this latter interpretation was made. The inscriptions on the original minarets of the Mosque of al-Hakim were equally loaded with Shi'i connotations. For example, on the western minaret the middle band contained Qur'an 11:73, which includes the words *Ahl al-Bayt*, literally 'the people of the house', meaning the family of the Prophet.[37]

Some of the inscriptions on the Mosque of al-Aqmar (built in 1125) are as equally explicit as those of the Mosque of al-Hakim. For example, the pierced medallion directly over the mosque's entrance has in the centre the names of Muhammad and 'Ali, and around them a circular inscription with Qur'an 33:33: 'O *Ahl al-Bayt*, God only desires to put away from you abomination and to cleanse you.'[38] This verse not only mentions the *Ahl al-Bayt*, but also brings to mind two events associated with the life of the Prophet often attested to by Shi'is generally. The first is the

Prophet's quoting of the verse when identifying the *Ahl al-Kisa'* ('People of the Cloak'), namely Fatima, 'Ali, and their sons al-Hasan and al-Husayn. The second is its use by the angel Gabriel when the Prophet's body was being prepared for burial, at the very moment Abu Bakr, rather than 'Ali, was being appointed the first successor to the Prophet.

Two further inscriptions on the façade of al-Aqmar should be noted. On the bevelled corner of the façade, in three little niches, appears Qur'an 16:128. In the top niche is the first part of the sura: 'Verily God is with'. In the bottom right niche is the second part of the sura: 'those who are God-fearing'. In the bottom left niche is the third part of the *sura*: 'and those who are doers of good'. In full it reads: 'Verily God is with those who are God-fearing and those who are doers of good'. But the placement of roundels on each side of the top niche means that the message can also be read as: 'God is with Muhammad and 'Ali'.[39] Another inscription which should be noticed is in the centre of the hood of the flat arch on the left hand side of the façade, where we find the name of 'Ali surrounded by five linked 'Muhammads'.[40] In sum, these inscriptions attest to the importance of both Muhammad and 'Ali in Fatimid theology.

Coinage and circular inscriptions

According to Irene Bierman, the design of Fatimid coinage is also significant for its articulation of the central tenets of Ismailism, and particularly the centrality of the imam. Bierman points to the Fatimid adoption of the so-called 'bull's eye', or concentric circle design, as an example of this view.[41] The new Fatimid capital, al-Mansuriyya, outside the city of Qayrawan, founded in 948, was circular and had the palace of the Imam al-Mansur (r. 946–953) in the centre. The next Fatimid Imam, al-Mu'izz (r. 953–975), produced a novel type of concentric circle coin design, which had a central raised dot surrounded by a series of concentric circles containing bands of inscriptions, hence the 'bull's eye' name given to these issues. Coins with concentric circles remained in use throughout the Fatimid period. The use of circles, concentric circles and 'bull's eyes' were, it seems, allusions to the Ismaili view of the centrality of the imam, and gave graphic expression to the Fatimid Ismaili, saying: 'Belief embodies Islam, but Islam does not embody belief.' In other words: 'A believer [i.e. an Ismaili/follower of the Ismaili imam] is a Muslim, but a Muslim is not necessarily a believer [i.e. an Ismaili].'[42]

That circular inscriptions were of royal and religious importance under the Fatimids is shown by a number of pieces of evidence. First are the coins with concentric circles of inscriptions discussed above. These have obvious regal as well as religious overtones, since coins were minted in the name of the ruling caliph-imam. Second, we know from a story told by the fifteenth-century historian, al-Maqrizi, that such circular inscriptions were of wider importance under the Fatimids. According to him, in the year 973, the Caliph al-Muʿizz put on display in his palace a gift destined for the Kaʿba in Mecca. Al-Maqrizi calls it a *shamsa*, a small sun, and says that it consisted of an openwork golden ball stuffed with pearls and gems, displayed inside a circle of Arabic writing. The inscription was the *Surat al-Hajj* or *Sura* of the Pilgrimage, written in emeralds, and the whole was on a background of red brocade, twelve spans by twelve spans in measurement.[43] Third, as mentioned above, in the roundel above the entrance door to the mosque of al-Aqmar, a circular inscription surrounds the names of Muhammad and ʿAli, and contains the words of Qurʾan 33:33.[44] Hence, we can be confident that, for the Fatimids, circular inscriptions had significance in both royal and religious contexts.

It is also important to note that Fatimid inscriptions on the various objects described above are all read anti-clockwise, or 'on the inside'. This form of circular inscriptions had been used even before the Fatimid period. The earliest may have been a stone plaque in the Aqsa Mosque in Jerusalem, recorded by Ibn al-Faqih, and perhaps dating from the reign of al-Walid I (r. 705–715). Situated to the right of the *mihrab*, it had written on it, apparently in a circle, the name of Muhammad.[45] Certainly, circular inscriptions occur on a group of ninth-century wooden panels, now in the Museum of Islamic Art in Cairo and the Louvre.[46] Around a cruciform design of four trefoils are the words *fa-sayakfikuhum Allah*, 'God will be sufficient for you against them' (Qur'an 2:137). The panels come from an unknown context, so their precise purpose and the purpose of the inscriptions are uncertain. Arabic being read from right to left, these inscriptions go anti-clockwise, with the main elements of the letters on the inside of the circle and the uprights of the letters radiating outwards. This seems to have been the usual way of designing a circular inscription in early Islamic times. Such inscriptions, 'read on the inside', occur, for example, on the four bronze door-plates in the name of the Habbarid *amir*, 'Abdallah b. 'Umar (r. 883–913), which were found at al-Mansurah in southern Pakistan.[47] They also occur on the three roundels decorated with pseudo-kufic inscriptions, which decorate the door of the tomb of Bohemond of Antioch in Bari in southern Italy.[48]

Decorative motifs

Caroline Williams has demonstrated that decorative motifs were used by the Fatimids in the same way as inscriptions: to articulate their theology.[49] For example, a recurring theme of Ismaili doctrine is that of *nass*, the explicit designation of an imam by his predecessor through special religious knowledge and divine guidance, which is believed to have been first invested by the Prophet in 'Ali. This knowledge is often symbolized as light and thus lamps. For example, Rashid al-Din b. Shahrashub (d. 1192), a Shi'i author, includes in his book, *Manaqib al Abi Talib* ('On the virtues of the family of Abu Talib'), the following epithets for al-Husayn: 'the lamp of those who trust in God', 'the lamp of the lofty family ties', 'the shining full moon', 'light of the Fatimid family' and 'a part of the light', and the same author quotes a poem composed by al-Husayn himself, in which he says: 'My father is a sun, my mother a moon, and I am the star, the son of the two moons; my grandfather was the lamp of guidance.'[50] The words *'ana qamr'* ('I am a moon') are also used as the decorative repeat motif on a Fatimid textile fragment in the Ashmolean Museum's Newberry Collection,[51] and were this to be read with reference to Ibn Shahrashub's poem, it would be a clear reference to Fatima.

Light symbolism pervades the decorative motifs used on the
mosque of al-Aqmar, whose façade was originally designed to
mirror the three *mihrab*s woven into the *kiswa* (cover) of the
Ka'ba at Mecca. The niche on the top left of the façade is decorated with a mosque lamp hanging in an arch. On its spandrels
are two roundels, one bearing the name Muhammad, the other
the words 'and 'Ali'. Below the lamp is an open grille which radi-
ates from a central six-pointed star. This combination of images
clearly refers the viewer to Qur'an 24:35: 'God is the Light of the
heavens and the earth; the likeness of His Light is as a niche
wherein is a lamp, the lamp in a glass, the glass as it were a glit-
tering star.' However, it is worth noting that early Sunni and Shi'i
Qur'anic exegetes equated the Light of God with the Prophet.
That this is the interpretation intended here is supported by the
fact that the light is coupled with the names of Muhammad and
'Ali, i.e. the two recipients of God's Light.[52] According to
Williams, the light symbolism here may also be an allusion to a
hadith of the Prophet popular with Shi'is, which states: 'The stars
are a pledge to the world that it will not be drowned, and my family are a pledge to the community that it will not go astray.'[53]
Similarly, the two large keel-arches which survive on the façade
of the mosque of al-Aqmar, with their central roundels containing the names of Muhammad and 'Ali, also radiate divine light.
The other arches, niches and roundels which decorate the façade
take up the same theme. These include a six-petalled rosette at
the centre of the niche, to the left of the point of the arch above
the main entrance.[54] The same message is repeated by the conch-
shaped hoods of the *mihrab*s in many of the twelfth-century
Fatimid Ismaili mausoleums of Cairo: Umm Kulthum (built in
1122); the *mashhad* of Sayyida Ruqayya (built in 1133); the
mausoleum of Muhammad al-Hasawati (built in c. 1150); and the
mausoleum of Yahya al-Shabih (built in c. 1145).[55]

Geometry and numbers

One of the most striking aspects of the Fatimid decorative programme was its use of geometric forms, especially stars and

rosettes, often accompanied by repeating inscriptions in particular numerical sequences. Thus we find pentagrams, a variety of
interlaced six-pointed stars, segmented six-pointed stars and
plain six-pointed stars, six-petalled rosettes, a curvilinear seven-
pointed star, eight-pointed rosettes, eight-pointed interlace stars,
plain eight-pointed stars, eight-pointed star and cross designs,
ten-pointed stars made of two interlacing pentagons, and fifteen-
petalled rosettes and fifteen-pointed interlaces.

For example, the use of pentagrams appears on the northern
minaret of the Mosque of al-Hakim[56] (where ten-pointed stars
made of two interlacing pentagons also occur),[57] in the *mihrab*
spandrels of the oratory in the western minaret of the same building,[58] and among other designs on the splayed arch of Bab
al-Futuh (built in 1087), one of Cairo's gates.[59] As we have already
seen, a star made up of the name of Muhammad five times (written with a strong linear emphasis), and with the name of 'Ali in
the centre, occurs in the middle of the medallion of the main hood
of the left-hand arch on the Mosque of al-Aqmar.[60] The use on Bab
al-Futuh is probably not particularly noteworthy, but, to judge
by the other choices, a five-pointed star must surely have had
particular significance.

The number six was also evoked. Particularly noteworthy is the
fact that the roundel at the focal point of the main *mihrab* in the
mashhad of Sayyida Ruqayya contains the name of 'Ali surrounded six times by the name of Muhammad, which provides
the logical source for the six-pointed star design in the same position on the portico *mihrab*s.[61] The *mihrab*s of the mausoleum of
Yahya al-Shabih also focus on a roundel containing a six-pointed
star.[62] Hence, we may without difficulty see a six-pointed star
design as a symbol of the divine light emanating from God
through 'Ali, with his special place in Ismaili theology and Shi'ism
more generally.

Seven was also used. Indeed, early on, the Ismailis were given
the appellation 'Seveners' in relation to the belief of a portion of
the early community in the rightful succession of seven imams,
the first being 'Ali and the seventh being Isma'il, the son of Ja'far
al-Sadiq (d. 765). However, it was alleged that they also upheld the

view that there are seven pillars of Islam, two in addition to the five of the Sunnis: purification and allegiance to the imams.[63] Furthermore, according to certain Ismaili thinkers, seven days of creation prefigured each prophetic cycle since Adam: Muhammad was the sixth major prophet, and the seventh 'day' was at hand with the triumph of Ismailism.[64] In art, a seven-pointed star is not easy to design, hence perhaps its rarity in Fatimid art. Nevertheless, one example is known, a curvilinear seven-pointed star on the northern minaret of the Mosque of al-Hakim.

Eight-pointed stars were also used. An example on the same minaret in the Mosque of al-Hakim shows the words 'from the shadows into the light', inscribed in the centre of an interlaced eight-pointed star, which surely emphasizes the meaning of the inscription. There is an additional occurrence of two interlaced eight-pointed stars on the façade of al-Hakim's mosque (as opposed to its minaret). The prominent location of these latter stars makes it all the more likely that they had some special visual significance.[65]

Finally, another element in the Fatimid decorative programme is the stylized geometric form. For example, a plant form in a diamond can be found on the façade of the Mosque of al-Aqmar,[66] just below the niche with a lamp discussed earlier. Williams suggests its use was aimed to evoke a tradition of the Prophet, which states: 'Hasan and Husayn are my two sweet-smelling herbs in the world.'[67] This offers a fascinating explanation of its presence in such a conspicuous place, particularly if the mosque originally had a symmetrical façade, with the left wing repeated on the right-hand side of the entrance; this would have given two such plants: one for al-Hasan and one for al-Husayn.

To summarize, Fatimid architectural decoration in the form of inscriptions and decorative motifs had a strongly symbolic quality. These appear to emphasize Ismaili Shi'i tenets of the centrality of the imam, links to the Prophet and 'Ali, and reflect discussions about cosmology and theology taken up by various thinkers during Fatimid times.[68]

Artistic responses to the Fatimids

A Muslim dynastic power which demonstrates its beliefs so strongly through visual symbols is unlikely to pass away without some sort of visual reaction from its successors, especially if they hold different religious views. And it is clear that the Fatimids' Sunni successors did, indeed, rework Fatimid symbols for their own ends. This can be seen in a variety of contexts, e.g. six-pointed stars became common motifs in Mamluk and related metalwork.[69] A particularly noteworthy example is the interlaced rectilinear six-pointed star around a central six-petalled rosette star, which occurs twice on the neck of the candlestick of Muhammad b. Sadr al-Din Yusuf b. Salah al-Din in the Nuhad Es-Said collection.[70] Here, as a result of the six almond-shaped drops in the external interstices of both stars, there can be no doubt that the motif is used to symbolize light. But under Mamluk patronage, light is now linked directly to the ruling Sultan, insofar as his titles appear between the two sun motifs.

This candlestick demonstrates a further link with the Fatimid heritage in its use of strapwork interlace between the rosettes on its body, shoulder and candleholder. Strapwork was used in 1125 on the semi-circular back of the *mihrab* niche in the mausoleum of Umm Kulthum.[71] Here, it forms interlaced crosses and eight-pointed stars as a background for the roundels containing the names of 'Ali and Muhammad, which must again symbolically direct the divine light on the worshippers. A similar but more general usage of strapwork is to be seen on the dome of the Karatay Madrese in Konya (built between 1251 and 1253), where it forms the background to the sun or star symbols of the heavens:[72] none of the star symbols now bears the name of Muhammad or 'Ali. On the Nuhad Es-Said candlestick, too, the strapwork has lost its personal message, but the overwhelming effect of the stars in their cosmic setting, and of the light which they emit, is indisputable.

Another motif which stands out in the Egyptian and Syrian context of Mamluk metalwork is the epigraphic sun-disc. The most striking example is that on the magnificent incense-burner in the Nuhad Es-Said collection, made for the Sultan Nasir al-Din

Muhammad (Ibn Qala'un) (r. 1294–1340),[73] but it is relatively
common on metalwork of the period. Hitherto, there seemed to
be no precedent for such a design, although there was an obvious
visual connection with the sun and light. In this regard, it is
important to note that the roundel on the incense-burner is set in
a cusped roundel. The Fatimids used cusps around their *mihrab*
arches, a feature which emphasizes the idea of light moving from
the *mihrab* (and the name of Muhammad and 'Ali) towards the
worshipper. Hence, this too was part of the Fatimid symbolic
repertoire associated with light, and could therefore be conve-
niently reworked by using it alongside a royal inscription to
indicate the Mamluk Sultan as the light of his subjects.

Turning then to the inscriptions on the incense-burner, it is evident that, unlike those of the Fatimid period, which as mentioned
above are read anti-clockwise or 'on the inside', these inscriptions
are read clockwise or 'on the outside'. Various questions immediately arise about this switch, including: how did the anti-clockwise
inscription turn into a clockwise inscription, and why was this
change made?

The earliest evidence of a movement to reverse such inscriptions seems to come from Anatolia, where a unique tile-work
inscription in the Alaeddin Cami, Konya, gives the titles of the
ruler read on the outside. This inscription dates from 1220–
1221.[74] Interestingly, it is part of a culture which used interlaced,
five-pointed star patterns for inscriptions, just as the Fatimids did.
Except that here the stellar inscriptions bear, alongside God and
the Prophet, not the names of members of the family of the
Prophet, but the names of the four 'Rightly Guided Caliphs'.
Examples are to be seen on the Cifte Minareli Medrese at Erzerum
(built in c. 1250) and in the Beyhekim Mescit in Konya (built
between 1270 and 1280).[75] The significance of this may become
clearer when we turn back to the Mamluk scenario.

From the reign of Baybars, or perhaps from the ensuing couple
of decades, i.e. from around 1260 onwards, comes what is probably the earliest example of an Egyptian or Syrian inscription read
completely on the outside. This example is on an embroidery in
the Ashmolean Museum, where the word *al-'izz*, 'glory', forms the

surround for a lion typical of Baybars's period.[76] Next, chronolog-
ically, come the royal inscriptions which decorate the ceiling of
the mausoleum of the Sultan Nasir al-Din Muhamamad (Ibn
Qala'un) (built in 1285),[77] and from the very end of the century
the inscription in the dome of the mausoleum of Zayn al-Din
Yusuf (built in 1298).[78]

The circular inscription read on the outside, having been established in architectural settings, then began to be used regularly on
inlaid metalwork. It occurs on four magnificent pieces dating
from the reign of Ibn Qala'un: a Qur'an box in Berlin,[79] a *kursi* in
Cairo,[80] a Qur'an box in Cairo,[81] and the incense-burner in the
Nuhad Es-Said collection. Following his death it is found on a
splendid rosewater sprinkler of al-Nasir Hasan (second r. 1356–
1363),[82] and on a candlestick in his name,[83] and thereafter on a
number of royal or emiral objects, where it illustrates the decline
in sultanic authority during the later Bahri Mamluk period.[84]

A fascinating parallel to the Mamluk situation presents itself in
the coinage of early fourteenth-century Iran. The Ilkhanid Sultan
Uljeitu (r. 1304–1316) inherited a coinage designed under his
predecessor, Ghazan Khan (r. 1295–1304), but following his conversion to Shi'ism he changed that design.[85] A typical coin of
Uljeitu has a circular obverse which contains an expanded profession of Shi'a faith, with the inclusion of the phrase "Ali is the friend
of God", and the blessings of the twelve imams around the margin
are read on the inside. On the reverse the Sultan's name and titles
fill the hexafoil, and the margin contains the mint, the date and a
traditional Qur'anic phrase (9:112). But when we come to Abu
Sa'id's reign (r. 1317–1335), and the return to Sunnism, we find on
his coinage, dating from 1322–1323, and 1323–1327, respectively,
that the names of the first four caliphs, which are placed in the four
segments outside the central square, are written to be read on the
outside,[86] while other marginal inscriptions on these issues are read
on the inside. In other words, there may have been a deliberate policy of changing the direction of the circular inscriptions away from
their Shi'i usage, particularly that of the Fatimid Ismailis, in order
to make the return to Sunnism visible symbolically, as well as in the
actual names used in the inscriptions.

To summarize, the Fatimids developed a broad vocabulary of inscriptions and symbols to demonstrate their doctrinal positions as Shi'is, and their claim to be descendants of 'Ali. The efficacy of their artistic programme must have been acknowledged by their contemporaries and successors, because Fatimid symbols and artistic methods of doctrinal representation were re-used, but in a modified fashion. Indeed, because the Fatimid artistic programme was so demonstrably Ismaili Shi'i, their Sunni successors either 'neutralized' it by omitting significant words from inscriptions, or by multiplying the motifs employed in the decorative programme, or by reversing the inscriptions altogether. The latter technique made absolutely clear that they held theological views diametrically opposed to those of the Fatimids, and this inadvertently gave birth to a distinctive Sunni artistic programme. At the outset of this chapter, I suggested that, in Islamic art, Sunnism is only definable in the negative. Yet, in this historical instance, the Fatimids' desire to articulate their beliefs through art demanded a concise response from their Sunni successors. As a result, we have a rare instance of Sunnism developing an artistic language, which made reference to that of its predecessors, but was clearly distinguishable as different in order to be read by its adherents and its adversaries alike.

Conclusion

This chapter has investigated some of the features which appear to differentiate Sunni, Shi'i and Sufi buildings, manuscripts and other works of art, which, through their function, form, contents or decoration, demonstrate their distinctive doctrinal position within Islam. It has used the case of the Fatimid Ismailis to demonstrate a uniquely comprehensive approach to the formation and expression of Islamic art, which was meant to convey a particular interpretation of Islamic doctrine and was subsequently altered to convey an alternative doctrinal position. However, this chapter has also noted some of the ambiguities which can make interpreting doctrinal attributions in Islamic artistic expressions difficult. In particular, the veneration that both Shi'is and Sunnis have for the *Ahl al-Bayt* frequently muddies the waters. To take a specific example, in 1534, following his conquest of Iraq, the Ottoman Sultan Suleyman the Magnificent, went on pilgrimage to the tomb of 'Ali at Najaf, an act of piety which his rival Shah Isma'il I had undertaken some years previously. But no one would suggest that Suleyman, like Isma'il, was a Shi'i. And the calligraphic discs in the Selemiye Cami in Edirne, built by Sultan Selim II between 1569 and 1757, bear not just the names of the Prophet and the four 'Rightly Guided Caliphs', but also those of al-Hasan and al-Husayn. This generalized veneration of the *Ahl al-Bayt* suggests that Muslims do share doctrinal common ground, their differences notwithstanding.

6

The Contestation and Resolution of Inter- and Intra-School Conflicts through Biography

R. Kevin Jaques

Although not much is known about the early formation of the Shafi'i and Hanafi *madhhab*s, two of the four schools of Sunni Muslim law,[1] it is clear that these schools developed over the course of several centuries and were established by jurists who lived at least 100 years or more after the deaths of their respective eponymous founders, Muhammad b. Idris al-Shafi'i (d. 820) and Abu Hanifa (d. 767). In fact, the Shafi'i *madhhab* does not appear to have begun to take a coherent form until Ibn Surayj (d. 918) drew together a large number of students who followed the legal curriculum he laid down.[2] Similarly, the Hanafi *madhhab* was probably established by the followers of Abu al-Hasan al-Karkhi (d. 952).[3]

As the legal schools were in the process of forming, scholars sought to create identities for themselves that marked them off as different from those seeking to perpetuate the doctrines of other teachers. This became especially vitriolic in Egypt, where those who coalesced around the doctrines of Abu Hanifa became the official state representatives of Abbasid policies. During the mid ninth century, the Abbasids enforced a theologically inspired inquisition (*mihna,* c. 833–850) that required all state officials to articulate the created view of the Qur'an.[4] In the aftermath of the collapse of the *mihna*, there followed a backlash against the Hanafis in Egypt that led to deep feelings of distrust and rancour between adherents of the school and others, especially the Shafi'is.[5]

In the context of these tensions, scholars used various strategies for sorting out and contesting inter- and intra-school identity.

One important, though poorly understood, method was the use of biographies written by historians who were also members of each school. Over the centuries that followed the *mihna*, Shafi'i and the Hanafi historians employed and augmented the biographical traditions that developed around the scholars of each school in Egypt, and in other regions, as a means to defining the boundaries between the two groups.

The use of biography to create ideas of identity occurred at the same time that it became one of the most important literary genres in Muslim historiography. Biography served a variety of functions, depending on the kind of text for which it was composed, and was, above all, shaped for a variety of rhetorical purposes that may go unnoticed without a detailed examination of the methods of argumentation used therein, and the relationships drawn between the various ideas, institutions and people mentioned in the text. The present paper will examine how historians used the biographical traditions that developed around the early Shafi'i scholar Abu Ibrahim Isma'il b. Yahya al-Muzani (d. 878) in the formation and maintenance of inter- and intra-school identity between the Shafi'i and Hanafi *madhhab*s; especially important in this regard were the biographical clusters that link al-Muzani to the early Hanafi scholar Abu Ja'far Ahmad b. Muhammad al-Tahawi (d. 933).

The formation of biographical traditions

Medieval Arabic-Muslim prosopographical texts became quite common by the thirteenth century. Although there are prosopographical elements in most genres of Arabic-Islamic historiography, the *mu'jam* and *tabaqat* genres came to form the core of the prosopographical genre.[6] *Mu'jam* texts are usually quite large 'compilations' of biographical entries, dedicated to the lives of famous and infamous people from a variety of walks of life. Texts such as al-Dhahabi's (d. 1348) *Siyar a'lam al-nubala*[7] catalogue the important people in each Islamic century, up to the author's time, who were important in the formation of the Islamic community. *Tabaqat* works are more specific than *mu'jam* and are dedicated to listing the intellectual authorities in a range of religious professions including law, theology, medicine, lexicography, grammar, poetry, philosophy and *hadith* studies.[8] While *tabaqat* texts tend to be smaller than most *mu'jam*, they became more widely published and used in the medieval period than biographical compilations. This was a result of the crises of the late Abbasid and Mamluk periods, when *tabaqat* became important in establishing orthodoxies, as religious authorities increasingly came under attack for their perceived failures as guides for the Muslim community.[9]

All prosopographical texts, whether they are *mu'jam*, *tabaqat* or found in other historiographical genres, are composed of usually brief biographical entries. Each entry generally contains the 'proper' name (*ism*) of its subject, and may include: a *nasab* (genealogy); the *kunya* (nickname), frequently the name of an oldest son; a *nisba* that refers to a place of origin, a trade for which the individual was well known, or some affiliation to a school, guild or trade; and a *laqab*, a nickname that refers to some characteristic by which a person becomes known (such as a physical deformity), or a religious name such as 'al-Shihab al-Din' ('the Shooting Star of Religion') or 'al-Sayf al-Din' ('the Sword of Religion'). Entries also include dates of birth and death if known, and the locations where the individual lived, travelled, worked or died. A scholar's biography may mention the name of his teachers, students, subjects studied or taught, books written, controversies and positions held; there are also usually references to characteristics, skills, abilities, attributes and virtues, or the lack thereof. If an entry is dedicated to a notable or political leader, it frequently lists the positions held, the events in which he or she were directly involved, his or her familial connections, and an appraisal of the individual's position in history.

Despite the often detailed information contained in a biographical entry, such texts should be viewed as points of departure in investigating the life-histories of a particular person. In other words, biographies often refer to 'parallel' information found in other biographical entries that may embellish the primary biographical account, adding to the 'texture' of the overall narrative presentation of the life of the primary biographical subject. Thus, a biographical entry is part of a cluster of narratives and cannot be read as a stand-alone entry in a given text.

Figure 1 illustrates a typical cluster of biographical entries and how they relate across a text. To help demonstrate the complex relationships between biographies, and why it is important to read all entries referring to a person, the hypothetical cluster is presented for an individual known as 'Yusuf' (the primary biography), with four parallel biographies for individuals known as 'Ahmad' (referent 1), ''Ali' (referent 2), 'Muhammad' (referent 3) and 'Idris' (referent 4). As the arrows indicate, in the primary entry for Yusuf there are references to Ahmad, 'Ali, and Idris. Muhammad is not mentioned in the entry for Yusuf, but Yusuf is referred to in Muhammad's biography. By referring to Ahmad, 'Ali and Idris in Yusuf's entry, the author intends for the reader to examine their biographies for information that may shed light on Yusuf's character, abilities or reputation(s). For instance, an author might say, 'Yusuf studied law with Ahmad'. To understand the importance of this comment, it is necessary to read the biography for Ahmad to see how the author depicts him, in order to ascertain what the initial comment means for the overall view of Yusuf. If the author describes Ahmad as a weak scholar, this would tend to diminish Yusuf's overall reputation. If the author describes Ahmad as a great scholar, then the contrary can be the case. The use of cross-references by authors is an important component in the accumulation of 'intellectual capital' that indicates important things about a person's standing in comparison with implicit standards of knowledge, virtue, integrity, piety, manliness or womanliness, virility and courage.[10]

The links between biographies will be referred to here as 'hypertextual clusters'. A hypertextual cluster has several layers and it is frequently necessary to trace through the many layers of the cluster to ascertain the network of implications that the author is seeking to make. For instance, an author might say: 'it is said that Yusuf was well known as a scholar of *hadith*. He was appointed deputy judge under Idris.' This kind of rhetorical strategy will be referred to as an 'association'. An association occurs when

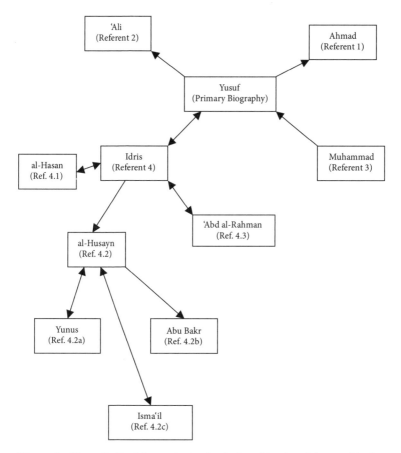

Figure 1. **Hypothetical hypertextual relationships in a biographical cluster**

an author links material together so that he can imply certain ideas without having to directly comment on the qualities of an individual. In this instance, the author comments in the biography for Idris that 'Idris was involved in a dispute with al-Husayn'. In turn, the biography for al-Husayn states: 'al-Husayn accused the jurist Idris of bribery when he was chief judge of Aleppo.' The author does not, however, state in the biography for al-Husayn that he was considered a reliable source. To ascertain the implications of al-Husayn's accusation for the author's presentation of the overall quality of Yusuf, it is necessary to look at the various entries in which al-Husayn is mentioned. In this case, the author presents Abu Bakr, someone he describes as being one of the great scholars of the age, as claiming that 'there was no one among the jurists of Syria more respected than al-Husayn'. Such testimony for someone so removed from the primary biography would still have the effect of diminishing the reputation of Yusuf, not only as a jurist but also as a scholar of *hadith*, because of the associations the author draws between Yusuf's activities as a judge and his work with prophetic traditions. By criticizing the character of Idris (and by supplying evidence for the correctness of his assessment), the author implies that, because Yusuf served as his deputy, he too might have been disreputable. Also, by placing the reference to *hadith* scholarship next to a comment designed to call Yusuf's reputation into question, the author seeks to draw the reader to the idea of Yusuf's implied corruption, and to link it to his role as a scholar. Thus, it is necessary to examine the clusters of biographies that are hypertextually linked within a text to understand how the author seeks to present any given individual.

As Figure 2 illustrates, it is equally important to consider the biographical traditions that developed over long periods of time, which came to include disparate kinds of material. Authors developed alternative views, depending on the material to which they had access, the kinds of groups in which they participated, how they understood the subject of the biography to affect the history of their groups or their own standing in those groups, and the extent to which they believed in the accuracy of the material based on their own intellectual, political or religious commitments. For most of the subjects of Muslim biography, it is generally assumed that at least *some* of the material is based on actual eyewitness accounts.[11] Depending on how early the individual lived in Islamic history, it is possible that some of these eyewitness accounts entered directly into the biographical tradition. Other eyewitness accounts were passed along in oral reports with varying degrees of accuracy. Initially, authors built their biographical clusters from eyewitness accounts that were communicated to the author orally by the witnesses themselves, or more frequently by

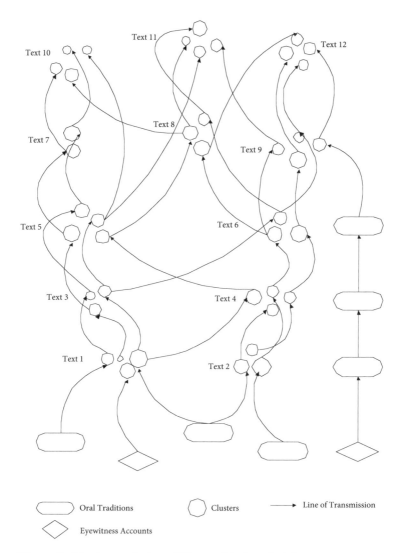

Figure 2. The transmission of biographical material

transmitters. They rarely, however, give verbatim quotations of the material they received. Instead, authors interpreted that information, combining it with other material to shape the biography to cast the individual in particular ways. Later authors continued this process, constructing their biographies from earlier written entries and possibly from oral accounts, combining information and interpreting it in different manners. Often, authors commented on material, which over time became part of the biographical tradition, sometimes being taken as historical information by later writers.[12]

All of this means that we have little by way of unbiased and unvarnished historical information about people who lived in early and medieval Islamic times. For instance, we know that al-Muzani was born sometime in the late eighth century, most likely in Egypt. He may have studied *hadith* in his teenage years, but we have no record of him studying law. He does, however, appear to have been deeply devoted to asceticism and to pious acts. Sometime around 814 or 815, Muhammad b. Idris al-Shafiʿi migrated from Baghdad to Egypt with a small group of followers. Shortly after he arrived, al-Muzani began to associate with al-Shafiʿi or his group. He is said to have studied law with al-Shafiʿi, but what this meant is unknown. By the time al-Shafiʿi died in 820, al-Muzani appears to have formed a group of his own followers, although what he taught is also unclear. He and his followers may have been loosely associated with other people who had studied with al-Shafiʿi in Egypt, although it is unlikely that they referred to themselves as Shafiʿis at this time. Over the next sixty years, al-Muzani continued to teach and transmit *hadith*, although how much of either he actually did is also unknown. When he died in 878, he left behind a small group of students and devotees. These scholars developed his ideas and appear to have produced a number of texts in his name, the most famous of which is the *Mukhtasar*.[13] The *Mukhtasar* is itself a rather obscure text, one that indicates that, while many of the ideas in the manuscript originated with al-Muzani and al-Shafiʿi, they were nevertheless revised and expanded by al-Muzani's students and intellectual descendants, who, for reasons unknown, actively sought to be included within the Shafiʿi school that was coalescing around the name of al-Shafiʿi and his writings, as they were developed by scholars into the early tenth century.[14]

An important aspect of the developing al-Muzani biographical tradition was the cluster of biographies that depicted his relationship with Abu Ja'far Ahmad b. Muhammad al-Tahawi (d. 933). Al-Tahawi was born sometime in the early ninth century in Egypt. His father appears to have been a judge of some repute and in his teenage years he began to study with al-Muzani, who may have been his maternal uncle, although whether he studied law, *hadith* or both with the older scholar is uncertain. For reasons of which accounts vary, after a short time, al-Muzani and al-Tahawi parted ways and al-Tahawi became a follower of the Hanafi school. He is credited with many books on *hadith*, history and law, several of which have come down to modern times. He may have become a deputy judge in the early tenth century, but it is unclear how long he served in this position. He had a number of students, although it appears most of them were involved in the transmission of *hadith* and only parenthetically in law. He died in 933.[15]

The above biographical sketches are based on the earliest sources available for both scholars. Over the centuries, their biographies were intertwined by members of the Shafi'i and Maliki schools to promote inter-school polemics. The al-Muzani biographical tradition seems to have driven much of the material used in the al-Tahawi tradition, since al-Muzani was considered by many historians, who also happen to have been Shafi'is, to be the more important authority. Between the tenth and early thirteenth centuries, the main purpose for depicting the al-Muzani/al-Tahawi relationship seems to have been inter-school conflicts and the development of Hanafi, and later Shafi'i, identity.

The early formation of the al-Muzani/al-Tahawi biographical tradition

The earliest known biography of al-Muzani was written by his student Ibn Abi Hatim (d. 938). It describes al-Muzani as a *hadith* scholar who transmitted prophetic traditions from a number of people, including al-Shafi'i; it does not, however, mention the study of law. Ibn Abi Hatim also describes al-Muzani as someone deeply engaged in asceticism.[16] Al-Tahawi is not mentioned in the biography, nor does he receive an entry of his own; this, however, is likely due to the fact that he died after, or approximate to, the completion of the text. Ibn Abi Hatim seems to be uninterested in the debates over school formation. His purpose in writing the text was to list those whom he considered important in the transmission of *hadith*.

The next biography written for al-Muzani was composed a few years later by 'Abd al-Rahman b. Ahmad al-Safadi, better known as Ibn Yunus (d. 958) in his *Tarikh al-Misriyin*. Ibn Yunus was the grandson of Yunus ibn 'Abd al-A'la (d. 877 or 878), who is said to have been one of al-Shafi'i's students in Egypt, and a contemporary of al-Muzani.[17] It is unknown if Ibn Yunus associated with the students of al-Shafi'i or al-Muzani, or whether he studied some other school of law, although it is likely that he knew al-Muzani (in his youth), al-Tahawi and Ibn Abi Hatim.[18] His brother, 'Abd al-A'la ibn Ahmad (d. 958), is described as a Hanafi jurist who was a companion of al-Tahawi.[19]

As does Ibn Abi Hatim, Ibn Yunus presents al-Muzani as an extremely pious person engaged in forms of asceticism, who was 'one of the best people of God [who] ... had many virtues'.[20] Unlike Ibn Abi Hatim, however, Ibn Yunus describes al-Muzani as being a companion (*sahib*) of al-Shafi'i, who was so close to his master that al-Muzani was buried in a grave near his.[21] Ibn Yunus goes on to say that al-Muzani 'was trustworthy in *hadith* and there is no dispute about him. He was [also] skilled in law'.[22] While neither Ibn Abi Hatim nor Ibn Yunus mentions al-Tahawi in their entries for al-Muzani, Ibn Yunus provides the earliest known biography for al-Tahawi, from whom he heard several of the elements found in his entry for the Hanafi jurist.

Ibn Yunus quotes al-Tahawi directly concerning his relationship to al-Muzani. He says:

> I first studied religious science from al-Muzani. I studied according to the doctrine of al-Shafi'i. I did this after two years and [then] Ahmad b. Abi 'Imran came to us as a judge over Egypt. So I became his student and I studied his doctrine. I studied law according to the opinion of the Kufans. I gave up (*taraktu*) my first doctrine. I saw al-Muzani in a dream and he said to me, 'O Abu Ja'far, *i'tasabtuk*, O Abu, Ja'far, *i'tasabtuk*'.[23]

In this first version of his 'conversion' to Hanafi thought, al-Tahawi does not give a reason as to why he left al-Muzani. Ibn Yunus assumes that his readers are aware that al-Tahawi had been a student of al-Muzani, and had at some point transferred his allegiance and become a member of the Hanafi school, because he does not attempt to fill in any of the background for their relationship. He is only interested in describing the circumstances of their separation.

This kind of rhetorical strategy is common in biography and occurs in a range of prosopographical genres.[24] The purpose for glossing historical details is two-fold: it allows the author to save space by not having to provide background information and, more importantly, it also permits authors to create new impressions about the individual under review by shaping circumstances through inferences to events, attitudes and relationships, without having to deal with them in a historical context. This is frequently done by adding new details or by combining narrative elements. He demonstrates this by simply saying that, after studying with al-Muzani for two years, al-Tahawi began to study with Ibn Abi 'Imran (d. 893) when he arrived in Egypt. Ibn Yunus assumes the actual causes of the break are known, or that various versions of the event may have been widely disseminated in Egypt, and he chooses not to address these stories directly but seeks to temper, or perhaps implicitly champion, a particular narrative by fashioning the story to include a rather terse account of the cause for the split (the arrival of Ibn Abi 'Imran), and, most significantly, to follow it with an account of the dream.[25]

Ibn Yunus's account of al-Tahawi's dream is significant because it sheds light on how the author viewed al-Tahawi's rejection of al-Muzani. Although it is unknown if the dream was supposed to have occurred while al-Muzani was still alive, the author implies that he was dead, otherwise al-Muzani could have come to him directly. In the dream, al-Muzani says from beyond the grave to al-Tahawi: '*Ya Aba Ja'far i'tasabtuk, ya Aba Ja'far i'tasabtuk.*' *I'tasaba* is the eight form of the verb "*asaba*' and means to 'gang up', or to 'form a group'. It can also mean to break ranks with someone after being close to them in a fraternal alliance.[26] Ibn Yunus presents al-Muzani as declaring: 'O Abu Ja'far, I break with you, O Abu Ja'far, I break with you.' The use of the phrase speaks to the pain of ending a close relationship, of being jilted by a close friend or associate for another. Al-Tahawi is also presented as a social climber, as someone who switched allegiances, not because of doctrinal preferences but because Ibn Abi 'Imran 'came to us as a judge over Egypt'. As such, Ibn Yunus casts al-Muzani as the wounded party who comes to al-Tahawi and, in an alternative form of reality, speaks a deep truth about the pain of the break between teacher and student.

Ibn Yunus implies that al-Tahawi had done something wrong in leaving his teacher and going to Ibn Abi 'Imran. Hanafi scholars, however, attempted to promote a motif that marks al-Tahawi as the wounded party. This is found for the first time, almost a century after Ibn Yunus, in the *Akhbar Abi Hanifa wa ashabihi* by Abu 'Abdallah al-Husayn b. 'Ali al-Saymari (d. 1045). Al-Saymari says that al-Tahawi:

> rose to become a leader of the companions of Abu Hanifa there (in Egypt). He studied religious science from Abu Ja'far b. Abi 'Imran and from Abu Khazim, the judge, and from others. He originally studied law (*tafaqqaha*) according to the opinion of al-Shafi'i. The Master Abu Bakr Muhammad b. Musa al-Khwarzmi transmitted to us, he said, 'The reason he came over to the opinion of our companions is that Abu Ibrahim said to him one day, "By God may nothing come of you." So Abu Ja'far was angered by that and had disdain for him (*anifa li-nafsihi*).' He went over to Abu Ja'far b. Abi 'Imran. So the first of what he wrote of his books was a short work (*mukhtasar*) in which he put into order the book of al-Muzani. So after he completed it he said, 'May God have mercy on Abu Ibrahim. If he were alive he would perform the expiation for his oath'.[27]

In this account, the cause of the break is al-Muzani's apparently unjustified rebuke of al-Tahawi, who is not only angered by al-Muzani's criticism, but develops disdain (*anifa li-nafsihi*) for al-Muzani as a result. Al-Saymari goes on to link the anger al-Tahawi felt to his composition of a short work (*mukhtasar*) on the text of al-Muzani, in which he sought to correct the text of his former teacher. Al-Saymari then directly ties the demand for expiation to the conclusion of his reworking of the *Mukhtasar*, saying that al-Tahawi called for it 'after its completion'.[28]

The most apparent meaning of al-Tahawi's demand for expiation is that he, by composing his own short work, had overcome al-Muzani's curse; he had produced a significant work, which was, according to al-Saymari, 'the first of what he wrote of his books'. The rhetorical power of associating the completion of al-Tahawi's commentary on al-Muzani's *Mukhtasar* to the demand for expiation, however, should not be overlooked for two reasons. First, by linking al-Muzani's apparently unjust criticism of al-Tahawi with al-Muzani's *Mukhtasar*, al-Saymari indicates that the sin that al-Muzani committed was greater than just his rebuke of al-Tahawi. Second, by connecting the *Mukhtasar* to the demand for expiation, al-Saymari injects into al-Tahawi's words an implicit argument that al-Muzani's purpose for writing the *Mukhtasar* went unfulfilled and that, were he alive at that time, he would be forced to carry out expiation for that sin as well.

The purpose to which al-Saymari seems to refer is found in the brief introduction of al-Muzani's *Mukhtasar*, where he says:

I condensed this book from the *'ilm* (knowledge, probably meaning texts)[29] of Muhammad b. Idris al-Shafi'i, may God be pleased with him, and from the meaning of his doctrine (*qawl*).[30]

Al-Saymari presents al-Tahawi as saying that al-Muzani's *Mukhtasar* is not based on the texts and doctrine of al-Shafi'i. Given that al-Muzani had a significant number of followers and intellectual descendants in Egypt among those who formed the early core of the Shafi'i school, including such important and influential scholars as Ibn Surayj, such a claim is a highly polemical argument that the Shafi'i school was not faithful to the doctrines of its eponym.

That al-Saymari would want to depict the break between al-Muzani and al-Tahawi as more dramatic and hurtful for al-Tahawi, and that al-Muzani was not faithful to the doctrines of al-Shafi'i, is not surprising, given that the *Akhbar Abi Hanifa wa ashabihi* was composed, in many regards, as a defence for the Hanafi school.[31] Where Ibn Abi Hatim and Ibn Yunus were close to al-Muzani, or at the very least neutral in the debate between school boundaries, al-Saymari was a Hanafi who was concerned with describing and promoting Hanafi scholars. The break, thus, becomes one arena in the polemics of school consolidation for the Hanafis, and in the following centuries for the Shafi'is as well.

Shafi'i responses to early Hanafi presentations of the 'break' narrative

At about the same time that al-Saymari wrote his biography of al-Tahawi, we find the first reference to a familial relationship between al-Muzani and al-Tahawi. This occurs in a biographical entry found in the *Kitab al-irshad* by Khalil b. 'Abdallah al-Khalili (d. 1058), a *hadith* scholar of some repute.[32] Written almost 150 years after al-Muzani's death, al-Khalili states that 'the *musnad* of al-Shafi'i would not have been transmitted from al-Muzani if not for the son of his sister al-Tahawi the Hanafi'.[33] Al-Khalili goes on to say:

> I heard 'Abdallah b. Muhammad the memorizer say, 'I heard Ahmad b. Muhammad al-Shuruti say, "I said to al-Tahawi, 'Why do you contradict your maternal uncle and choose the opinion of Abu Hanifa?' He said, 'I used to see my maternal uncle continually studying the books of Abu Hanifa, because of that I transferred to him.'"[34]

Al-Khalili does not appear to assume that the reader knows that al-Tahawi was al-Muzani's nephew, because he makes a point of mentioning their relationship in three different places: once in the context of textual transmission, and twice in the context of the break narrative.

Nowhere, however, in al-Khalili's biography of al-Muzani is the relationship between the uncle and nephew described as acrimonious. Al-Tahawi is presented as being a dutiful transmitter and student of al-Muzani, one who, far from producing a correction to the text, had great respect for al-Muzani's *Mukhtasar*, which, according to al-Khalili, al-Tahawi describes as 'beginning as a virgin not to be deflowered (*faqad sara bikran la yuftaddu*)'; in other words, as a pure and unadulterated work.[35] Al-Khalili seems to include the reference to al-Tahawi as a means of responding to pre-existing debates about the student/teacher relationship and seeks to ameliorate the negative assertions of those who sought to use the break as a means of criticizing al-Muzani.

Al-Khalili's purpose for composing the *Kitab al-irshad* is to outline authorities in the transmission of *hadith*. In his biography of al-Muzani, he goes to great lengths to present him as a trustworthy and reliable transmitter.[36] Following his description of al-Tahawi's transfer from al-Muzani, al-Khalili says, 'for al-Tahawi the books he wrote were about *hadith*'.[37] Al-Khalili, however, must not have considered him to be an important transmitter because he does not provide a biographical entry for him. Al-Tahawi's status in the *Kitab al-irshad* rests in large part on his relationship to al-Muzani, which portrays him as one who, while leaving al-Muzani, still sees his teacher as an important and influential thinker. He is a link in the authentic transmission of al-Muzani's ideas and perhaps, more importantly, to the doctrines and ideas of al-Shafi'i.

Following al-Khalili, and up to the mid thirteenth century, there are at least three Shafi'i biographies that discuss variations on the break between al-Tahawi and al-Muzani that are designed to respond to Hanafi narratives, which place al-Muzani as the wounding party. The first of these was written by the great Shafi'i jurist Abu Ishaq al-Shirazi (d. 1075). In his *Tabaqat al-fuqaha'*, al-Shirazi seems to follow al-Saymari's account of the break in his biography for al-Tahawi.[38] To understand how al-Shirazi seeks to portray the episode, however, it is necessary to compare biographical entries for the two men. Al-Shirazi describes al-Tahawi as becoming a leader (*ra'is*) of the Hanafis in Egypt. He goes on to say that al-Tahawi:

studied religious science from Ibn Abi ʿImran and from Abu
Khazim and others. He was a Shafiʿi, studying from Abu Ibrahim
al-Muzani. So he said to him, 'by God, may nothing come from
you.' So Abu Jaʿfar became angry at that and went over to Abu Jaʿ-
far Ibn Abi ʿImran. After he wrote his *Mukhtasar* he said, 'May God
have mercy on Abu Ibrahim, if he were alive he would perform the
expiation for his oath.' He wrote *Ikhtilaf al-ʿulamaʾ, al-Shurut,
Ahkam al-Qurʾan*, and *Maʿani al-athar*. He was born in 238 [852
CE] and he died in the year 321 [933 CE].[39]

Although al-Tahawi was a leader of his school, no greatness is
implied in the passage. He studied religious science (*ʿilm*), but no
specific fields or qualifications are mentioned. In comparison, al-
Muzani is described as:

> an ascetic, a scholar, a *mujtahid*, an intense debater and argumen-
> tative; he dove into the sea of precise meanings. He wrote many
> books: *al-Jamiʿ al-kabir, al-Jamiʿ al-saghir, Mukhtasar al-
> mukhtasar, al-Munthur, al-masaʾil al-maʿtabarah, al-Targhib
> fiʾl-ʿilm*, and *Kitab al-wathaʾiq*. Al-Shafiʿi said, 'al-Muzani is the
> champion of my school of thought'.[40]

When compared with al-Muzani, al-Tahawi seems a minor
scholar. Al-Muzani wrote 'many books', al-Tahawi just four
(although he wrote far more books than al-Shirazi lists); al-
Muzani was 'an ascetic, a scholar, a *mujtahid*, an intense debater
and argumentative, and he dove into the sea of precise meanings',
al-Tahawi is given no such praise; and while al-Muzani was
the champion of the Shafiʿi school, al-Tahawi seems rather indeci-
sive, switching from one school to another. Although al-Shirazi
does not say that al-Muzani was justified in swearing at al-Tahawi,
he implies that, given al-Muzani's elevated status, he could not
have erred.

   The books that al-Shirazi attributes to al-Tahawi are also
designed to point to his closeness to the Shafiʿi school, even after
his break from al-Muzani. Each of these works draws heavily on
the statements of al-Shafiʿi, as they were transmitted to him by

al-Muzani and other Shafi'i scholars. In his *Ahkam al-Qur'an*, for instance, al-Tahawi transmits *hadith* and other material from al-Shafi'i and his students over 500 times (al-Shafi'i is the single largest contributor), roughly one third of all the transmitted material in the text.[41] Citing these texts, among the long list of works known to have been composed by al-Tahawi, is meant to draw the reader back to the idea that he was still close to the Shafi'i school, and that his turn to the Hanafis, while important, had more to do with personal problems he had with al-Muzani and was not a rejection of the school itself.

Perhaps most significant in Abu Ishaq's retelling of events is his alteration of the context of al-Tahawi's demand for expiation. It will be recalled that, following al-Muzani's rebuke and al-Tahawi's defection to Ibn Abi 'Imran, al-Saymari claims that:

> the first of what he (al-Tahawi) wrote of his books was a short work (*mukhtasar*) in which he put into order the book of al-Muzani. So after he completed it he said, 'May God have mercy on Abu Ibrahim. If he were alive he would perform the expiation for his oath'.[42]

Abu Ishaq, however, truncates the account by stating:

> after he (al-Tahawi) wrote his *Mukhtasar* he said, 'May God have mercy on Abu Ibrahim, if he were alive he would perform the expiation for his oath'.

Here, Abu Ishaq al-Shirazi removes any reference to the work of al-Muzani or that al-Tahawi's text was a correction of it. By expunging the association drawn by al-Saymari, Abu Ishaq seeks to eliminate any link between the *Mukhtasar* of al-Muzani and the connotation of sin or error as implied by al-Saymari. The demand for expiation in Abu Ishaq is solely connected to al-Muzani's curse and nothing else.

The following century, the Shafi'i scholar and historian Ibn 'Asakir (d. 1176) attempted to harmonize the various accounts into a comprehensive and coherent whole, and, in doing so, to present al-Muzani as the wounded party. In his *Tarikh madinat Dimashq*, Ibn 'Asakir provides a biography for al-Tahawi, who, he says, travelled to Damascus briefly in 881–882. He begins his discussion of the break by quoting al-Shirazi's quote of al-Saymari (with the implicit polemics of his comparison in mind) and then attempts to combine the accounts given by Ibn Yunus and al-Saymari, with significant alterations of their original versions. He, quoting al-Tahawi, says:

> I originally wrote down *hadith* from al-Muzani and I studied according to the doctrine of al-Shafi'i. After two years Ahmad b. Abi 'Imran came as a judge over Egypt. So I became his companion and studied according to his doctrine. I studied according to the opinion of the Kufans. I gave up my first doctrine. I saw al-Muzani in a dream and he said to me, 'O Abu Ja'far, I break with you, O Abu Ja'far, I break with you.'[43]

Here, Ibn 'Asakir carefully alters the account given in Ibn Yunus. Al-Muzani is portrayed primarily as a *hadith* transmitter; and although al-Tahawi says that he first studied the 'doctrine of al-Shafi'i', it is by no means clear that al-Muzani was his teacher. Where Ibn Yunus implies such a relationship, Ibn 'Asakir's interpolation of the statement that he 'wrote down *hadith* from al-Muzani' suggests that al-Tahawi may have studied Shafi'i law from others. This is particularly evident because al-Tahawi is not quoted as using the phrase "*anhu*' ('under him') following the verb '*akhadhtu*' ('I studied'). By not saying 'I studied under him', meaning al-Muzani, Ibn 'Asakir leaves open the possibility that he studied with other Shafi'i scholars.

The suggestion that al-Muzani was only or even primarily a *hadith* transmitter to al-Tahawi provides a different context for the dream narrative mentioned earlier. Al-Muzani's statement, 'O Abu Ja'far, I break with you, O Abu Ja'far, I break with you', becomes a statement of personal pain at the ending of a relationship and is not the result of a rejection of his legal ideas or those of the eponym.

Ibn ʿAsakir goes on to say:

> I report that [the Ibn Yunus narrative] because he [al-Tahawi] gave
> up the Shafiʿi school because one day al-Muzani said in his pres-
> ence concerning a question, '*Wa Allah la tuflihu abadan*.' So he
> became angry from what al-Muzani said and he went over to Abu
> Jaʿfar b. Abi ʿImran. He became a proponent of the statements of
> Abu Hanifa until he became a leader in it. So after that he went to
> the tomb of al-Muzani and he said, 'May God have mercy on you,
> O Abu Ibrahim. If you were alive you would perform expiation for
> your oath.'[44]

Again, Ibn ʿAsakir subtly changes the account of the break drawn
from al-Saymari to cast al-Muzani more favourably. He says that
the context for the break was one in which the teacher and the student were given a legal issue to resolve; whether this was a
pedagogical device or an actual legal question is not clear. Al-
Muzani, exasperated that al-Tahawi was either taking too much
time to resolve the issue or unable to answer the question satisfac-
torily, says in a fit of pique, '*Wa Allah la tuflihu abadan*'. This is
significantly different from al-Saymari's description of the statement that has al-Muzani saying, '*Wa Allah la jaʾa minka shayʾ*' (By
God, may nothing come from you), without any apparent justification. Instead, Ibn ʿAsakir has al-Muzani utter the much more
harsh phrase 'By God, you will never prosper'. The implication of
the oath in the context of al-Tahawi's inability to resolve a legal
problem is that al-Muzani doubted his student's legal abilities and
that al-Tahawi had no native talent for the law.

If Ibn al-ʿAsakir were to have ended his discussion there, he
might be understood to be presenting al-Tahawi as the wounded
party. But, by immediately stating that al-Tahawi became a leader
of the Hanafi school after first arguing that he was not capable of
answering a legal question in al-Muzani's presence, Ibn ʿAsakir is
implying that the Hanafi school is inferior to that of the Shafiʿis;
that their method is easier and less rigorous. In a system of
thought that prized the struggle of legal discovery (the basic

meaning of *ijtihad*), taking refuge with an easier school is a serious criticism indeed.

Al-Tahawi's demand for expiation is also quoted, although without reference to al-Saymari's discussion of the completion of al-Tahawi's correction of al-Muzani's *Mukhtasar*. Instead, it occurs after al-Tahawi became the leader of the Hanafi *madhhab* in Egypt. It creates an image of an al-Tahawi consumed by anger; who, at his first opportunity, goes to al-Muzani's grave to condemn his former teacher. Furthermore, the demand for expiation and the dream narrative are held in tension, since it is unclear which was supposed to have come first. If the dream, with al-Muzani's declaration of pain at the break-up of their teacher-student relationship, comes first, then al-Tahawi's demand for expiation at the man's grave looks mean-spirited and even childish. If the demand for expiation came first, then al-Muzani's visitation would seem to be a complete rejection of al-Tahawi's comment. Either way, al-Muzani is presented as the wounded party and al-Tahawi as the churlish transgressor.

Inter-school conflict and the al-Muzani/al-Tahawi tradition

A century after Ibn 'Asakir seemed to resolve the issue of al-Tahawi's supposed rejection of al-Muzani, another Shafi'i scholar, known as Ibn Khallikan (d. 1282), composed a biographical dictionary entitled *Wafayat al-a'yan wa-abna' abna' al-zaman*.[45] The *Wafayat al-a'yan* was designed to be a comprehensive account of the elite men and women in Muslim history up to his time. Because his focus was greater than just *hadith* scholars, the Shafi'i school, the legal profession, or the history of a particular city, his biographical entries drew on a wider range of sources. In his biography for al-Muzani, however, he is also influenced by the desire to contextualize Shafi'i scholars within the larger framework of the history of the school and their approximation to what was perceived to be its core doctrines.

Ibn Khallikan's biography of al-Muzani was written in the milieu of debates about the place of al-Muzani in Shafi'i history that came about because of the publication of the *al-'Aziz fi sharh al-wajiz* by Abu al-Qasim al-Rafi'i (d. 1226 or 1227), and its commentary *Rawdat al-talibin* by Muhyi al-Din al-Nawawi (d. 1278).[46] The *'Aziz* and the *Rawdah* became the two most important legal compilations of Shafi'i law written in the medieval period. Both texts were devoted to explicating the divergent opinions of the great legal authorities of the Shafi'i school, and led to debates within the *madhhab* over the place of al-Muzani and other jurists as authoritative transmitters of al-Shafi'i's authentic opinion.[47] Although there had been intensive debate about al-Muzani prior to al-Rafi'i and al-Nawawi, their texts brought to the fore long-festering doubts about the authority of the Egyptian scholar and his closeness to al-Shafi'i.[48]

Ibn Khallikan begins his entry by quoting, without attribution, Abu Ishaq al-Shirazi. Although Abu Ishaq al-Shirazi initially wrote his biography as a defence of the Shafi'i school, Ibn Khallikan, as do later scholars such as al-Subki, al-Dhahabi,[49] Ibn Qadi Shuhbah and Ibn Hajar al-'Asqalani,[50] use material from al-Shirazi's entry for al-Muzani as a statement for his inclusion in the mainstream of the school. Particularly evocative of this desire is the quotation found in al-Shirazi, in which he attributes to al-Shafi'i the statement that 'al-Muzani is the champion of my school of thought'.[51]

He then states:

> When he settled a problem and consigned it to his *Mukhtasar* he stood up in the prayer niche and prayed two stanzas of thanks to God. Abu al-'Abbas Ahmad Ibn Surayj said, 'The *Mukhtasar* of al-Muzani left the world a virgin, not to be deflowered. It is one of the foundational books in al-Shafi'i's school of thought, may God be pleased with him. According to its example they [the jurists] arrange [their books] and according to its discussion they [the jurists] interpret and comment'.[52]

There are a number of elements in this passage that stand out as examples of Ibn Khallikan's attempt to pull al-Muzani into the mainstream of the school. First, there is the linking of the composition of the *Mukhtasar* to prayer. The earliest biographies of al-Muzani focused on his piety and asceticism. Associating the *Mukhtasar* to al-Muzani's ritual practice is designed to create an image of purity that goes against accusations of his duplicity, found in texts such as Abu Bakr al-Bayhaqi's *al-Manaqib al-Shafi'i*. Al-Bayhaqi (d. 1066), an important Shafi'i scholar, argues that al-Muzani spread lies about al-Shafi'i and was not trustworthy in the transmission of *hadith*, and thus, by implication, unreliable in the transmission of al-Shafi'i's authentic opinion.[53] By drawing the reader back to early Shafi'i descriptions of al-Muzani as the paragon of pious devotion, Ibn Khallikan is attempting to blunt the vitriolic accusations of al-Bayhaqi and others who desire to remove him as a school authority.

The second feature is the long quotation that Ibn Khallikan attributes to Ibn Surayj. Ibn Surayj is an extremely important figure for Ibn Khallikan. Quoting Abu Ishaq al-Shirazi's biography for the scholar, Ibn Khallikan says that Ibn Surayj was 'among the great Shafi'is and leaders of the Muslims'.[54] The passage attributed to Ibn Surayj is, therefore, meant to vouch for the importance of the *Mukhtasar* for the Shafi'i school and to rebut the claims made by the Hanafi al-Saymari, and the Shafi'is al-Nawawi, al-Isnawi and others, that the text should not be thought of as representing anything but the opinion of al-Muzani.[55]

Another feature that makes the reference important for the debate about al-Muzani's place within the structure of the school is that Ibn Khallikan attributes the comment 'the *Mukhtasar* of al-Muzani left the world a virgin, not to be deflowered' to Ibn Surayj. It will be recalled that al-Khalili, in the *Kitab al-irshad*, originally attributed the remark to al-Tahawi, rendering it as 'beginning as a virgin not to be deflowered'.[56] The similarity of the quotations and the change in attribution does not, however, appear to be accidental. Ibn Khallikan read al-Khalili's text and quotes extensively from it in his entry for al-Tahawi.[57] He knew that the quotations were similar, and seems to have placed it in the text in order to evoke al-Tahawi and his break from al-Muzani without having to do so directly. He does this so that he can, by comparison, elevate the stature of al-Muzani even higher, although in this instance, not for the purpose of inter-school rivalry, but to argue that al-Muzani was a great scholar of *hadith* and, by implication, a reliable transmitter of al-Shafi'i's thought.

This rhetorical move is evident because Ibn Khallikan follows the quotation from Ibn Surayj, and the implicit reference to al-Tahawi and all of that it brings to mind, with the introduction of the story of al-Muzani and the Hanafi judge Bakkar b. Qutaybah (d. 884). He states that:

> when the Hanafi judge Bakkar b. Qutaybah was appointed chief judge of Egypt and travelled there from Baghdad, he wanted to meet with al-Muzani and [waited] for a while in the discussion group. He did not have any success. So during a get-together one day at a funeral prayer, Bakkar said to one of his companions, 'Ask al-Muzani something until I hear him speak.' So that person said to him, 'O Abu Ibrahim, in the *hadith* [collections] there are [traditions] that prohibit wine (*nabidh*) and [traditions] that permit it also. Why does the prohibiting take precedence over the permitting?' So al-Muzani said, 'No one among the community of learned scholars opines that wine was prohibited during the time of ignorance and then permitted. The agreement came down that it was permitted. [Its] prohibition [afterwards] was supported by sound *hadith*.' He (Bakkar) thought [al-Muzani's explanation] was correct. This is from irrefutable evidence and was according to the pious intention.[58]

There are several reasons for Ibn Khallikan to introduce this story into the al-Muzani biographical tradition and to place it next to a comment meant to evoke al-Tahawi. First, Bakkar b. Qutaybah was a famous Hanafi scholar of *hadith* who is said to have written a book outlining how al-Shafi'i refuted the legal arguments of Abu Hanifa.[59] To have such a famous scholar of *hadith* seek out al-Muzani in order to test his abilities is meant to demonstrate that al-Muzani was an important *hadith* transmitter. Secondly, that Bakkar would approve al-Muzani's reasoning based on his knowledge of *hadith* is designed to prove that those who criticize the scholar as a weak transmitter, and thus not reliable as a source for al-Shafi'i's doctrines, are simply wrong.

Finally, there was a close association between Bakkar and al-Tahawi. Al-Tahawi cites Bakkar 149 times as a source of traditions in his *Ahkam al-Qur'an*, one of the largest non-Shafi'i contributors to the text. The reference is meant to point readers to the entry for al-Tahawi, not only for what it says about the rivalry between the two, but also for what it suggests about al-Muzani in the post-Rafi'i era of Shafi'i legal thinking.

Ibn Khallikan's biography for al-Tahawi begins, as it did with al-Muzani, with an unattributed quotation from al-Shirazi, complete with the story of al-Muzani's statement that 'by God, may nothing come from you', al-Tahawi's angry rejection, and his demand for expiation. He immediately follows this, however, with the statement:

> Abu Ya'la al-Khalili mentions in the *Kitab al-irshad*, in the history of al-Muzani, that al-Tahawi mentioned that he was the son of a sister of al-Muzani, and that Muhammad b. Ahmad al-Shuruti said, 'I said to al-Tahawi, "Why do you contradict your maternal uncle and choose the opinion of Abu Hanifa?" He said, "I used to see my maternal uncle continually studying the books of Abu Hanifa, because of that I transferred to him"'.[60]

This is the first reference to al-Tahawi being the nephew of al-Muzani since al-Khalili originally asserted it 200 years earlier. For reasons that are not clear, it fell out of the biographical tradition until it is resurrected by Ibn Khallikan. Ibn Khallikan, however, places the authority for the reference with al-Tahawi himself, something that was not original to the *Kitab al-irshad*.[61] By associating the break with a familial relationship, Ibn Khallikan is attempting to present the event as more important and tragic, one in which not only did al-Muzani seem to insult al-Tahawi, leading to the rupture of the teacher-student bond, but also of the much more serious blood relationship. Over the next 175 years, seven other scholars refer to al-Muzani as the maternal uncle of al-Tahawi (see Table 1). Why this element suddenly became important in depictions of their relationship is uncertain. It is possible that, in the post-Rafi'i period of biography, especially for the Shafi'is, it was a useful tool

Table 1. Common Narrative Elements in the al-Muzani/al-Tahawi Cluster

Author	Nephew	Oath	Expiation	Dream	Bakkar	'Adalah	Method
Ibn Yunus				X			
al-Saymari		X	X				
al-Khalili	X						
al-Shirazi		X	X				
al-Sam'ani							
Ibn 'Asakir		X	X	X			
al-Rafi'i	(sister)						X
Yaqut b. 'Abdallah				X			
al-Nawawi	(sister)						X
Ibn Khallikan	X	X	X		X	X	
al-Dhahabi							
(*Siyar*)	X	X	X	X	X	X	X
(*Tarikh*)	X	X	X	X	X	X	X
al-Safadi	X	X	X				
al-Yafi'i	X	X	X		X		X
Ibn Kathir	X	X	X			X	
al-Isnawi	(sister)						X
al-Subki					X		X
al-Qurashi	X	X					
Ibn Qadi Shuhbah							X
al-'Asqalani	X	X	X		X		

for referring to the debate over al-Muzani's qualities as a *hadith* transmitter, in the same way that al-Nawawi, al-Isnawi (who used it to imply the negative view) and Ibn Khallikan (who used it to support the positive view) used such allusions.

Al-Tahawi's more gentle explanation for the break, used by al-Khalili to soften the split between the two, is exploited by Ibn Khallikan to draw very different conclusions. Ibn Khallikan holds al-Muzani's apparent insult of al-Tahawi and the latter's acrimonious demand for expiation in tension with the kinder explanation given by al-Tahawi, causing the reader to consider the implications of the two presentations. Why, the reader is forced to ask, would al-Tahawi want to portray the break as a simple matter of juristic preference and not resulting from al-Muzani's comment?

Ibn Khallikan provides an answer in the following section of his entry, where he implies that al-Tahawi may have acted improperly in accepting several administrative appointments under the Fatimids. According to Ibn Khallikan, al-Tahawi was first appointed court secretary under Abu 'Ubaydallah Muhammad Ibn 'Abdah (d. 924), when he was 'utterly destitute' (*su'lukan*), but due to the generosity of Ibn 'Abdah, he became quite wealthy. This comment, in itself, can be taken as a criticism, since accusations of bribery were a common trope in biographical discussions of judges.[62] Then, according to Ibn Khallikan, when Ibn 'Abdah was replaced with the judge Abu 'Ubayd 'Ali b. al-Hasan b. Harb (d. 931), al-Tahawi gained a new advocate who attempted to appoint him to the position of inspector of witnesses (*'adalah*).[63] A number of the official court witnesses (*shuhud*) complained because they believed that combining the two positions would put too much power in al-Tahawi's hands. The witnesses appear to have blocked the nomination for some time until a group of them went on the pilgrimage and, in their absence, Abu 'Ubayd was able to bring the promotion to completion.[64]

Ibn Khallikan combines the elements of the biography to make al-Muzani's comment about al-Tahawi seem almost prophetic. In a sense, when al-Muzani says 'may nothing come from you', he is portrayed as foreshadowing the accusation of al-Tahawi's later bribery and impropriety. Al-Tahawi's demand for expiation, in this light, appears to be the supreme act of hubris, as damning as the unseemliness of which he is accused. While this could be understood as a manifestation of the earlier pre-Rafi'i inter-school rivalry, it is unlikely to have been the case. Although Ibn 'Abdah was a Hanafi jurist, his replacement, and the one who brings about al-Tahawi's second promotion that causes such controversy, was a Shafi'i.

Ultimately, Ibn Khallikan goes to great lengths to build the stature of al-Muzani as a scholar, person and judge of character. He combines elements that he inherits from the biographical tradition and adds new material to construct an image of al-Muzani that seeks to refute those who, to various degrees, want to present al-Muzani as being a weak transmitter of *hadith*, or an outright fabricator. Although he is interested in al-Tahawi, his main purpose in presenting his entry is to contribute to the reputation of his teacher, whose rejection is designed to foreshadow his later corruption.

The resolution of inter-school rivalries

Over the next several centuries, various authors emphasize different aspects of the cluster of traditions that developed around al-Muzani and al-Tahawi (see Table 1). All of these narrative elements predate the contribution of Ibn Khallikan and, in one way or another, respond to the interpretation of events that he details. Al-Dhahabi (d. 1348),[65] al-Safadi (d. 1363),[66] al-Yafi'i (d. 1367),[67] Ibn Kathir (d. 1373),[68] al-Nuwayri (d. 1372),[69] al-Qurashi (d. 1374–1375)[70] and Ibn Hajar al-'Asqalani (d. 1449),[71] among others, utilized various aspects of the al-Muzani biographical tradition to create specific images of both scholars.

In most cases, the old inter-school rivalries that characterized the pre-Rafi'i biographical tradition were suppressed in preference to intra-Shafi'i polemics. The one notable exception to this is the *Jawahir al-mudi'ah fi tabaqat al-Hanafiyah,* by al-Qurashi.[72] As the title implies, al-Qurashi composed the text as a self-conscious defence of the Hanafi school. He draws on various elements of the al-Muzani/al-Tahawi cluster, adds new material, and changes particular phrases in another attempt to recast al-Tahawi as the wounded party.

Ultimately, the kinds of divisions that characterized the early dynamics of inter-school conflict seem to have been suppressed or to have been replaced by a new cooperation between schools. Fifteenth-century scholars commonly studied outside their own legal communities and worked closely with scholars across *madhhab* boundaries. Scholars such as the historian Ibn Qadi Shuhbah (d. 1448) studied with and taught students from the Hanafi and Hanbali schools,[73] something that scholars in previous periods may not have been encouraged to do.

7

Traditions of Reform, Reformers of Tradition: Case Studies from Senegal and Zanzibar/Tanzania*

Roman Loimeier

Introduction

When Ibrahim Niass, a Senegalese *shaykh* of the Tijaniyya *tariqa* (Sufi brotherhood), claimed, in the 1930s, to be the supreme Sufi saint, the *ghawth al-zaman* (reformer of the age), he was soon attacked by leading scholars of the competing Qadiriyya *tariqa* in Northern Nigeria. The *shaykh*s of the Qadiriyya rejected Ibrahim Niass's claim to spiritual supremacy as false on account of his well-known love for money and accused him of just being a 'successful farmer'. In the debate that ensued between the Tijaniyya and Qadiriyya *tariqa*s, Abubakar Atiku, a leading *shaykh* of the Tijaniyya from Kano, took up Ibrahim Niass's defence by arguing that the *ghawth al-zaman* always assumes the character of his time.[1] That is, a *ghawth* was not defined by specific behavioural features or his *zuhd* (asceticism), a conventionally classical measure of a man's piety. Rather, the veracity of his claim was demonstrated by his material success, a measurement more commensurate with contemporary times: obviously, the greater his wealth, the greater would be his *baraka* (power to confer God's blessing).

The major argument in this dispute, namely that saints assume the character of their times, may be translated easily into the larger context of movements of reform in Muslim societies, insofar as such movements also assume the character of their times. As a

* I am grateful to Zulfikar Hirji, Réné Otayek, Scott Reese and Benjamin Soares for their comments on this chapter.

whole, traditions of reform in Muslim societies display a staggering diversity and betray numerous fluctuations over time and space. This poses difficulties for an analytical study of the various phenomena that can be placed under the rubric of reform.[2] In order to overcome the problem of conceptualization and analysis of reform, I propose to examine reform not through programmes (of reform), but rather as 'processes of change with a particular programme and orientation' or, to be shorter, as 'change with a programme'. This definition of the term 'reform' understands 'reform' to be informed by, first of all, a normative (reformatory) discourse (an ideology, a programme) and, second, modes of programme-oriented agency which propose to translate a specific programme of change in a specific historical context into social realities.

Examining reform in this manner has four main advantages. First, it takes into consideration the internally dialectical character which movements of reform display over time. That is, in the name or guise of 'modernization', a particular instance of reform may seek to modify, completely change or eradicate established social, religious or political traditions, rituals, reforms introduced in the past, or the manner or form by which Muslim scholastic teachings are interpreted or taught. In a subsequent twist, the very same instance of reform, even if viewed as possessing a modernizing[3] spirit during its own time, sooner or later comes to be regarded as the established 'tradition'.[4] Adopting such analytical posture thus serves to examine the manner and extent to which a particular set of reforms converse with their own history.

Second, the examination of reform as 'processes of change with a programme' also allows for the study of modern reform movements that do not have a distinctive modernizing mission, such as movements of reform which claim to reinvigorate the faith and which could be defined to represent a 'scripturalist' or 'literalist' episteme.[5] For instance, Islamic movements of reform committed to a scripturalist episteme often reject supererogatory prayers, as well as the *dhikr* (meditative prayers in Sufi ritual) and the *mawlid* (the birthday celebration for the Prophet or a saint, or praise poetry/prayer associated with such a celebration), while simultaneously putting stress on the literal understanding of the Qur'an, and advocating the reform of particular rituals, of Islamic education, or the manner in which Prophetic traditions are incorporated into traditions of learning.[6]

Third, a broader examination of reform also allows for the inclusion of a spectrum of Sufi-oriented traditions of reform, which represent an 'esoteric' episteme. Although Sufi-oriented movements of reform are the central focus of many studies, they are often not viewed as forming part of a greater 'reformist' paradigm,[7] but as being opposed to 'reformist Islam'. The dilemma of dichotomous representations which position 'Sufi Islam' against 'reformist Islam' is exemplified in Eva Evers Rosander's introduction to *African Islam and Islam in Africa*.[8] Here, Evers Rosander associates 'African Islam' with Sufi contexts, and 'Islam in Africa' with reformist and activist tendencies, while subsequently modifying this position when referring to the importance of the Senegalese Sufi 'reformist' scholar Ibrahim Niass. The framework proposed in the present study, and the case material to be presented in its defence, challenges such a dichotomous representation of reform in Muslim societies.

Fourth, an inclusive examination of reform has the advantage of being able to escape politically biased perceptions of Muslim reform movements, which tend to indiscriminately portray them as basically radical, activist, 'fundamentalist' and militantly 'Islamist' expressions of 'political Islam', while opposing them with allegedly quietist, peaceful and accommodating expressions of 'Sufi Islam'. For example, the events of 11 September 2001, and the subsequent focus on 'fundamentalist' movements, have tended to emphasize these dichotomous interpretations of patterns of reform in Muslim societies. This reifies both types of expression, and renders one in opposition to the other.

Ultimately, most external representations of reform movements in Muslim societies fail both to account for the multiplicity of expressions which cover the spectrum between 'activist' and 'quietist' poles, and also to recognize the dynamic character of Muslim societies in which social actors actively position, negotiate and interpret ideas and materials coming from various places along the spectrum.

However, it is also important to recall that, within Muslim societies, dichotomous representations of reform and reformers often constitute an important means of 'othering' opponents in a local context. These processes are important to examine, insofar as they reflect emic perceptions of reality. These dichotomous representations are relational, and result from negotiation processes specific to a local context. They are often made operational or articulated for specific purposes, and consequently change ascription if the context changes. Hence, this chapter argues that, while reform movements have to be understood in terms of how they are situated in a matrix of international networks and media-based representations, they have more so to be interpreted in terms of how they are situated in local contexts, wherein their advocates attempt to translate their interpretations for reality on the ground. Thus the success or failure of particular reform movements is consequently defined by processes of negotiation in the local context and not so much by their degree of trans-local integration. It is only if a reform movement manages to 'translate' its programme into a multitude of local contexts, and to properly address the needs, anxieties, frustrations and aspirations of many different local populations by offering viable solutions to the nagging and often banal problems of everyday life, that it will gain acceptance and become a truly trans-local movement.

Finally, having evoked such a framework of study, it can be suggested that Muslim reform movements may be characterized by a large spectrum of expressions which attempt to translate specific interpretations of a 'great tradition',[9] such as the canon of Islam's sacred texts and norms of behaviour, into multiple local contexts wherein there is a constant process of negotiation, contestation and re-interpretation. This process has been defined by the anthropologist Talal Asad as being 'a constitutive part of any Islamic tradition'.[10] In the process of translation, contestation, negotiation and re-interpretation of a specific interpretation of the canon into different geographic, social, political and religious contexts, reform movements can be seen to develop distinctive positions, both with respect to their contexts as well as to other contemporary reform movements and/or historical traditions of reform: such reform movements have synchronic and diachronic dimensions which require careful examination. Thus, each tradition of reform is marked by distinctive contexts, distinctive markers of reform, and distinctive positions with respect to other traditions of reform. This chapter examines these multiple dimensions of reform as they have developed amongst Muslim societies in sub-Saharan Africa, particularly in Senegal and Zanzibar/Tanzania (see Table 1 for a summary).[11]

Senegal

Many scholars[12] associate the emergence of a Senegalese tradition of reform with Cheikh Touré (b. 1925) and the Union Culturelle Musulmane (al-Ittihad al-Thaqafi al-Islami, ITI, established in 1953). In fact, modern reformist ideas and actions in Senegal are much older and go back to the mid nineteenth century. In 1848, a Muslim civil rights movement started to develop in the Quatre Communes of St Louis, Gorée, Dakar and Rufisque in Senegal, which had French community status.[13] This Muslim civil rights movement fought for the public recognition of Muslim norms, customs and rites, as well as the use of Islamic personal law in courts of law. It was connected with the activities of Muslim intellectuals and scholars such as Ahmad Ndiaye Hann, Muhammad Seck and Ndiaye Sarr.[14] These *"ulama'* – *'citizens'* – developed a *modus vivendi* with French colonial rule by accepting work within institutions such as *qadi* courts and *madrasa*s, which had been established and defined by the French colonial administration.

In the early twentieth century, this Muslim civil rights movement acquired a new character by developing the typical features of modern French political associations. These 'associational' forms of organization were not only better suited to translate Muslim aspirations into the colonial context; they were also recognizable for French colonial administrators and thus easily identifiable as 'modern' religio-political movements.[15] In 1922, for example, a Union fraternelle des Pèlerins Musulmans de l'A.O.F. was established in Dakar in order to improve the conditions of the *hajj*. This was followed by the foundation of many other pilgrims' associations such as the Liwa' Ta'akhi al-Muslim as-Salih (Brigade de la Fraternité du Bon Musulman), founded in 1934 in St Louis, which in addition to organizing the *hajj* also campaigned for reforms in the area of Islamic education. In 1936, the French colonial administration estimated the number of these associations to be more than fifty in Dakar alone.[16] However, most of these types of association were confined to urban areas and essentially fought for limited goals such as the improvement of the pilgrimage, Islamic personal law or a distinctive Muslim code of dress. Notably, the majority of the members of these associations and, in particular, their leadership were also still affiliated with a *tariqa*, and, in most cases, this affiliation was with the Tijaniyya.[17]

Thus, the establishment of the al-Ittihad al-Thaqafi al-Islami (ITI) in 1953, under the leadership of Cheikh Touré, may be seen as a watershed in the development of modern reformist organizations in Senegal, only insofar as it was the first organization to develop an encompassing programme of reform which also had a distinctively anti-Sufi character. Undoubtedly, it is the ITI's programme of reform which has not only influenced all subsequent movements of reform in Senegal, but has also exerted influence on Muslim movements of reform in countries which neighbour Senegal.[18]

ITI's own reform programme and public discourse itself drew inspiration from North African traditions of reform, especially the Algerian Jam'iyyat al-'Ulama' al-Muslimin al-Jaza'iriyyin.[19] In addition, ITI cultivated a religio-political discourse which was not only critical of the French colonial administration policies, but also attacked the Senegalese *tariqa*s; in particular, those *marabout*s (religious leaders)[20] who cooperated closely with the colonial administration. Its polemics against alleged acts of *bid'a makruha* (reprehensible innovation) such as excessive spending for marriage ceremonies and burials, the practice of the *dhikr*, as well as specific features of local ritual practices such as the wearing of *gri-gris* (amulets), became another important element of ITI's public discourse. In these ways, ITI can be regarded as the first tradition of reform in Senegal which turned against the 'esoteric episteme' as it had developed locally.[21] At the same time, ITI established Senegal's first reformist journal, *Le reveil islamique*, and propagated the theatre as a new form of expression of religious and political thought in Senegal's public sphere.[22] ITI's use of these 'modern' mass public mediums of expression indicates that it sought to sever links with the local esoteric tradition and its leadership, who ruled through personal networks, contacts and influence, and maintained their authority through genealogical ties and personal charisma. The new forms of expression cultivated by the ITI also show that the ITI was trying to woo the urban, literate and Western-educated Muslim populations which had started to grow considerably in size in the 1950s.

A closer examination of Cheikh Touré, as well as ITI's reform programme, indicates that the situation as presented above was not so clear cut when considering the implementation of their programme of reform in social and political terms: neither Cheikh Touré nor ITI thus categorically refused to cooperate with the (colonial) state, or condemned Sufism as a whole. Thus, Cheikh Touré never completely relinquished his ties with the Tijaniyya.[23] At the same time, Cheikh Touré and his followers were prepared to work with the state when specific issues of reform, such as the struggle against 'obsolete social and religious customs', could be linked with respective state policies of reform. This strategy is not uncommon. Muslim reformers have often supported the strategies of development as propagated by colonial or post-colonial administrations; in particular, when these strategies of development were presented as a kind of 'Islamic state' reformism. For instance, Islamic state reformism was characterized by its modernizing orientation, as in Mamadou Dia's policies of development in Senegal in the early 1960s, and was often directed against established religious scholars such as the *marabouts* of the *tariqas*.[24]

In the 1960s and 1970s, Muslim reformist organizations in Senegal largely lost their political autonomy and were incorporated into state-controlled associations such as the Fédération des Associations Islamiques du Sénégal (FAIS). Associations such as FAIS were again controlled by young *marabouts* of the Tijaniyya and Muridiyya *tariqas*, who were closely associated with the ruling party, Senghor's Union Progressiste Sénégalaise (UPS). In this period of time, loyalist Muslim functionaries, essentially regarded as 'reformers in the pay of the state', came to increasingly influence Muslim (and *étatist*) discourses on modernization and social development. As a result, leading members of *tariqa*s such as the late Khalifa Général of the Tijaniyya in Senegal, Shaykh Abd al-Aziz Sy (d. 1997), labelled Muslim reformers who supported these state-informed policies of modernization as '*islamologues fonctionnariés*' or 'Islamists in the pay of the state'.[25]

Only in the late 1970s were Muslim reformers able to free themselves of state control and establish new organizations such as the Jama'at 'Ibad ar-Rahman (JIR) and the Harakat al-Falah (HF). Today, the JIR may be regarded as Senegal's most important reformist organization, even though it has not managed to break the overwhelming authority and power of the Tijaniyya and Muridiyya *marabout*s. Initially, the JIR continued the reformist discourse of the ITI with respect to *bid'a* . In the late 1980s, the JIR seems to have realized, however, that the struggle against the *marabout*s and the *tariqa*s was largely counterproductive on account of the ongoing popularity of the *marabout*s. As a consequence, the JIR has suspended, since the early 1990s, its polemics against the religious leaders of the *tariqa*s and redirected it against the state. Thus, the JIR has managed to escape the dilemma of being accused of creating *fitna* (disruption, chaos, anarchy) by fighting against fellow Muslims.

More recently, the JIR seems to cultivate a public discourse which concentrates on topics such as the alleged moral decay of contemporary Senegalese society and issues such as drug abuse, prostitution and some of the nefarious effects of modernization, which may easily be pinned on the secular state and its inability to provide for balanced social development. At the same time, the issues of *bid'a* and the *marabout*s have stopped being the targets of JIR's criticism. Rather, the JIR, like other contemporary reform movements, concentrates on the development of modern Islamic schools and social activities, particularly those which aim to incorporate youth and women. In fact, the JIR (like Cheikh Touré and the Harakat al-Falah) now focuses largely on education. Its

Plate 1 Opening page of the *Monajat* of Hazrat 'Ali, Isfahan 1010/1601, Gulestan Palace Library no. 2251 (*Golestan Palace Library. A Portfolio of Miniature Paintings and Calligraphy*, Tehran 2000, p. 76)

Plate 2   Rug depicting Nur 'Ali Shah and Mushtaq 'Ali Shah, Kashan 1221/1806,
Tanavoli Collection (P. Tanavoli, *Kings, Heroes and Lovers*, Scorpion Publishing, London
1994, no. 54)

Plate 3 Silver coin of Shah Tahmasp II (1135–45/1722–32), minted in Tabriz, including the words, '*'Ali wali allah*', and the names of the 12 imams, Ashmolean Museum (Photo: Ashmolean Museum)

Plate 4   Mosque of al-Aqmar façade (Photo: Creswell Archive, Ashmolean Museum, no. 1010)

Plate 5   Embroidered fragment decorated with the words '*ana qamr*', Fatimid period; Ashmolean Museum, Newberry Collection, accession number EA 1984.402 (Photo: Ashmolean Museum)

Plate 6 Candlestick in the name of Muhammad b. Sadr al-Din Yusuf b. Salah al-Din, copper alloy inlaid with silver and gold, early fourteenth century; Nuhad Es-Said Collection (Photo: Nuhad Es-Said Collection)

Plate 7   Mihrab, mausoleum of Umm Kulthum, Cairo 519/1125 (Photo: Creswell
Archive, Ashmolean Museum, no. 3883)

Plate 8   Incense-burner of Sultan al-Malik al-Nasir Muhammad Ibn Qala'un, brass
inlaid with silver and gold, Cairo early fourteenth century; Nuhad Es-Said Collection
(Photo: Nuhad Es-Said Collection)

Plate 9 Embroidered fragment decorated with a repeating 'al-ʿizz', Cairo, c. third quarter of the thirteenth century; Ashmolean Museum, Newberry Collection, accession number EA 1984.44 (Photo: Ashmolean Museum)

educational efforts have stimulated, in the 1990s, the establishment of numerous reformist Islamic schools, which not only teach
established Islamic sciences such as Arabic, Qur'an and *hadith*,
but also stress the importance of 'marketable skills'[26] as well as the
education of girls and women. The success of these new schools
has again forced the *tariqa*s to follow suit with educational programmes of their own, which reproduce this trend in the
development of modern Islamic education.

Since the mid nineteenth century, Senegal has thus seen the
emergence of a distinctive 'associationist' tradition of reform. This
tradition spans five generations, and includes reformers who
attempted to translate multiple colonial and post-colonial modernities into their own context, by adopting, amongst others,
associationist forms of organization and expression. These
reformers legitimized their reform programmes with reference to
scholastic traditions which have developed outside Senegal in
places such as Algeria, Egypt, Libya, Saudi Arabia and Iran, and
they have evoked the scholastic canon of the Salafiyya movements
of reform (including the Wahhabiyya) in these locations.

Senegal has also seen the development of a 'second tradition' of
reform, however, which was more closely linked with locally
based *tariqa*s (see also the chart at the end of this article for a
comprehensive overview of the different traditions of reform
mentioned in the text). The reformers of this second tradition
referred to sources of inspiration which developed in the
Senegalese context,[27] or the established centres of the Tijaniyya in
Morocco and Algeria. Like their predecessors, these reformers
also attempted to translate multiple colonial and post-colonial
modernities into their context, while remaining true to Sufi
modes of organization and expression. It is important to note that
each tradition of reform and its respective chain of reformers
developed in constant interaction and dialogue with each other;
'associationist' movements of reform have influenced Sufi-
oriented movements of reform, and vice versa.[28] Equally, the
development of these traditions of reform in Senegal was not only
influenced by particular programmes of reform, but also by the
way in which the representatives of a specific generation of

reformers articulated their position in relation to another tradition of reform and/or a preceding generation of reformers.[29] The extent to which similar processes informed the development of specifically Sufi-oriented reform movements in Senegal is discussed below.

It is generally recognized that the 'venerable forefathers' of modern Sufism in Senegal are Ahmad Bamba (d. 1927) for the Muridiyya, or al-Hajj Malik Sy (d. 1922) and Abdallah Niass (d. 1922) for the Tijaniyya. These 'grand *marabouts*' struggled to find 'paths of accommodation'[30] with Senegal's colonial administration. After their respective deaths, a new generation of '*marabouts-fils*' emerged, who attempted to come to terms with the legacy of their fathers by either following the patterns of accommodation (with colonial rule) established by their fathers, or by trying to develop their own notions of accommodation. In addition, bitter disputes over the question of succession and *irshad* (spiritual guidance) developed. Such struggles were informed by 'dialectics of positioning' within the individual branches of a *tariqa* and the different maraboutic families.[31] These dialectics of positioning used religious, social and political issues to negotiate between *marabout*s, the maraboutic clientele and the colonial administration. Muhammad Niass's (d. 1959) succession to Abdallah Niass (d. 1922) was thus opposed by Ibrahim Niass (d. 1975), while Mansur Sy's (d. 1957) (and, later, Abd al-Aziz Sy's (d. 1997)) succession to Abubakar Sy (d. 1957) was opposed by Cheikh Tidiane Sy.[32] Within the Muridiyya, Muhammad Mustafa Mbakke's (d. 1945) succession to Amadou Bamba was opposed by Cheikh Anta Mbakke (d. 1941), while Falilou Mbakke's (d. 1968) succession to Muhammad Mustafa was opposed by Cheikh Ahmad Mbakke (d. 1978).[33]

Cheikh Tidiane Sy's aborted succession to his father, Abubakar Sy, in 1957, attests to the longevity of family disputes in Senegal over several generations and their religious and political implications. Cheikh Tidiane Sy was the son of the second Khalifa Général of the Sy branch of the Tijaniyya, Abubakar Sy (d. 1957), through al-Hajj Malik Sy's first wife, Rokhaya N'Diaye, and Abubakar Sy's third wife, Astou Kane. Abubakar Sy, however, had two half-brothers, Mansur (d. 1957) and Abd al-Aziz (d. 1997), by a different mother, namely Safiétou Niang, al-Hajj Malik Sy's second wife, who had come to dominate the house of the family in Tivaouane. In the dispute over succession to Abubakar Sy in 1957, first Mansur and then Abd al-Aziz managed to divert the succession from the direct patrilineage, i.e. from Abubakar Sy to his son Cheikh Tidiane Sy, and established the dominance of the 'Niang' branch of the Sy family as against the 'N'Diaye' branch.

The family dispute has continued ever since, and is today in the hands of the third generation of sons, grandsons, nephews, great-grandsons and grand-nephews of al-Hajj Malik Sy. Today, Sérigne Mustafa Sy represents the N'Diaye branch, whereas since 1997, the present Khalifa Général of the Sy family, Mansur Sy (a son of Abd al-Aziz), represents the Niang branch. This fifty-year-old family dispute shows that politics (of reform) may be subordinated in substantial ways to family history, and that political and/or religious disputes possibly mask other agendas. For instance, in the late 1950s, Cheikh Tidiane Sy not only introduced a different date for the *gammu* (annual family pilgrimage) to Tivaouane, but was also willing to cooperate with Cheikh Touré and ITI in order to fight the second branch of the family in both religio-symbolic as well as political terms.[34]

With respect to their relationship with the state, the second-generation *marabouts-fils* also developed a spectrum of different positions, which ranged from being 'close to power' and mere 'acceptance' of the state's role to 'withdrawal' from the state, and to active and militant opposition to the state. For instance, Abd al-Aziz Sy Jr., a leading *marabout* of the Tijaniyya and son of the Khalifa Général of the Sy branch of the Tijaniyya, came to assume a leading role in state-controlled Islamic associations, while many *marabouts* of the Muridiyya, including the Khalifa Général, Abdul Lahatte Mbakke, adopted attitudes of 'conspicuous indifference' with respect to the affairs of the state. In this regard, the community of Ceerno Mouhammadou Seydou Ba in Madina Gounass/ Casamance, as established in 1935, became famous for its policy of self-isolation. Whereas, at the other end of the spectrum, Sidi Lamine Niass or Abdoulaye Khalifa Niass gained notoriety for their spectacular critique of Leopold Sédar Senghor's policies of development and their call, in the late 1970s, for a 'jihad' in the context of the foundation of a new religio-political party, the 'Hisbollah'.[35]

While the second generation of '*marabout-fils*' dominated Sufi-oriented discourses from the 1930s into the 1970s, a new generation of '*marabouts-petit-fils*'[36] emerged in the 1980s. This new generation of 'grandson-*marabouts*' was also referred to as '*marabouts mondains*',[37] a term which refers to the worldly nature of the activities and the appearance of a number of third-generation *marabout*s such as Modou Kara Mbakké, a grandson of Mame Thierno Birahim Mbakke (a younger brother of Amadou Bamba), who established a Mouride youth movement, the Mouvement Mondial pour l'Unicité de Dieu (MMUD), which claims to have 500,000 supporters.[38] Another example of a '*marabout mondain*' is Sérigne Moustapha Sy, a son of Cheikh Tidiane Sy, who did not hesitate to address his young followers and disciples in the outfit of a rocker and music-star, while showing off, at the same time, his cosmopolitanism in scholarly diatribes against the moral decay of the Senegalese government in Wolof, French and Arabic. The usage of these three languages served to prove his rootedness in Islamic scholasticism (Arabic), modernity (French) and local tradition (Wolof).[39]

The generation of '*marabouts-petit-fils*' also developed the first youth movements within both the Tijaniyya and the Muridiyya *tariqa*s: the Da'irat al-Mustarshidin wa-l-Mustarshidat (DMM) for the Tijaniyya, as well as the Mouvement Mondial pour l'Unicité de Dieu (MMUD), the Hizbut Tarqiya (HT) and the Matlaboul Fawzaini (MF),[40] which have all emerged from the Muridiyya. These youth movements were marked by their associationist character and their distinctive style of approaching audiences. In addition, the DMM, the MMUD and the HT came out in support of modern expressions of youth culture such as music and sports, and Senegal's popular bands and musicians such as Youssou Ndour, Baba Maal and Ismail Lô, as well as the plethora of Dakar's rap-bands, reflected this turn to the youth in their texts, which have since assumed a remarkably religious character.[41]

The new Sufi-oriented movements of reform, such as the DMM or the HT, were characterized thus by the fact that they have adopted modern types of organization and expression which had been the domain of associationist movements of reform such as the ITI. Also, the generations of sons and grandsons have continued to pursue independent strategies with respect to politics, and seem to be increasingly prepared to question the authority of the 'fathers'; as expressed, for instance, in the *ndiggël* (Wolof: command) of the Khalifa Général of the Muridiyya.

The *ndiggël* of the Khalifa Général, in particular the *ndiggël politique*,[42] had been questioned for the first time in 1988 when a number of young Muridiyya *marabouts*, as well as many of the Muridiyya youth, were no longer prepared to follow the *ndiggël* of Khalifa Général Abdou Lahatte Mbakke and to vote for the Socialist Party in the presidential elections of that year. Rather, they supported the leader of the opposition, Abdoulaye Wade.[43] Abdou Lahatte Mbakké's successors, Abdou Khadre Mbakke (1989/ 1990) and Saliou Mbakke (since 1990), have since abstained from proclaiming a *ndiggël politique*, and more recent efforts to impose one have failed dramatically, as in the case of Modou Kara Mbakke, in 1999, who had asked his followers to vote for the Socialist Party in the 2000 presidential elections.[44]

The most prominent youth 'wings' of the Tijaniyya and the Muridiyya, the DMM and the HT, have also undergone a series of developments which reflect their efforts to negotiate specific religious, political and social issues, as well as personal disputes, within their respective *tariqa*s. The DMM was established in the middle of the 1970s as a youth movement of the Tijaniyya and was led, from 1976, by its Sérigne Mustafa Sy, a son of Cheikh Tidiane Sy. In the 1980s, the DMM became a major movement of support for President Abdou Diouf.[45] However, in 1993, Mustapha Sy organized a complete political *volte-face* and switched support to Abdoulaye Wade, Abdou Diouf's challenger in the 1993 presidential elections. In a short period of time, the DMM became one of the most outspoken movements opposed to Abdou Diouf. DMM protests against him led to riots in Dakar, which in turn led to Mustafa Sy's imprisonment in 1993. The DMM was interdicted in early 1994. In 1995, the movement was rehabilitated and subsequently renewed, albeit briefly, its support for Abdou Diouf.

When Abd al-Aziz Sy, the Khalifa Général of the Tijaniyya, died in 1997, Cheikh Tidiane Sy's efforts to finally rise to the position of the supreme leader of the family misfired again. The old feud between the two branches of the Sy family, as represented by Sérigne Mustafa Sy and the new Khalifa Général, Mansur Sy, resurfaced. As a consequence, Mustafa Sy and the DMM decided to renew their support for Abdoulaye Wade's call for *sopi* (change). In the run-up to the elections of 2000, Mustapha Sy decided to switch political allegiances yet again and to support the Parti de l'Unité et du Rassemblement (PUR), as established by Khalifa Diouf.[46]

While the DMM has been the most prominent youth movement within the Tijaniyya, the Hizbut Tarqiya (HT) had a similar role within the Muridiyya. The HT was founded in 1978 in Dakar as a Mouride students' *da'ira* (circle) under the name of 'Dahira des Étudiants Mourides de Dakar' (DEM),[47] which was under the patronage of the Khalifa Général of the Mourides, Abdou-Lahatte Mbakke. The movement became very popular in a short period of time and emerged as a major youth organization of the Muridiyya, led by Atou Diagne. When the rival Association des Jeunes Mourides was dissolved in 1986 by Abdou Lahatte Mbakke for being too outspoken, the DEM became even more important for the organization of the Mouride youth.[48] In 1992, the DEM was renamed Hizbut Tarqiya by the new Khalifa Général, Saliou Mbakke. In the 1990s, the influence of the Hizbut Tarqiya grew to such an extent that it was asked, in 1995, to organize the 1996 *magal* (pilgrimage festival) of Touba.[49] The HT subsequently appropriated an increasingly larger role in the management of the *tariqa*, not only with respect to the organization of the annual *magal*, but also in the representation of the Muridiyya in Senegal's public sphere and even with respect to access to the Khalifa Général. The increasing prominence of the movement (and the shutting out of other groups) was resented and regarded as a form of defiance and disrespect by a number of third-generation *'marabouts petit-fils'* of the Mbakke family. Their objections cited the rise of a non-Mbakke group to leading ranks within the *tariqa*,[50] as well as certain HT attitudes which publicly rejected the authority of the younger generation of Mbakke *marabout*s and, thus, implicitly, the principle of gaining inherited authority. When members of the Hizbut Tarqiya eventually refused Moustapha Saliou, the son of the Khalifa Général, Saliou Mbakke, access to his own father, the Khalifa Général disowned the group in July 1997.[51]

The recent fragmentation of established modes of authority within the Tijaniyya and Muridiyya *tariqa*s in Senegal can be attributed to the merging and blending of different modes of organization and expressions of reform over several generations. It cannot be said that such processes are confined to either 'Sufi' or 'reformist' traditions, but clearly inform a range of Muslim traditions and groups at various junctures in their respective histories. At the same time, references across both 'generations' and 'traditions' clearly emerge as a pattern of religious disputes in the Senegalese context. Contemporary reformers thus fight the '*islamologues fonctionnariés*' by referring to the first generation of non-Sufi-oriented reformers, in particular Cheikh Touré, who followed a similar argumentative pattern: in order to attack the *marabout*s of his time, especially those who collaborated with the colonial state, he established legitimizing links not only with the dissident *marabout*s of his time, but also with the generation of fathers of the '*marabouts-fils*' of his time, namely Ahmad Bamba and al-Hajj Malik Sy. A major element of Cheikh Touré's discourse was to present contemporary *marabout*s as corrupt, while depicting the founding fathers of both Tijaniyya and Muridiyya in Senegal, i.e. the 'grand *marabout*s', as good Muslims whose straight path had been abandoned by their own sons. Not surprisingly, trans-generational legitimizing references may also be identified within both the Tijaniyya and the Muridiyya. While the case of Cheikh Tidiane Sy has already been presented above, the leader of the Hizbut Tarqiya, Atou Diagne, has recently challenged the third generation of leading *marabout*s of the Muridiyya, by claiming that leadership within the Muridiyya must not necessarily be linked with the Mbakke family. That is, any *murid* could become the Khalifa Général and the direct allegiance with Ahmad Bamba (and not loyalty to his grandsons) was more important for the *murid*s than loyalty towards the '*marabouts petit-fils*'.[52]

East Africa

Senegal's histories of Muslim reform traditions and processes are comparable to those of coastal East Africa. Like Senegal, coastal East Africa had a tradition of Sufi-oriented reformers that dates to the late nineteenth century. These include the Qadiriyya and the Alawiyya *tariqa*s, as represented by Shaykh Uways al-Barawi (d. 1909), Sayyid Ahmad b. Sumayt (d. 1925), Abdallah Ba Kathir al-Kindi (d. 1925) and Sayyid Habib Salih (d. 1937). This first generation of reformers introduced new rituals such as new forms of *dhikr* and the celebration of the *mawlid al-nabi* (the birthday of the Prophet), and advocated reforms in Islamic education. As in Senegal, the first generation of Sufi-oriented reformers of coastal East Africa also tried to come to terms with colonial rule (established in this region by Germany and Britain) and to find paths of accommodation within it. Some of the above-mentioned scholars worked for the colonial administration as *qadi*s (judges), teachers and clerks. At the same time, as in Senegal, some scholars became increasingly aware of reformist discourses outside of their local context. In particular, scholars such as Sayyid Ahmad b. Ali Mansab (d. 1927) or Burhan Mkelle (d. 1949) took note of reformist discourses led by prominent Salafis in Egypt.[53] As a group, this first generation of Sufi-oriented reformers influenced religio-political debates in East Africa from the 1880s to the late 1920s.

From the 1930s to the 1950s, a new generation of Sufi-oriented reformers, such as Sayyid Umar b. Sumayt (d. 1976), Sayyid Umar Abdallah (d. 1988) and Shaykh Hassan b. Ameir (d. 1979), began to modify established modes of reform. Like their predecessors, they stressed the importance of Islamic education and directed modern Islamic schools. A poignant example of their activities was the establishment of the Muslim Academy in Zanzibar in 1951 and its subsequent administration by Sayyid Umar Abdallah, a well-known religious scholar affiliated with both the Alawiyya and Qadiriyya *tariqa*s. The Muslim Academy represented a different approach to Islamic education insofar as it was no longer marked by teacher-master oriented forms of learning in the *madrasa*, but by institution-oriented forms of learning in a new type of school, the *ma'had* (institute). As was the case with the Senegalese '*écoles franco-arabes*', these new forms of learning adopted Western European concepts of education, even when combined with traditional Islamic disciplines. This new orientation brought about several changes: 'marketable' skills were given more stress than 'social' skills;[54] the blackboard replaced the *lauh* (wooden plank); a curriculum and a timetable replaced individual learning; the charismatic scholar-educator was eclipsed by a largely depersonalized educational apparatus consisting of school buildings, a body of teachers and curricula.[55] Essentially, the temporal rhythms of the *madrasa*, that focused on individual progress and timing, was gradually replaced by the regimented schedule of *ma'had*-school-time that stressed standardized and synchronized learning. The application of these new temporal structures to the educational system served to marginalize the 'esoteric episteme' identified with the previous generation of reformers.

In 1964, Zanzibar and Tanganyika formed the Union of Tanzania under the leadership of Julius Nyerere (President from 1964–1985, d. 1996). In the context of Nyerere's *ujamaa* (community) policies,[56] there emerged a group of Muslim bureaucrats, often linked to the Qadiriyya and the Shadhiliyya *tariqa*s, who supported state-informed policies of reform and tried to translate state-informed programmes of modernization into an 'Islamic code'. By the 1970s, scholars such as Abdallah Chaurembo and Adam Nasibu came to form a group of Tanzanian '*islamologues fonctionnariés*', organized in a party-linked association called Baraza Kuu la Waislamu Tanzania (BAKWATA) (Supreme Council for Tanzanian Muslims). These 'BAKWATA *shaykhs*' managed to marginalize the most outspoken representatives of the earlier tradition of reform, such as Shaykh Hassan b. Ameir who was the most respected *shaykh* of the Qadiriyya *tariqa* and Mufti of Tanzania until 1968, and who had opposed Julius Nyerere's policies.[57] But despite their efforts, the Tanzanian '*islamologues fonctionnariés*' largely failed to influence the public discourse in their societies on Islamic reform.

As was the case in Senegal, it is misleading to assume that *tariqa*s in Tanzania formed a homogeneous block over time. Rather, the disputes between *shaykh*s of the Qadiriyya and the Shadhiliyya *tariqa*s in the late 1960s and the 1970s, which led to the foundation of BAKWATA,[58] show that the *tariqa*s were split into a number of networks, some who supported the state, and others, such as Shaykh Nur ud-Din Hussein (b. 1924–1925), who opposed it or tried to keep their distance. Shaykh Nur ud-Din's example also shows that an independent and, at times, critical position with respect to the state in Tanzania was not a privilege of activist Muslim groups, but was also cultivated by scholars who represented the 'esoteric' episteme.

Since the late 1950s, Shaykh Nur ud-Din has become the leader of the Shadhiliyya *tariqa* in contemporary Tanzania and is renowned for his politically independent positions. He studied with local *shaykh*s in Tanzania and at al-Azhar in Cairo, before settling in Lindi, Southern Tanzania, in the early 1950s. At Lindi, he started a *madrasa* and worked in different professions, such as secretary for a mangrove wood company, before he started his own business as a trader of dried fish. In 1965, he was put under arrest for allegedly plotting against Nyerere, and spent eight months in prison in Mtwara. After his release from prison he settled in Tanga and resumed his trading and teaching activities, and established a new *madrasa* in Korogwe, near Tanga. In 1980, he moved to Dar es Salaam and established another *zawiya* and *madrasa* in the Kariakoo quarter. In 1992, he set up the 'Hajj Trust', a private company that specialized in the organization of the *hajj* for Tanzanian (mainland) pilgrims. Although, formally, the organization of the *hajj* had been the privilege of BAKWATA, through his 'Hajj Trust' Shaykh Nur ud-Din became a household name in virtually every large town in Tanzania. Through such activities, Shaykh Nur ud-Din has become one of the most respected religious scholars in contemporary Tanzania. Furthermore, he has gained status because he is seen to be independent from BAKWATA. In addition, Shaykh Nur ud-Din has gained national importance as the leader of the Baraza Kuu la Jumuiya na Taasisi za Kiislamu (Supreme Council of Islamic Organizations and Institutions in Tanzania), established in 1992. This organization is a 'Shadhili' NGO, based in Dar es Salaam at Kariakoo. Recently, the Baraza Kuu has assumed control over the 'Tanzania Islamic Centre' at Magomeni, one of Tanzania´s most prominent 'Islamic centres', and was involved in an initiative to take over BAKWATA-controlled mosques in Dar es Salaam.[59] Shaykh Nur ud-Din and the Baraza Kuu also represent a new generation of Sufi-oriented scholars who have adopted associationist/NGO modes of organization. Among these are, apart from the Baraza Kuu, the Katiba ya Jumuiya Zawiyatul Qadiriyya Tanzania (Constitution of Qadiri Associations of Tanzania), an NGO established in 1990 at Arusha by Shaykh Muhammad Nassor and Shaykh Muhammad Abd ar-Rahman Dedes. While the Katiba cooperates closely with the Tanzanian state, the Baraza Kuu has cultivated links with some activist groups opposed to the state.

Parallel to these developments, Tanzania, like Senegal, has been home to reformers who have attempted to translate multiple (non-Muslim) modernities into their local contexts, while adopting associationist modes of organization and expression and fighting against those who advocated the 'esoteric episteme'. Reformers such as Shaykh al-Amin b. Ali al-Mazrui (d. 1949) and, later, Sayyid Hamid b. Ahmad Mansab (d. 1965) and Shaykh Abdallah Salih al-Farsi (d. 1982) rejected some features of the locally established Sufi-oriented traditions of religious practice, particularly the *dhikr* or specific forms of *mawlid*.[60] Shaykh al-Amin b. Ali al-Mazrui also advocated new and modern approaches to Islamic education and established the first reformist newspapers such as *al-Islah*. Despite a rather general critique of the colonial situation as such, they were prepared, however, to work for the colonial (and post-colonial) administration. In particular, they sought to define specific projects of development within the framework of the colonial system.

After Tanzania's independence and in the wake of Nyerere's *ujamaa* policies, some disciples and students of Shaykh al-Amin b. Ali al-Mazrui and Shaykh Abdallah Salih al-Farsi started to develop even more radical and activist positions with respect to Sufism and the post-colonial state. This new generation of reformers were characterized by their staunch, albeit individualistic and unorganized, opposition to the post-colonial state. Among them, scholars such as Shaykh Saidi Musa, Ahmad b. Hamid Mansab (d. 1977), Ali Rashad or Muhammad Mansab (d. 2002) cultivated new regional orientations towards Sudan, Saudi Arabia and Iran. However, their attitudes failed to hold sway over local populations.

Since the 1980s, a younger generation of activist Muslims has been able to gain larger audiences. This generation of activist Muslims, as represented by Shaykh Nassor Bachu in Zanzibar and Ally Bassaleh in mainland Tanzania, have started openly to fight against state-paid Muslim functionaries. By intensifying the critique of the post-colonial state and by adopting increasingly militant forms of action which include new forms of public preaching (*mihadhara*), often inspired by Christian Pentecostal forms of preaching,[61] they have managed to exert a greater influence over local populations than earlier generations of reformers. An important feature of this new generation of Muslim reformers is that they have established activist organizations, such as Uamsho (Reawakening) or the Ansar as-Sunna, which are independent of BAKWATA. Also, they have somewhat redirected their attacks away from Sufi scholars towards the state and the Christian churches operating in the region.

The generational dimension and the importance of legitimizing references

When comparing the reform movements of Senegal and East Africa, a common pattern of development emerges in which there is dialectical interaction of not only reform movements with their respective social and political contexts as well as between different reform groups, but also between different generations within a particular tradition of reform. With regard to the latter, one generation of reformers follows its predecessor, responding to established norms of thought and practice. Each generation of reformers is linked by specific and distinctive 'markers' of reform and may consequently be clearly identified with a particular tradition of reform. The markers of reform are the specific ways in which reform is translated into social contexts and acquires relevance in everyday life. Some of these markers include:

1. specific texts which are seen as key texts;
2. distinctive theological, political or social positions, as presented in the respective texts;
3. a distinctive use of media, as developed in the twentieth century in the cultivation of newspapers and pamphlets, the radio, cassettes, the TV and the internet;
4. distinctive positions with respect to ritual issues (i.e. rejection/advancement of *dhikr*, *mawlid*, cultivation of *tajwid*);[62]
5. specific approaches to language (i.e. Arabic, local/vernacular) and specific disciplines in the canon of Islamic learning (i.e. preference of *hadith* over *fiqh*; *tajwid* over *mawlid*);
6. stress on exclusivity or inclusiveness of the respective movement;
7. cultivation of specific trans-local links (i.e. Egypt, Iran, Saudi Arabia, Libya);
8. different formative biographical experiences (i.e. struggle for independence, struggle against colonialism and the post-colonial state);
9. specific modes of teacher-disciple relationships, as well as specific concepts of education and orientation of the curricula (i.e. charismatic education/institutional learning, social skills/marketable skills, different temporal regimes; see above); and
10. distinctive positions with regard to the state, other reformers, opponents or society.

Sooner or later, however, these markers of reform may be adopted as 'cross-overs' by another tradition of reform and a subsequent generation of reformers. For example, cross-overs have been a major feature of Sufi-oriented traditions of reform in both Senegal and Tanzania, which have adopted, as we have seen above, a number of organizational features from associationist movements of reform. The same is true for associationist movements of reform, which have adopted 'Sufi' modes of expression as, for instance, the way in which *tajwid* ceremonies are organized in *dhikr*-like reunions. At the same time, Muslim movements of reform may adopt (consciously or unconsciously) specific modes of preaching, media-use or approaches to texts from non-Muslim religious or political movements. Such trans-religious cross-overs are clearly visible in the development of 'Pentecostal Islam' in South Africa, Tanzania and Nigeria.[63]

The different generations and traditions of reform are also characterized, as described above, by disputes which contribute thus to define the distinct character of a specific generation of reformers. These disputes between both contemporary and/or those between 'new' and 'old' movements of reform are linked with specific strategies of argumentation, which are again marked by 'legitimizing references' cultivated by the different groups. These legitimizing references may assume a trans-local, trans-historical, trans-traditional or trans-generational character, all of which attest to the pluralistic character of reform in Muslim contexts.[64] More specifically:

1.   A group of reformers may try to establish or activate a (new) trans-local link with a spiritual centre of the same tradition of learning (such as Baghdad for the Qadiriyya or Fes for the Tijaniyya), which had, until then, been unknown, irrelevant or neglected in a specific local context, in order to marginal-ize competing sub-centres *within* the same tradition.[65] Reformers may also establish trans-local links with a centre of authority, which represents *another* interpretation of reform.[66]

2.   A group of reformers may establish a trans-historical (and often rather virtual) link to the canon of referential texts and/or a new interpretation of these texts (by stressing *hadith* more than *fiqh*, for instance, by quoting a hitherto neglected yet classical author), or by referring to the venera-ble forefathers, *al-salaf al-salih*, or, most often, the *sunna* of the Prophet.[67]

3. A group of reformers may come to establish trans-traditional legitimizing links to another tradition of reform.
4. Finally, a group of reformers could establish a trans-generational link within the same tradition of reform to the generation of the fathers or grandfathers to give legitimacy to their cause. Such a trans-generational link serves to recall not only a respected tradition of thought (as with trans-traditional references), but also the memory of a respected personality, a saint, a respected scholar or a *mujtahid*.

In disputes between distinctive traditions of reform, trans-generational dialectics are particularly important when a new generation of reformers tries to bring an established tradition of reformers into disrepute by referring to an (allegedly sound) tradition established by a previous generation. For example, in East Africa, the present generation of activist Muslims opposes the generation of state-paid Muslim reformers ('BAKWATA-Muslims') by making reference to scholars such as Shaykh Hassan b. Ameir (d. 1979), the former Mufti of Tanganyika and Tanzania and major leader of pre-independence Muslim religious scholars. Even though Shaykh Hassan b. Ameir was known to have been affiliated with the Qadiriyya, i.e. a *tariqa* which was otherwise attacked by contemporary Muslim activists as representing both *bid'a* and 'BAKWATA- (i.e. government) Islam', Shaykh Hassan b. Ameir's legacy could easily be presented as yet another example of Tanzanian anti-Muslim policies, as Shaykh Hassan b. Ameir had indeed been victimized, since the mid 1960s, by both Nyerere and a generation of post-independence 'BAKWATA-Muslims'. The trans-generational link between contemporary reformers in Tanzania and a major figure of Muslim reform of the 1950s and 1960s thus also had a distinctive trans-traditional character.

A major case for the cultivation of trans-traditional, trans-historical, trans-generational, as well as trans-local, legitimizing references in East Africa is a dispute between two major *shaykhs* of the Qadiriyya, Shaykh Abd al-Aziz b. Abd al-Ghani al-Amawi (d. 1896) and Shaykh Uways al-Barawi (d. 1909), in the late nineteenth century. Shaykh Uways was from Brawa.[68] He was one of the few East African scholars of the Qadiriyya *tariqa*, who managed to visit Baghdad, the spiritual centre of the Qadiriyya, in the 1870s and 1880s. After his return home from Baghdad, in 1883, he claimed a leading role in the local scholarly establishment on account of his great scholarship and his direct connections with the Qadiriyya centre at Baghdad. While the claim was rejected in his native Brawa, it found considerable recognition in other parts of East Africa, in particular at Zanzibar, which soon became a major centre of his activities.

After the late 1880s, his specific interpretation of the teachings of the Qadiriyya became popular, especially among converts to Islam. These teachings were connected with a number of distinctive religious practices, in particular the *zikri ya kukohoa* (meditative prayer of the cough), a *dhikr* implying respiratory exercises of rhythmic inhaling and exhaling (i.e. *anfas*, lit. breath). These new *dhikr* practices were soon attacked as a *bid'a* by senior scholars of the Qadiriyya and particularly Shaykh Abd al-Aziz, who was, at the time, the paramount scholar of the Qadiriyya. The rapid spread of Shaykh Uways's movement must have been seen as a threat by Shaykh Abd al-Aziz. In one of his polemical poems against the *zikri ya kukohoa*, Shaykh Abd al-Aziz claimed that the *zikri ya kukohoa* resembled the '(pre-Islamic) African dance' and 'spirit possession cults' such as Ngoma, Lelemama or Pepo, where women have a leading role. He writes: '*Mashekhe mnaosoma, na vitabu kufunuwa; dhikiri yenu ni ngoma, kadiri itavyokuwa; hiyo ima lelemama, au pepo kimamvuwa; wapi ilikozuliwa, ibada ya kukohoa?*' (Oh you scholars, read and discover your (own) books; your *dhikr* is nothing but *ngoma*, think! Why is it like that? Your *dhikr* might even be a kind of *lelemama* or *pepo*; where was this worship of coughing invented/born?).[69]

It is important to stress, however, that Shaykh Abd al-Aziz had also introduced, in the 1860s, another form of the *zikri*, namely the *zikri ya dufu* (meditative prayer of the drum),[70] which had also been attacked, by the established scholars of that time, as a *bid'a makruha* (a reprehensible innovation). Despite this, Shaykh Abd al-Aziz did not hesitate to attack the *zikri ya kukohoa* in the 1890s as a reprehensible innovation, and more particularly as a form of mixing '(pre-Islamic) African' customs with Islamic practice. Yet, while the Amawi branch of the Qadiriyya depicted the *zikri ya kukohoa* as a *bid'a*, it was nothing new for Shaykh Uways, who had witnessed this form of the *dhikr* when he was studying in Baghdad where the *zikri ya kukohoa* formed part of Qadiri tradition. The attacks on the *zikri ya kukohoa* as a *bid'a* can be regarded as a function of local religious disputes, with their respective strategies of legitimization and delegitimization.

The critique of specific forms of Sufi teachings and rituals is often connected thus with dialectics of competition among religious scholars over questions of religious authority in rather local contexts of dispute, even if the discursive elements activated for the legitimization of specific religious positions are quoted from greater, trans-local and perhaps even universal discursive traditions, canons or frames of reference.[71] As such, these discursive traditions and strategies of argumentation have residual character and may be activated any time in comparable constellations of dispute, should the need arise.

This residual character is exemplified in the continuity of the Uways versus al-Aziz debate in the 1940s, by Shaykh Abdallah Salih al-Farsi (d. 1982). By quoting the polemical poem which Shakyh al-Amawi had composed to attack the *zikri ya kukohoa* practices of Shaykh Uways in the 1890s, Shaykh Abdallah Salih advanced his own struggle against the *zikri ya kukohoa* practices of another Qadiriyya scholar, Shaykh Mahmud b. Kombo from Makunduchi, Zanzibar (d. 1968).[72] Shaykh Abdallah Salih could point out thereby, in a very scholarly and clever way to the Qadiris of his time, that even well-known and respected Qadiri scholars of the past, such as Shaykh al-Amawi, had criticized these ritual excesses.

In his polemics against the *zikri ya kukohoa*, Shaykh al-Farsi never mentioned, however, that Shaykh al-Amawi had written, in the 1860s, as has been mentioned above, a treatise in defence of the *zikri ya dufu*, although this practice could as easily be attacked as a *bid'a* as the practice of the *zikri ya kukohoa*. Although Shaykh Abdallah Salih's reference to al-Amawi's poem was thus totally out of its temporal context, it was absolutely set within a context of similar epistemological patterns of confrontation. In each case of conflict, different legitimizing links of trans-local, trans-historical and/or trans-traditional character were cultivated: to Baghdad, in Shaykh Uways's case against Shaykh al-Amawi in the 1890s; and to an earlier tradition of Islamic learning, represented as being more authentic Qadiri than contemporary practices, in the case of Shaykh Abdallah Salih's attack against Shaykh Mahmud in the 1940s.[73]

The disputes between these religious scholars and these traditions of reform clearly show that interpretation and presentation of, for instance, a specific ritual in the respective texts and discourses of a specific period of time, as orthodox or unorthodox, as Islamic or un-Islamic, as African or Arab, may not only be rather deceptive, as being based on legitimizing considerations. At the same time, these disputes should be seen to be set within respective contexts of dispute and the negotiation of claims for leadership and hegemony of definition (*Deutungshegemonie*) with respect to ritual, religious or political issues. As a consequence, the interpretation of the issues at stake as well as the legitimizing references and links may change any time, if the context changes. The fact that trans-local, trans-historical, trans-traditional or trans-generational links may be cultivated for strategic purposes, such as the legitimization of specific religious claims of superiority of one tradition over another in contexts of conflict, also points to the basic instrumentability (*Instrumentalisierbarkeit*) as well as the interpretationability of traditions and texts, or the canon (of Islam, of Islamic teaching) as such. This strategic '*disponabilité*' of traditions, texts and the canon again disproves essentialist reductions of Islam and Muslim societies.[74]

Conclusion

Based on the case studies discussed here, it can be suggested that traditions of reform have evolved not only in a dialectical process of interaction with the respective context of time and region (space) and each other, but also in a generational mode of interaction with preceding traditions of reform, in a dialogue with the past.[75] Such preceding traditions of reform may be quoted (and activated for a contemporary context) in trans-traditional, trans-historical, trans-generational and trans-local terms. As a consequence, distinctive generations and traditions of reform can only be identified and analysed, after the programmes and markers of reform have been analysed in their respective discursive, spatial and historical contexts. The interplay between traditions, texts and the canon through space and over time disproves essentialist reductions of Islam and Muslim societies, confirming Talal Asad's basic assumption of the contested and pluralist nature of Islam and Muslim traditions and movements, and enabling us to overcome obsolete yet convenient dichotomous constructions of Muslim societies.

Table 1. Traditions of Reform

Traditions of Reform I: The 'Sufi-oriented' Tradition in Senegal

Tariqa	Muridiyya
Generation *'père'*	Ahmad Bamba
Generation *'fils'*	Muhammad Mustafa Mbakke (Khalifa Général) vs. Cheikh Anta
	Falilou Mbakke (Khalifa Général) vs. Cheikh Ahmad
	Abdou Lahatte Mbakke (Khalifa Général)
	Saliou Mbakke (Khalifa Général)
Generation *'petit-fils'*	Atou Diagne (HT) vs. Moustapha Saliou
	Modou Kara Mbakke (MMUD)

Tariqa	Tijaniyya	
Generation *'père'*	al-Hajj Malik Sy	Abdallah Niass
Generation *'fils'*	Abubakar Sy	Muhammad vs. Ibrahim Niass
	Abd al-Aziz vs. Cheikh Tidiane	Ahmad Khalifa, Sidi Lamine
Generation *'petit-fils'*	Mansur Sy vs. Moustapha Sy	Hassan Cissé

Traditions of Reform II: The 'Associationist' Tradition in Senegal

Formative period (1840s–1900s)	Muslim civil rights movement
Early associationist period (1900s–1940s)	*Hajj* associations
UCM (1950s)	Cheikh Touré
State-informed reform (1960s and 1970s)	FAIS and others
Contemporary associationist period (since 1980s)	Jama'at 'Ibad ar-Rahman, Harakat al-Falah

Traditions of Reform III: The 'Associationist' Tradition in Tanzania

Formative period (1920s–1940s)	Shaykh al-Amin b. Ali al-Mazrui
Late colonial period (1950s–1960s)	Shaykh Abdallah Salih al-Farsi
State-informed reform (1970s)	BAKWATA
Activist groups (since the 1980s)	Ansar as-Sunna, Uamsho (Nassor Bachu)

Traditions of Reform IV: The 'Sufi-oriented' Tradition in Tanzania

Early colonial period (1880s–1930s)	Shaykh Uways vs. Shaykh Abd al-Aziz (Qadiriyya)
	Sayyid Ahmad b. Sumayt, Bakathir al-Kindi,
	Habib Saleh (Alawiyya)
Late colonial period (1940s–1960s)	Sayyid Umar Abdallah, Shaykh Hassan b. Ameir
	Burhan Mkelle, Shaykh Hassan Badawi
	Umar b. Sumayt (Alawiyya)
BAKWATA period (1970s)	Abdallah Chaurembo
Associationist period (since the 1980s)	Shaykh Nur ud-Din (Shadhiliyya) Muhammad Nassor (Qadiriyya)

8

Justifying Islamic Pluralism: Reflections from Indonesia and France

John R. Bowen

Popular perceptions to the contrary, Islam has a long and strong history of recognizing that questions of norms and laws have many legitimate possible answers. Beginning in the eighth century, scholars developed different ways of interpreting the sacred texts. Some scholars emphasized the use of reason and analogy in applying scripture to everyday life, while others gave greater weight to the well-documented statements and actions of the Prophet Muhammad. To these differences in interpreting scripture were added differences in societies and cultures in the Muslim world. In their practical jurisprudence (*fiqh*), Muslim jurists and judges took account of local norms and practices to the extent that these did not violate God's commands. As Muslims took their religion outside the Arabian homeland, these cultural differences increasingly shaped and differentiated the emerging traditions of normative and legal reasoning.

Eventually, these traditions became distinct legal schools (*madhhabs*). Although these schools differ on many important matters of ritual and social norms, most Muslims have considered these differences in interpreting scripture to be legitimate, the differences that inevitably arise when fallible humans attempt to read the signs left by God.[1]

By the early twentieth century, some Muslim scholars had sought to move beyond the recognized *madhhabs* and create new understandings of Islamic law, ones that would be better suited to the conditions of life in the modern world. These scholars argued that Muslims should return to scripture, or to the objectives (*maqasid*) of scripture, rather than to their literal meaning. These modernist or reformist positions ran counter to the older practices of Islamic jurisprudence, and elicited counter-arguments; the debates continue to the present day.[2]

Today, Muslim public intellectuals continue to debate the possibilities and limitations of normative and legal pluralism within Islam, i.e. the co-existence of distinct sets of Islamic norms, which may or may not be given the force of law, in the Muslim world.[3] They do so not only in societies of a relatively recent Muslim presence, such as in North America and Europe, but also in Egypt, Saudi Arabia, Indonesia and elsewhere. Many are asking whether Muslims should base their actions on the traditions of jurisprudence or whether they should rethink Islam in terms of its broader principles, and, if so, what those principles should be. In Europe and North America, they consider whether, in the absence of Islamic institutions, Muslims ought to adapt to and participate in non-Muslim banks, courts, and schools, or whether they should create Islamic substitutes for these institutions.

In what follows, I will focus less on specific proposals for adaptation or innovation than on ways Muslim public intellectuals seek to justify their positions. I draw on current debates amongst Muslims in Indonesia and France to present three quite distinct ways of understanding and judging the co-existence of competing norms in Islam, what I shall refer to as the general issue of normative pluralism. Indonesia and France share more than one might suspect, from a centralizing political structure recently challenged by demands for decentralization to a general sense that Islam, although long established in the one place, recently arrived in the other, brings new values and cultural forms that should be adapted to the country. In both places, this sense of discord has given rise to new and creative efforts to rethink Islamic traditions of normative and legal reasoning.

These new ways of thinking are challenged by those who advocate continuing long-established forms of jurisprudence, and these challenges produce, in turn, justifications for innovation. In what follows, I distinguish between three forms these justifications have taken. The first takes a pluralism of cultures as offering a justification for a pluralism of Islamic norms. Those who make this argument point to the cultural differences between the homelands of Islamic jurisprudence in the Arabic-speaking world and other lands settled by Muslims (in this case, Indonesia), arguing that the traditional legal schools were informed by the culture of Arab society, and urge that new Islamic norms be developed, ones that would be more appropriate to the different cultural values in other societies.

The second form of justification, in a sense the obverse of the first, points to the dominant non-Muslim character of other new lands of Muslim settlement (in this case, Europe) to claim exemptions from Islamic rules for Muslim residents of those areas. This justification on the basis of social necessity or 'emergency' (*darurat*) is highly controversial, in that it depends on the idea of distinct realms, the Islamic and the non-Islamic, defined in a way that is both religious and political, and because it denies the universal applicability of jurisprudence. Finally, a third argument opposes making distinctions based on regions, not because these thinkers wish to apply traditional Islamic jurisprudence everywhere, but because they propose that Muslims rethink norms and laws on the basis of general principles. All three forms of justification have their roots in long-standing positions taken by Muslim scholars, but all three incite considerable controversy today.

Cultural pluralism as justification in Indonesia

Indonesia is both the largest Muslim society in the world and one that is particularly distant from Middle East cultural traditions.[4] Islam came to Indonesia and most of Southeast Asia by way of trade and cultural exchange, and was adopted and adapted with local conditions in mind. But Indonesian Muslim scholars have kept up a lively exchange of ideas with scholars in the Middle East over the centuries. Due to their multiple interactions with the Middle East and other parts of the Muslim world, Indonesians have been well aware of the general diversity of the Muslim world, the dominant legal schools, as well as their own, internal cultural diversity.

This internal diversity is usually talked about in terms of *adat*, a word that has strong connotations of localism, although of course it comes from Arabic. In Indonesia, *adat* can refer to the rules or practices of social life, to feelings and a sense of propriety, or to a somewhat thinner sense of tradition and custom. Or it can mean 'customary norms' as opposed to Islamic law or state law. It also has a narrower sense of '*adat* law' (*hukum adat*), an expression whose systematic use dates from the period of Dutch colonial rule. To the extent that colonial rulers in the Dutch East Indies wished to rule indirectly, they tried to determine what the local laws might be, and those they consolidated into what they termed *adatrecht* (*adat* law). Dutch (and to a lesser extent Indies) anthropologists and administrators compiled manuals of the laws in each '*adat* area' in the Dutch East Indies, and in some regions judges continue to rely on these colonial-era manuals in making decisions. Thus, Indonesian *adat* differs from '*urf*', as it is known in most other Muslim societies, in that it is seen as an alternative to Islamic law, as having sources distinct from Islam, namely in local practices, and as existing in the form of distinct, often written, codes.[5] In all its uses, it signals the fact that Indonesia's many local societies have their own ways of resolving disputes, conducting marriages, and so forth.

Islamic law as such also has a long history in Indonesia. Certain '*ulama*' gave legal opinions, usually based on Shafi'i teachings, and heard disputes, usually about divorce, and more rarely about inheritance. The Dutch created a set of (European-styled) Islamic tribunals on Java to hear a limited range of Muslim cases. But Islamic courts were only slowly integrated into the Indonesian legal system; a uniform system of Islamic courts, known as Pengadilan Agama ('Religious Courts'), was created only in 1989, and a code of Islamic law was promulgated by Presidential decree in 1992.

Some local systems of *adat* and some tenets of Islamic law have conflicted with a third set of norms, namely the general sense that women and men had equal claims on property and in married life. In general, Southeast Asian societies are marked by relative gender equality: women and men work together in the fields, in child care, and in trading and education. Islamic law, by contrast, offered women a post-divorce payment rather than a share of property, and gave men rights to initiate divorce not also possessed by women. *Adat* was not always any different; some systems gave only sons rights to land, although more rarely women inherited, most famously among the Minangkabau people of West Sumatra.

Beginning in the 1930s, women's groups demanded equal property rights for women and reform of marriage and divorce laws. After independence, the Indonesian Supreme Court proclaimed that a new, post-Revolutionary 'living *adat*' held the equality of men and women as a notable principle. Others tried to develop a new Indonesian tradition of Islamic jurisprudence, and they did so by pointing to the cultural specificity of Indonesian values and practices *vis-à-vis* the Arab world.

One such Muslim jurist was Professor Hazairin, of the University of Indonesia Law School. Hazairin had been trained as a scholar of *adat* law, but also taught Islamic law. In the 1960s, he turned his attention increasingly to Islamic law. He urged his fellow jurists to develop an 'Indonesian *madhhab*', based on the bilateral principle that rights to property extend through sons and daughters. He argued that Islamic inheritance law contains general and universal principles, notably the principle that both women and men inherit property, and also specific rules. The rules derive from the Arab culture within which early jurists wrote, and in a different time and place they may be discarded, he argued. Hazairin's approach to jurisprudence betrays a type of cultural pluralism.

For example, Hazairin pointed out that according to classical *fiqh*, by which he meant specifically the Shafi'i school, after certain fixed shares of an estate have been awarded, the remainder of the estate is divided in such a way that agnatic relatives (related through males) take priority over uterine relatives (related through females). Arab jurists decided on this priority because Arab society was patriarchal. For Hazairin, this is confirmed by the fact that Iran-based schools of Shi'i jurisprudence do not favour agnatic over uterine relatives. Both legal traditions are appropriate for the society with which they are concerned. He states:

> The Sunni approach is correct because it is in accord with their Arab society and so is the Shi'i one because it fits their society's needs. I believe that had there been a Minangkabau [West Sumatran] person among the Messenger's apostles, that person would have constructed a *fiqh* for his group that would have met the demands of the Qur'an and Sunna but then would have favoured not the agnates but to the contrary the uterine relatives according to the maternal *adat* of the Minangkabau.[6]

Hazairin's pluralist approach to jurisprudence was adopted by his students, many of whom became the leading architects of *fiqh* reform in the 1980s and 1990s. Indeed, a number of these students are today's older generation of law professors and Supreme Court justices. They draw on Hazairin's argument in advocating current reforms, including the 1992 Compilation of Islamic Law. One of the scholars who formulated the Compilation – Professor Muhammad Daud Ali – describes how he and others drew on history and culture in determining the new rule that orphaned grandchildren should inherit the share their parents would have received:

> We took as our primary sources the text of the Qur'an and Sunna. But in practice we were flexible because the Qur'an, as we all know, is not a law book, nor is the *hadith*. They are the 'mother books' containing fundamental messages for people everywhere and throughout time ... [We] always considered the conditions under which verses were revealed and *hadith* pronounced. In this way the general principles contained in these two sources could be developed according to the changing conditions of time and place.

> If something was not fixed in the text of Qur'an and *hadith* but was felt to be among the needs of Muslim society today, we developed a 'new line of law', such as the right of a child to take over the status of a predeceased parent when an estate is divided. We used the *fiqh*

principle of *al-'adatu muhakkamat, adat* that is good can be made into (Islamic) law – for community property, for example, which is not regulated in the Qur'an or *hadith*, nor in the jurists' books, but is to be found in the *adat* of Muslim Indonesians and lives in the legal consciousness of Muslim society in our country.[7]

The '*fiqh* principle', mentioned by Professor Daud Ali, sometimes is cited in the form of '*adat* is *shari'a* that is made into law' (*al-'adah shari'ah muhakkamah*). It is [often] a basis for declaring certain local social practices to be Islamic law, as well as positive law, if they do not conflict with tenets of the Qur'an or *hadith*. However, the application of the principle incites two sorts of problems.

The first problem is to do with the historical baggage of the Dutch colonial 'reception doctrine', the principle that Islam could be the law of the land only if already 'received' into *adat*. Here is where Hazairin's culturally pluralist critique/approach to jurisprudence becomes apparent. That is, if all *fiqh* can be shown to depend on local practices, as well as on sacred texts, then those Indonesian practices, that differ from Arabian ones can serve as the basis for a new *fiqh*.

In a discussion with me in 1994 about marital property, Professor Daud Ali justified the Compilation's rule of equal division of marital property after divorce or death by drawing on a general Islamic principle of equity, plus the social practices in Indonesia, that underlie a local sense of justice. His Hazairin-style argument combines empirical reality with Islamic values. He states:

> We differ from classical jurisprudence on common property. The *fiqh* texts say that the wife takes care of the house and of her husband's wealth, and if she divorces she leaves with nothing. Well maybe in Arabia the wife does not do anything, but in Indonesia it is not like that. If a man takes up a machete to go out to the fields, his wife comes with him, carrying a bundle on her back. So she has contributed to the wealth, either by working on the fields or by taking care of the family, and she should receive some of the

inheritance – and then we set specific amounts. Here we differ
from *fiqh*, we take account of culture.

In his explanation of the new rule, Daud Ali recognizes that
Islamic law as transmitted in *fiqh* books already included Arab-
world customary law and customary practices, and for that reason
can be further modified to converge with Indonesian norms. This
understanding of custom's place in *fiqh* allows him to admit the
Indonesian practices (men and women working together), indicative of a general sense of gender equity (equal work means equal
rewards), as constituent elements of Islamic law.

Now, the type of reasoning articulated by Professor Daud Ali
could in theory lead to the creation of slightly different Islamic law
rules for different parts of Indonesia, such that each society could
potentially have its own *fiqh*. Indeed, in practice, judges often
gauge the acceptability of specific articles of the Compilation of
Islamic Law in terms of local sensibilities. Muslim judges in
Indonesia's Aceh province told me that they tried not to apply the
new *fiqh* doctrine about 'replacement heirs', for example, because
it was not in tune with the opinions and practices of most
Acehnese people. Since early 2002, Aceh has been empowered to
exercise a great deal of freedom in passing its own laws, now
called '*kanun*', and to base them on '*shari'a*' based on local ideas of
what *shari'a* should be. Although it is as yet unclear what the
content of these laws will be, the 'culturalist' argument already
accepted by many of Indonesia's Muslim public intellectuals
would justify a set of Aceh-specific interpretations of Islamic
norms. Here we have a whole new level of potential pluralism of
Islamic law, sanctioned by an already embedded Indonesian tradition of interpretation.

Living in 'non-Muslim lands' as justification in Europe

The cultural pluralism discussed above superficially resembles
another, older set of distinctions Muslims have made between the
application of law in Muslim lands and in non-Muslim lands; such

a distinction has been the basis for a series of recent influential legal opinions regarding Muslims in Europe.

In Europe, many Muslims encounter a very different social setting for Islam than in their home countries. For example, Muslims living in France encounter conflicts between two sets of demands.[8] On the one hand, to be accepted as French, as part of an 'Islam of France', they must be French in speech and comportment, regulate their lives under secular laws and in accord with broad, European legal norms, and respect the norms of *laïcité*, meaning that religion must be left in the private sphere. On the other hand, the religious lives of many of them are defined through public events of worship, through study and prayer in Arabic, and through participation in trans-Mediterranean networks of scholarship and education that readily connect to the Arab worlds of the Middle East and North Africa. This particular form of cultural pluralism is thus quite distinct from that experienced by Indonesians (and, for that matter, from that experienced by Muslims in Britain or the United States). That is, while Indonesians living in Indonesia have tended to see themselves as distant and distinct from the Arabian culture in which Islamic jurisprudence was formed, Muslims in France are not only close to the Arab world, they are very often part of it.

The vast majority of the five million or so Muslims living in France either immigrated to France or were born there of immigrant parents. Most consider themselves to be in the process, not of assimilating to pre-existing French norms and values, but of creating a distinctive kind of cultural citizenship, one in which they can claim identities as both Muslims and French. On the one hand, they declare themselves completely at home with ideas of freedom of religious expression and equality before the law, the institutions of French society, and the French value of *laïcité*, or the neutrality of the state with respect to religion. On the other hand, they proclaim their identities as Muslims, who follow their best understanding of the commands that God has given them. In order to develop these understandings, they often turn to the writings and speeches of Muslim authorities living outside Europe, and who for the most part write about Islamic norms from the perspective of someone living in a Muslim-majority country.[9]

In this context of multiple references and sources of authority, Muslims living in France, and more generally in Europe, have developed two broad approaches to the problem of pluralism. The first approach posits that Europe is outside the Muslim world, and poses quite specific challenges to Muslims, challenges that may require exceptions to Islamic law for the greater good of protecting Islam. This approach remains within the intellectual framework of Islamic jurisprudence, in that it grounds decisions on judgements made within one of the traditional legal schools. The second approach is to urge that Muslims focus on the principles (*maqasid*) of Islam, and that these principles can be retained even as one moves away from traditional jurisprudence.

Let me begin by discussing the first of these two approaches. The notion that there is a 'Muslim world' was developed within Islamic thought in terms of a contrast between two realms or abodes, the *dar al-Islam* or 'abode of Islam', versus the *dar al-harb* or 'abode of war', a distinction which meant approximately 'Muslim societies' versus all others. The distinction was developed by scholars in the early centuries of Islam to distinguish between countries ruled under Islamic law and all others, where, presumably, Muslims would not be free to worship.[10]

Today, many Muslims find discomfort in this way of viewing the world. Such a position raises the following questions: How is one to define 'Muslim societies'? Does one look to the correctness of the government, the piety of the people, or simply the fact that most people living in the country profess Islam as their religion? Is a majority-Muslim country whose government represses its people and prevents the free expression of religious ideas to be considered part of *dar al-Islam*? Conversely, why should countries not governed by Islamic laws, but where Muslims are free to worship, be considered as belonging to an 'abode of war'?

Some Muslims have proposed alternatives. Referring to the protection given to religious minorities by international law, some scholars have proposed *dar al-'ahd* (abode of treaty) as a better way of designating non-Islamic states that offer religious freedom.

Others have proposed *dar al-da'wa* (abode of predication) or *dar al-shahada* (abode of witness), emphasizing the possibilities open to Muslims in these lands.[11]

Such proposals raise a number of questions for Islamic jurisprudence. If conditions in a European country are markedly different from those in a Muslim one, should Muslims living in Europe live by different religious rules than those in, say, Qatar or Egypt? Should there be a separate jurisprudence for Muslims in such situations, a *fiqh* for Muslim minorities? If so, where does one draw the line between the two types of societies? If not, must adaptations of *fiqh* in Europe also be applicable in a Muslim country for them to be considered religiously valid?

Let me consider one recent example in this regard. One of the more pressing questions for some Muslims in Europe is whether they can take out loans at interest to purchase homes. A general prohibition against lending or borrowing at interest would seem to prevent them from so doing. However, in the late 1990s some Muslims living in Europe put the question to the European Council for Fatwa and Research, a collection of jurists of various nationalities who now reside in Europe.[12] Notably, the Council is led by the highly influential Egyptian jurist Shaykh Yusuf Qardawi, currently of Qatar. In 1999, the Council issued its response as a *fatwa*, a non-binding legal opinion issued by a qualified person or group. Therein, the jurists stressed that the prohibition on usury does mean that Muslims everywhere should take steps to avoid borrowing from banks that charge interest, and should devise alternative ways of financing homes, such as paying more than the stated price but in instalments. However, if Muslims in Europe could not practise such alternatives, then they could take out a mortgage for a first house. The jurists cited two considerations. First, the doctrine of extreme necessity (*darurat*) allows Muslims to do what otherwise is forbidden under compulsion or necessity. Why is home ownership a necessity? Renting keeps the Muslim in a state of uncertainty and financial insecurity. Owning a house allows Muslims to settle in close proximity to a mosque, and to modify their house to accommodate religious needs. Moreover, said the Council, Muslims living in Europe had reported to the Council that mortgage payments are equal to or lower than rents.

The jurists also referred to a principle that, while in non-Muslim countries, Muslims may make contracts that violate Islamic law. The principle is found in the Hanafi legal school, and consistent with one interpretation of the Hanbali school.[13] The jurists justify the principle by arguing that Muslims cannot change the institutions that dominate life in their host countries and thus are not responsible for the existence of an interest-based financial system. If they were forbidden to benefit from banking institutions, then Islam would be weakening their social life, which would contradict the principle that Islam should benefit Muslims.

The ruling does not seek to justify the practice of lending at interest. Such lending remains prohibited *in principle*. Instead, it states that Muslims living in Europe are exempted from the prohibition because of a combination of empirical circumstances: the importance of owning a house, the high level of rents, and the absence of viable alternatives. These circumstances allow the jurists to apply the principles that necessity allows for exemption, and that Muslims may use otherwise invalid financial instruments when they live in 'non-Islamic countries'.

The ruling generated considerable interest among Muslims living in Paris, even though many of those individuals either were far from being able to apply for a bank loan, or because they were only in Europe for a brief period of study, and would probably return to their home country to seek work and raise a family. They found the ruling important because it implied that Muslims in Europe could legitimately create a new set of Islamic rules, valid only in Europe. This heady possibility excited some and disconcerted others.

Among supporters of the ruling is one of the members of the European Council, Dr Ahmed Jaballah, who explained to me that the Council decided that Muslims could best provide for their children by moving out of poor neighbourhoods and buying houses. He stated: 'The only way to improve family life is to move out, and the loan helps them do that. But many in the

Muslim world objected to the *fatwa* because it approved interest. They do not understand what social life is like here.'[14]

The immediate problems of social life in Europe are on the minds of Muslims who attend public discussions of Islamic law, and help to explain the interest many take in a particular question concerning the history of jurisprudence. The question is as follows: If knowledgeable scholars studied the same texts, using the same methods and, indeed, often directly learning from each other, why should the four schools differ on important legal questions? Of particular interest is the scholarship of al-Shafiʻi, the founder of the legal school that bears his name. Imam Shafiʻi was the student of another great scholar, Imam Malik, whose name is attached to another legal school. Since one was the student of the other, how could it be that they differed?

This example comes up frequently in public discussions in France. Three examples will indicate the range of possible answers to this question. The first involves a network of writers and activists in Paris who advocate the reinterpretation of jurisprudence for Europe, and who are associated with the publication *La Médina*. In November 2002, I was one of several speakers on a panel sponsored by *La Médina*. A younger man in the rather small audience asked at one point how there could be differences in interpretation in Islam if the Qur'an and *hadith* were one. The moderator, one of *La Médina*'s editors, Abdelfattah El Halfaoui, explained:

> As you know well, Imam Malik was the teacher of Imam Shafiʻi. Imam Malik lived in Iraq and Imam Shafiʻi in Egypt. But if you read Imam Shafiʻi there are differences with his teacher, although you would expect them to be of the same opinion. Why? It is because when Imam Shafiʻi lived in Egypt he saw that they had traditions that were different from those in Iraq, Kufra, Saudi Arabia and so forth, and so he created a new approach, a new *rite*. He said that those people in Iraq, they have their own traditions, and many things, and Imam Malik, when he was there, had given responses on the level of *fiqh* that fit that place, but in Egypt, people were used to different traditions, and so he was obliged to create a new

approach. And now the question arises for Muslims in the United States or in Europe, the fact that Muslims are there is something new, and now, it is up to the learned people to interpret new laws, new *fatwa*s, according to the tradition. Because, the Muslims now in France or in Europe, are a minority community, living with different laws than in Muslim countries, and so we have to invent our response according to the region in which we live.

The moderator is not a scholar of Islamic law, but a well-educated Muslim involved in debate and publishing, and his response is one that many Muslims of similar orientation would offer to such a question. The response respects the legal schools, and attributes their differences to the diversity of social conditions: other fields, other *fiqh*s. Because understanding the scholarship of al-Shafi'i in this way does indeed lead logically to this general conclusion, scholars and publicists who do not share this point of view are quick to contradict this version of the distant past. I will cite two instances in Europe of this quick correcting of what is seen as a misunderstanding of history: one in a Paris mosque, and the other at an assembly in London.

The Adda'wa Mosque in Paris's nineteeth *arrondissement* is the site of weekly panel discussions during the year. Each one attracts close to 100 men and women, some of whom speak mainly Arabic, some French. The panellists usually include one or more experts on a topic from the Arabic-speaking world, and one or more non-Muslim speakers.

After having attended several of these panel discussions in 2001 and 2002, I was invited to participate on a panel in April 2002 on Islamic jurisprudence. Two speakers represented Islamic expertise from outside France. The better known of the two was Dr Mohamed Tawfik al-Bouti, who is the son and intellectual heir of the more famous Shaykh Mohamed Sa'id Ramadan al-Bouti, and currently serves as Chair of the Department of Islamic Jurisprudence at the University of Damascus, Syria. The second speaker was an Iraqi woman scholar, Dr Shiyma al-Sarraf, who has a degree in law from the University of Baghdad and a doctorate in Islamic thought from Paris III. In her remarks, al-Sarraf advocated the changing of legal opinions (*fatwa*s), though not *shari'a*, according to the 'conditions of the era', and, in passing, invoked the example of Imam Shafi'i and Imam Malik. When it was his turn, al-Bouti was quick to disagree with this idea, mentioning a different pair of *madhhab*s: 'When we compare al-Shafi'i to al-Hanafi, their differences are due not to the environment, the place or time, but rather to their respective methods of understanding the texts.' Al-Bouti then criticized another comparison that had been made earlier, between Islamic jurisprudence and Anglo-Saxon common law. The basis for the comparison was the shared sensitivity of the two systems to changes in social environments, but, again, al-Bouti saw the danger (from his perspective) in developing the analogy. The difference, he said, was that, while *fiqh* develops directly from the texts of Qur'an and Sunna, Anglo-Saxon laws 'tend to emphasize current reality, and when the reality changes the rules change. They [the laws] don't repair reality, they don't change behaviour, and they don't determine values.' A version of *fiqh* that did function along the lines of common law would simply mirror the conditions of a new region, something al-Bouti wants to prevent.

A similar, if harsher, version of the same criticism was made at the annual assembly of the Hizb ut-Tahrir in the London Arena on 15 September 2002. The Hizb ut-Tahrir originated in Central Asia as a militant political opposition group; although it has been banned in a number of countries, it is able to meet openly in London.[15] The organization argues that only with the re-establishment of an Islamic caliphate can there be a Muslim society, one in which Muslims can properly practise their religion.

At the assembly, attended by perhaps 10,000 people, the leaders of the associations appeared on stage towards the end of the day to address questions posed to them by people at the assembly, or people following it through video conferencing. The leaders all wore black suits and white, open-necked shirts, and made crisply argued responses in educated English tones to questions. The message, however, was one of absolute refusal of integration, as in the answers given to the following questions from the floor:

Question: Some people say that we should integrate; what is meant by that?

Answer: It does not mean learning English, wearing pinstripe suits, and eating fish and chips. Integration means abandoning basic values; if we do that then our sons will bring home boyfriends, and our daughters, girlfriends. They will send us to old folks' homes. Democracy is for infidels, because in Islam only the Prophet *s.a.w.* can legislate. We need to have the Caliphate to have rule according to Islam, and only when we have the Caliphate will Muslims live under Islam. We must stick to Islam pure and simple.

It is thus not surprising that, when someone asked 'Did not Imam Shafi'i change the *fiqh* that he advocated as he travelled from one country to another?', the answer was: 'No, he changed his jurisprudence only because he developed and deepened his understanding of *usul al-fiqh*, and not because he moved to a new place.'

Despite the radical differences among the positions taken by these intellectuals, they all propose that Muslims continue to develop normative guidelines based in the traditions of *fiqh*, and indeed in the traditional schools. Their disagreements concern whether or not the processes of legitimate divergence among those schools justify the enunciation of differing rules for Muslims living in Europe and Muslims living in lands with Muslim institutions.

However, not even those who advocate enunciating distinct rules for European Muslims justify such a claim on the grounds of cultural differences, as in the Indonesian case. After all, between what societies would such differences be found? Is there a 'French Muslim culture', to be distinguished in its Islam from an 'Arabian Muslim culture'? It would be difficult to make such an argument when Muslims in France are engaged in communication and movement across these political boundaries.

Principles versus jurisprudence as justification

Standing outside such contemporary debates are those Muslims in Europe who argue that Muslims should seek to focus on the broad principles of Islam and discard much of the legal tradition. This position takes on different forms, from a search for specific convergences between Islamic principles and European ones, to a more Islamic-focused study of the principles (*maqasid*) of Islam.

The well-known Swiss intellectual Tariq Ramadan, for example, considers Qardawi's approach to be a sort of '*bricolage*', an effort to 'lighten' *fiqh*, as he puts it, without rethinking it in European terms. Instead, Ramadan would look for European equivalents to Islamic practices. For example, many Muslims in France consider marriages to be religiously valid only if performed in a private, 'Muslim' context, after the legal marriage has been performed at city hall. For Ramadan, thinking in this way is to preserve the traditional forms of marriage without examining the nature of marriage itself, which is a contract: 'A civil marriage already is a Muslim marriage, I think, because it is a contract, and that is what a Muslim marriage is.' More generally, the European law of contracts corresponds to the Islamic law of contracts, and Muslims are just as obliged to respect contracts with non-Muslims as with Muslims: 'that is a universal element of *fiqh*, valid anywhere. This step allows us to accept much of European law.'[16]

The search for general principles as a bridge across cultural and legal divides is itself controversial, particularly when it takes the form of a search for general principles of Islam and recommendations that 'traditional' practices be discarded. One major advocate of this approach is Tareq Oubrou, the Imam of the Bordeaux mosque, who, in 2000 in the magazine *La Médina*, set out his views on the *halal* status of meat.[17] Now, providing meat from animals killed according to Islamic rules is an increasingly salient issue in France, both because of concern about the methods followed in everyday butchering, and because it has become very difficult for Muslims to have an animal 'properly' killed for the annual Feast of Sacrifice ('*Id al-Adha*). 'Proper' killing is generally taken to mean pronouncing a '*Bismillah*' at the moment of execution, the use of a sharp knife to quickly cut the throat, and draining all the blood from the animal. Some French activists and officials have insisted that stunning be used to prevent the pain of the throat cutting, but some Muslims have feared that stunning would kill the animal.

Oubrou intervened in this debate by insisting that the pronouncement of *Bismillah* had no effect on the legal status of the meat purchased by a Muslim. Rather, he argued that one should choose one's butcher based on his character, i.e. whether he prays, does not lie, and so forth. He also contended that, in any case, the Islamic rules were primarily justified by their hygienic rationale: 'Why does Islam refuse to eat meat that has not been cleansed of its blood? Precisely because the blood contains unhealthy germs.'[18]

In conversations with me in late 2002, Oubrou expanded upon his initial reasoning. He stated:

> *Halal* meat? That's different; people confuse the ritual act that is Abraham's sacrifice with an act that is not ritual, there is no 'kosherization' of killing the animal, it is not part of ritual (*ibadat*); it is part of ethics, of *mu'amalat*, that the animal be healthy. So the question is how best to kill, and the best way is to cut the transmission between the neurons and the rest of the animal, by cutting the throat, and evacuating the blood immediately; this is the most humane way to kill the animal, as it causes it to lose all feeling, because the oxygen stops. Secondly, letting out blood rids the animals of germs; I classify it in ethics, it is not to sacralize it; canonists do not require the pronouncement of the *Bismillah* at the moment of sacrifice. Of course, people will cite the Qur'an, but you must read the Qur'an; at the time, people sacrificed for idols, so as a reflex, the Qur'an asked them to do it in the name of God. The Prophet himself allowed Aishah an exemption from this rule. She told him that people had brought them meat and she did not know whether or not they had said the *Bismillah* or not before killing it, and the Prophet said, you say it before eating. It's really not the end of the world.[19]

Of course, many Muslims object to this reasoning. Oubrou's article in *La Médina* prompted at least one reader to object (in a letter published by the magazine in the following issue) that 'to think in that way is to empty Islam of its meaning, to reduce it to its surface appearance, and to turn aside from the object of all Muslim acts, namely the adoration of God'.

Similar considerations shape thinking about the sacrifice performed annually on *'Id al-Adha*, which is celebrated on the tenth day of the last month of the Islamic calendar. The day of the *'id* falls in the middle of the pilgrimage period, and pilgrims perform the act in the city of Mina near Mecca, while other Muslims carry out the sacrifice wherever they reside. Carrying out the sacrifice has become both important to the new generation of European-born Muslims, because it provides a way to publicly assert their identity as Muslims, and yet problematic, because it has become increasingly difficult to find appropriate places for sacrifice in urban France. In 2003, European rules on hygiene led the French government to forbid the temporary slaughterhouses that had been erected in earlier years. Some Muslims now substitute what they take to be an Islamically equivalent practice, usually either giving money as alms or paying to have an animal slaughtered by relatives in their (or their parents') country of origin. As Hakim El Ghisassi, the editor-in-chief of *La Médina*, explained to me in October 2002: 'Most Muslims already have stopped carrying out the sacrifice; they just give money at that time. It is those who do not practise Islam who have a problem; they want their cultural traditions to continue.'

For Oubrou, it is important to remind Muslims that performing the sacrifice is a recommended act (*sunna*), not a required one (*wajib*). It is much more important, he argues, to carry out the ritual prayer that is performed on the same day as the sacrifice. In our interview, Oubrou cited the problem of Muslims who neglect the required prayer while carrying out the optional sacrifice, and suggested:

Sacrifice may disappear in the second and third generations. First, because the cultural tradition of eating the meat together will

disappear, and, secondly, because the way people live, in apart-
ments, make it impossible to carry out the killing of animals. In any
case, the practice does not have the importance that Muslims give
it. The sacrifice has a symbolic importance, as part of the Muslim
tradition, Abraham's sacrifice. It is enough if the imam, or two or
three people in the Muslim community, sacrifice. But even if one
million Muslims do not sacrifice, it's not the end of world, given
that it is not an essential rite.

Although these lines of reasoning, particularly when formulated
by Oubrou, shock many other Muslims, they draw on older ideas
about the principles (*maqasid*) of Islam. For example, the writings
of the fourteenth-century scholar al-Shatibi have had a particularly important effect in shaping the ideas of many scholars in
France and elsewhere.[20] They are attractive and useful to those
Muslims in Europe and North America (and not only in those
regions) who wish to develop an Islam that offers justifications at
the level of a universalistic ethics. Universalistic justifications in
turn facilitate ecumenical dialogue and acceptance of Islamic
ideas by majority non-Muslim populations.

It may well be that this final type of justification, on the basis of
general principles, will offer a rallying point for Muslims who
wish to make a break with the traditions of classical jurisprudence, and yet also wish to develop Islamic justifications for their
actions and ideas. It remains to be seen, however, whether Muslim
public intellectuals can develop a sufficiently deep grounding of
these universalistic ideas in Islamic thought to satisfy those who
remain advocates of jurisprudence.[21]

Conclusions: Towards a sociology of
Islamic justification

The examples discussed above indicate that the positions taken by
Muslims, particularly public intellectuals, living in or comment-
ing on Europe differ in an important way from those taken by
their counterparts in Indonesia. While Indonesian Muslims point
to local customs and culture as both indigenous and Islamic, and

draw on a language of *fiqh* to argue that *adat* ought to be considered to be part of *shariʿa,* European Muslims cannot refer to custom and culture. For them, such references can only be made in Muslim-majority countries. Moreover, in Europe, such references provide no rhetorical or logical purchase. European legal traditions increasingly refer to universalistic principles, such as human rights; claims that custom in, say, Morocco dictates that a Muslim act in a certain way have no legal basis in Europe.[22]

Unlike their Indonesian counterparts, European Muslims straddle between worlds: they take part in transnational networks of Muslim scholarship, and they are residents, often citizens, of a European country in which most citizens are reluctant to accept the possibility that Islamic law might be recognized as having legal validity in that country. Hence, compared with the arguments of their Indonesian counterparts, Muslim European arguments for normative pluralism necessarily involve a move to a level of universality, whether that of traditional jurisprudence (from which one may or may not wish to grant exemptions for Europeans) or that of general principles. Ultimately, the differences in the social situations of Muslims in Indonesia and Europe inform their respective approaches to jurisprudence, and provide very different types of justification of these approaches.

These approaches suggest that Muslims in Indonesia and Europe are working with distinct sets of 'repertoires of pluralism', each with its own detailed supporting arguments, and each relatively well suited for particular social settings. I would suggest, however, that this set of repertoires is not limitless; indeed, it may be that the cases discussed above exemplify the most common contemporary responses to Muslim pluralism. In sum, the cases reveal how contemporary Muslim public intellectuals are approaching issues of normative pluralism in ways that both take account of current social settings and draw on long-standing forms of argumentation from within the Islamic traditions of jurisprudence and learning.

Notes

1. Debating Islam from Within: Muslim Constructions of the Internal Other

1   C. Geertz, 'The Uses of Diversity', *Michigan Quarterly Review*, 25:1 (Winter 1986), p. 112.
2   BBC Newsnight, 'British Cartoon Protests Debated', http://news.bbc.co.uk/1/hi/programmes/newsnight/debates/default.stm (accessed 27 August 2009).
3   S. P. Huntington, 'The Clash of Civilizations?', *Foreign Affairs*, 72:3 (Summer 1993), pp. 22–49; and S. P. Huntington, *The Clash of Civilizations and the Remaking of World Order* (New York, 1996), throughout, but especially at pp. 217–218.
4   The Muslim panellists in the first debate were: Anjem Choudary (Spokesman, Al-Ghuraba), Humera Khan (Co-Director, An-Nisa Muslim Women's Society), Tariq Ramadhan (Visiting Scholar, Oxford University) and Sayeeda Warsi (Vice-Chair, Conservative Party). The non-Muslim panellists were: Ann Cryer (Labour Party MP for Keighley) and Roger Knapman (Leader, United Kingdom Independence Party). The panellists in the second debate were: Dyab Abou Jahjah (Founder, Arab European League), Nazenin Ansari (Kayhan Iranian Newspaper, London), Tariq Ramadhan (Visiting Professor, Oxford University) and Sybrand Buma (Dutch Christian Democrats).
5   R. Weekes, ed., *Muslim Peoples: A World Ethnographic Survey* (London, 1978), still provides one of the most comprehensive worldwide surveys of Muslim groups; C. E. Bosworth, *The New Islamic Dynasties* (Edinburgh, 1996), provides a detailed list of the religio-political divisions into which Muslims are commonly divided; A. Nanji, ed., *The Muslim Almanac* (New York, 1995), contains tables (pp. xxiv–xxxv) showing the geographical distribution of Muslims around the globe.

6   The argument is made clearly in E. W. Said, *Covering Islam* (London, 1981), p. *l*.

7   See, for example, M. Mamdani, *Good Muslim, Bad Muslim: America, The Cold War, and the Roots of Terror* (New York, 2004).

8   A. Sen, *Identity and Violence* (New York, 2006), p. 19.

9   A. Sen, *Identity and Violence*, p. 182.

10 A. Sen, *Identity and Violence*, pp. 179–180.

11 See Camilla Adang, 'Belief and Unbelief', in J. D. McAuliffe, *Encyclopaedia of the Qur'an* (Leiden, 2001), Vol. 1, pp. 218–226; and Adang, 'Hypocrites and Hypocrisy', in J. D. McAuliffe, *Encyclopaedia of the Qur'an* (Leiden, 2001), Vol. 2, pp. 468–472.

12 See Frederick Mathewson Denny, 'Community and Society', in J. D. McAuliffe, *Encyclopaedia of the Qur'an* (Leiden, 2001), Vol. 2, pp. 367–386.

13 E. W. Said, *Orientalism* (New York, 1979).

14 V. Nasr, *The Shia Revival* (New York, 2006).

15 See http://ammanmessage.com/ (accessed 27 August 2009); see article by J. Pearl, 'Islam struggles to stake out its position', *International Herald Tribune*, Wednesday 20 July 2005, posted on http://www.iht.com/articles/2005/07/19/opinion/edpearl.php (accessed 27 August 2009).

16 J. Z. Smith, 'What a Difference A Difference Makes', in J. Neusner and E. S. Freichs, eds., *'To See Ourselves As Others See Us': Christians, Jews, 'Others' in Late Antiquity* (Chico, 1985), pp. 3–48, at pp. 14–15.

17 J. Z. Smith, 'Differential Equations: On Constructing the "Other"', in *Relating Religion: Essays in the Study of Religion* (Chicago, 2004), pp. 245–246; see also J. Z. Smith, 'What a Difference A Difference Makes', p. 47.

18 Significant among the examinations of the 'other' is Jean Paul Sartre's *Being and Nothingness: An Essay on Phenomenological Ontology*, H. E. Barnes, trans. (London and New York, [1943] 2003), especially at p. 283, and M. Merleau-Ponty's *The Phenomenology of Perception*, C. Smith, trans. (London & New York, [1945] 1962), especially at pp. 356–357.

19 See, for example, J. Derrida, *'Différance'*, originally published in the *Bulletin de la Société française de philosophie*, 62, No. 3 (July–September, 1968), pp. 73–101; M. Foucault, *Discipline and Punishment*, A. Sheridan, trans., (London, 1977).

20 See, for example, G. Spivak, 'Can the Subaltern Speak?', in C. Nelson and L. Grossberg, eds., *Marxism and the Interpretation of Culture* (Urbana, 1988), pp. 271–313.

21 Mohammed Arkoun, 'Rethinking Islam Today', *Annals of the American Academy of Political and Social Sciences* 588 ([1987] July 2003), pp. 18–39.

22 For a cogent and readable account of 'political pluralism' in its different guises, see R. Grillo, *Pluralism and the Politics of Difference: State, Culture*

and *Ethnicity in Comparative Perspective* (Oxford, 1998); the classic (but
consistently challenged) works on the subject of 'plural societies' are by J.
Furnivall, *Netherlands India: A Study of Plural Economy* (Cambridge, 1939)
and *A Comparative Study of Burma and Netherlands India* (Cambridge,
1948); for discussions which consider 'Islam' and 'Muslims', see R. Grillo,
Pluralism and the Politics of Difference, and B. Tibi, *Islam between Culture
and Politics* (New York, 2001); for the 'multi-culturalism' debate see, for
example, W. Kymlicka, *Multicultural Citizenship: A Liberal Theory of
Minority Rights* (Oxford, 1995); B. Parekh, *Rethinking Multiculturalism:
Cultural Diversity and Political Theory* (New York, 2000), particularly
Chapter 10; see also A. B. Sajoo's *Pluralism in Old and New States: Emerging
ASEAN Contexts* (Singapore, 1994); and A. A. Sachedina, *The Islamic Roots
of Democratic Pluralism* (Oxford, 2001), who takes up the task of locating
'pluralism', 'democracy' and 'civil society' within the Qur'an. Also see, in the
present volume, references cited by P. Brodeur and J. R. Bowen.

23 See S. Hashmi, ed., *Islamic Political Ethics: Civil Society, Pluralism, and
Conflict* (Princeton, 2002), especially Part III; F. Esack explores the issue of
a 'hermeneutic of inter-religious pluralism for liberation' from a theological
perspective in *Qur'an, Liberation & Pluralism: An Islamic Perspective of
Interreligious Solidarity against Oppression* (Oxford, 1997); A. Aslan's
*Religious Pluralism in Christian and Islamic Philosophy: The Thought of John
Hick and Seyyed Hossein Nasr* (Curzon, 1998) concerns similar issues, but
here Nasr represents the perspective of a particular branch of the Shi'i
Ithna'ashari exegetical tradition which favours a philosophical-mystical
reading of the Qur'an; for a critique of Hick, see Muhammad Legenhausen,
Islam and Religious Pluralism (London, 1999); M. Shatzmiller, ed.,
Nationalism and Minority Identities in Islamic Societies (Montreal, 2005).

24 R. Weekes, ed., *Muslim Peoples.*

25 E. Gellner, *Muslim Society* (Cambridge, 1981).

26 C. Geertz, *Islam Observed: Religious Development in Morocco and Indonesia*
(New Haven and London, 1968).

27 A. H. El-Zein, 'Beyond Ideology and Theology: The Search for the
Anthropology of Islam', *Annual Review of Anthropology*, 6 (1977), 227–254.

28 M. Gilsenan, *Recognising Islam: Religion and Society* (London and Sydney,
1982).

29 Some of the salient issues are addressed in D. Eickelman, *The Middle East
and Central Asia: An Anthropological Approach* (New Jersey, 2001), pp.
241–312. For further insight into the debate, see R. Tapper, 'Islamic
Anthropology and the Anthropology of Islam', *Anthropological Quarterly*,
68:3 (1995), pp. 185–193; the range of issues are cogently summarized in
R. A. Lukens-Bull, 'Between Text and Practice: Considerations in the

Anthropological Study of Islam', *Marburg Journal of Religion*, 4:2 (1999), pp. 10–20, D. M. Varisco, *Islam Obscured* (New York, 2005); and G. Marranci, *The Anthropology of Islam* (London and New York, 2008).

30 D. M. Varisco, *Islam Obscured* (New York, 2005), p. 161.

31 D. M. Varisco, *Islam Obscured*, p. 149.

32 D. M. Varisco, *Islam Obscured*, p. 161.

33 T. Asad, *The Idea of an Anthropology of Islam* (Georgetown, 1986).

34 Lila Abu-Lughod, 'Zones of Theory in the Anthropology of the Arab World', *Annual Review of Anthropology*, Vol. 18 (1989), pp. 267–306.

35 The seminar series on which this volume is based had a keynote session on diversity and gender/women in Muslim contexts; the presenter was unable to provide a transcript for publication.

36 See L. Holy, ed., *Comparative Anthropology* (London, 1987), and T. Ingold, ed., *Key Debates in Anthropology* (London, 1996), pp. 21–54.

37 T. Asad, *Formations of the Secular: Christianity, Islam, Modernity* (Stanford, 2003), p. 17.

38 D. Parkin, 'Comparison as Search for Continuity', in L. Holy, ed., *Comparative Anthropology* (London, 1987), pp. 52–69. It should be noted that, while there is no geographical proximity or common time period that binds the individuals or groups under discussion in the present volume (albeit the spatial distinction may be less applicable to contemporary life than it was in the past), the case studies presented herein do refer to people who explicitly and implicitly are Muslims.

39 D. Eickleman and J. Piscatori, eds), *Muslim Travellers* (London, 1990).

40 B. D. Metcalf, ed., *Making Muslim Space in North America and Europe* (Berkeley, 1996).

41 L. Manger, ed., *Muslim Diversity* (Richmond, 1999).

42 S. Headley and D. Parkin, *Islamic Prayer across the Indian Ocean* (Richmond, 2000).

43 A. B. Sajoo, *Civil Society in the Muslim World: Contemporary Perspectives* (London, 2002).

44 P. Crone, 'The Rise of Islam in the World', in F. Robinson, ed., *Cambridge Illustrated History of the Islamic World* (Cambridge, 1996), p. 13. The civil war involved some of the most famous personalities in Muslim history, including: 'Ali, the cousin and son-in-law of the Prophet who at the time of the war was the designated caliph; 'A'isha, the Prophet's favourite wife; and Mu'awiya, the third caliph Uthman's cousin. In the end, 'Ali was assassinated by the Kharijis for agreeing to arbitration with Mu'awiya, who subsequently took over the leadership of the community of believers under his family, the Umayyads. The events resulted in the establishment of various groups, each of whom had a different view on leadership: the Shi'is, who subsequently

divided into a number of groups over succession disputes about their own leadership, initially maintained that leadership and religious authority of the whole community was ordained by the Prophet to remain in his family through 'Ali; the Kharijis, who rejected hereditary claims, held that leadership of the community be determined through election; and those Muslims, who in time came to be known as Sunnis, who accepted the outcome of the civil war, focused more on the temporal aspects of the leadership, and eventually developed a notion of communal consensus and an elaborated system of jurisprudence with a number of legal schools.

45 F. Rahman, *Islam* (Chicago, [1966] 1979), p. 167 (following I. Goldziher), argues that the whole exercise of delineating 'sects' was flawed insofar as most of the groups identified in heresiographical treatises that took as their inspiration the *hadith* on divisions were not 'sects' in the strict sense of the word, but legal and theological schools.

46 A. S. Dallal, 'Ummah', in J. Esposito et al., ed., *Oxford Encyclopaedia of Islam in the Modern World*, Vol. 4, p. 270.

47 I have purposely not glossed this point in terms of 'minorities', insofar as discussions of minorities in states often assume that members of such groups have no differences between them, and that, in states where they are accommodated, minorities agree on who represents their concerns to the state.

48 For comparable views and ethnography, see M. Fischer and M. Abedi, *Debating Muslims* (Madison, 1990), pp. 287–314.

49 See, for comparison: A. Purpura, 'Portrait of Seyyid Silima from Zanzibar: Piety and Subversion in Islamic Prayer', in D. Parkin and S. Headley, eds., *Islamic Prayer across the Indian Ocean* (Richmond, 2000), p. 129.

50 Some have extended the meaning of *dar al-harb* to mean the 'abode of war'.

51 This term comes from Clifford Geertz, 'The Uses of Diversity', *Michigan Quarterly Review*, 25:1 (Winter 1986), p. 112.

52 Geertz, 'The Uses of Diversity', p. 122.

2. *Pluralism and Islamic Traditions of Sectarian Divisions*

1 Much of this essay is similar to another essay which has been published in the *Svensk Teologisk Kvartalskrijft*, Vol. 82 (2006), pp. 155–161. The material on the division into seventy-odd sects is abundant enough to fill a volume, and I hope to return to it in a later essay.

2 For references to these sources, see M. J. Mashkur, 'Introduction', *Haftad-o do millat* (Tehran, 1962), pp. 6–7; and A. Mahdavi-Damghani, *Hasil-i awqat* (Tehran, 2002), p. 615. Dr Mahdavi-Damghani's outstanding treatment of this subject has greatly aided me in writing the present study.

3   M. J. Mashkur, 'Introduction', p. 6.
4   K. Lewinstein, 'Studies in Islamic Heresiography: The Khawarij in Two
    Firaq Traditions', PhD Dissertation (Princeton University, 1989), p. 3, no. 3,
    including the quotation from Ibn Babawayh.
5   K. Lewinstein, 'Studies in Islamic Heresiography', quoting from the
    unpublished fifth-century *Asas al-maqalat* of Abu'l Ma'ah.
6   M. J. Mashkur, 'Introduction', p. 6.
7   A. R. Gaiser, 'Satan's Seven Specious Arguments: al-Shahrastani's *Kitab
    al-milal wa'l-nihal* in an Isma'ili Context', *Journal of Islamic Studies*, 19:2
    (2008), p. 186.
8   *Ahsan al-taqasim* (Leiden, 1906), p. 38, cited by K. Lewinstein, 'Studies', p. 3,
    no. 4.
9   Cited by M. J. Mashkur, 'Introduction', p. 7.
10 al-Ghazali, *Fada'il al-'anam min rasa'il hujjat al-Islam*, ed. Mo'ayyad
    Thabeti, Tehran 1333 AH, pp. 72–73. I owe this reference to an addendum
    by Dr Mahdavi-Damghani to his original article, which was published in
    Yadnamah-ye rashed, Tehran 2009, pp. 541–553. Dr Mahdavi-Damghani
    suspects that there is a missing segment of text, which would explain al-
    Ghazali's contention first that one sect is saved and then that forty-eight
    sects are saved.
11 al-Baghdadi, *al–Farq bayn al–firaq*, ed. M. Badr (tr. K. C. Seelye, *Moslem
    Schisms and Sects*), New York, 1920.
12 al-Razi, *Tafsir al-Fakhr al-Razi* (Cairo, 1985), XI, p. 219. My translation is
    slightly different from Goldziher's. See I. Goldziher, 'Le dénombrement des
    sectes mahometanes', in his *Gesammelte Schriften* (Hildesheim, 1968), II,
    pp. 409–410.
13 I. Goldziher, 'Le dénombrement', p. 410, where it is also noticed that some
    say 'sixty-odd'.
14 A. Mahdavi-Damghani, *Hasil-i awqat*, p. 618.
15 I. Goldziher, 'Le dénombrement', p. 411.
16 I. Goldziher, 'Le dénombrement', p. 410.
17 A. Schimmel, *The Mystery of Numbers* (New York, 1993) pp. 132, 263–264.
18 A. Schimmel, *The Mystery of Numbers*, pp. 264–266.
19 On heaven, see A. Mahdavi-Damghani, *Hasil-i awqat*, p. 617, quoting from
    Mishkat al-masabih no. 2821 from al-Tirmidhi. On hell, see Muslim, *Sahih*,
    ed. M. F. Abd al-Baqi (Cairo, n.d.), IV, pp. 2184–2185, the twenty-first
    hadith in *Kitab al-jannah*.
20 A. Schimmel, *The Mystery of Numbers*, p. 265; and A. Mahdavi-Damghani,
    Hasil-i awqat, p. 618.
21 al-Zamakhshari, *al-Kashshaf* (Riyadh, 1998), Vol. 3, p. 74.
22 al-Kulayni, *al-Kafi* (Tehran, 1982), Vol. 2, p. 199.

23 Hafiz, *Divan*, ed. S. Naysari (Tehran, 1993), p. 161.
24 My translation, influenced by that of R. A. Nicholson, *Masnavi*, Text
    (London, 1933), Book V, vss. 3214–3232, p. 205; Translation (London,
    1934), p. 194.
25 R. A. Nicholson, *Masnavi*, Text (London, 1940), p. 289.
26 R. A. Nicholson, *Masnavi*, Text (London, 1925), Book I, vss. 3288–3289,
    p. 302; Translation (London, 1960), p. 179. Here, the Nicholson translation
    is given without alteration.
27 Again, R. A. Nicholson's translation is given without alteration. Text
    (London, 1929), Book III, vss. 1496–1504, p. 85; Translation (London,
    1930), p. 84.
28 R. A. Nicholson, *Masnavi*, Commentary (London, 1940), p. 43.
29 R. A. Nicholson, *Masnavi*, Text (London, 1929), Book III, vss. 4719–4726,
    omitting 4722 and 4724, p. 270; and Translation (London, 1930), p. 263,
    given here without alteration.

3. *Being One and Many Among the Others: Muslim Diversity in the Context of South Asian Religious Pluralism*

1 See H. Oberoi, *The Construction of Religious Boundaries: Culture, Identity
   and Diversity in the Sikh Tradition* (Delhi, 1994), p. 11. Shafique Virani,
   whom I thank for this interesting information, has also found out that the
   Gupti Imamshahi community of Saurasthra (Gujarat) defines itself in the
   same words.
2 See H. Oberoi, *The Construction of Religious Boundaries*, pp. 9–12; and D-S.
   Khan, *Crossing The Threshold: Understanding Religious Identities in South
   Asia* (London, 2004).
3 See A. Shodhan, 'Legal Formulation of the Question of Community:
   Defining the Khoja Collective', *Indian Social Science Review*, 1 (1999), pp.
   139–140.
4 See D. Vasudha and H. Von Stietencron, eds., *Representing Hinduism: The
   Construction of Religious Traditions and National Identity* (Delhi, 1995),
   pp. 20–21.
5 P. Gottschalk's *Beyond Hindu and Muslim: Multiple Identity in Narratives
   from Village India* (Oxford, 2000) provides fascinating insights into the
   issues of plurality and pluralism which are discussed here.
6 The Ajlafs, as opposed to the Ashrafs, are supposed to be the members of
   converted communities, and are mainly artisans, whereas the four Ashraf
   groups claim descents from the Arabs, Persians, Mughals or Afghan
   noblemen (i.e. Sayyids, Shaykhs, Mughals and Pathans respectively; see
   no. 32).

7   For the idea of *sanatan dharm*, see, for instance, K. W. Jones, *Arya Dharm: Hindu Consciousness in 19th-century Punjab* (Berkeley, 1976).

8   A. Esmail, *The Poetics of Religious Experience: The Islamic Context* (London and New York, 1998), p. 30.

9   A. Esmail, *The Poetics of Religious Experience*, p. 47.

10 Y. Sikand, *The Origins and Development of the Tablighi Jama'at (1920–2000): A Cross-country Comparative Study* (Delhi, 2002).

11 Y. Sikand in *The Origins and Development*, quoting S. B. Freitag, 'The Roots of Muslim Separatism in South Asia: Personal Practice and Public Structures in Kanpur and Bombay', in E. Burke III and I. M. Lapidus, eds., *Islam, Politics and Social Movements* (Berkeley, 1988), pp. 115–145.

12 Y. Sikand, *The Origins and Development*, p. 24.

13 The concept of 'imagined communities' is developed for India by S. B. Freitag, 'Contesting in Public: Colonial Legacies and Contemporary Communalism', in D. Ludden, ed., *Making India Hindu: Religion, Community and the Politics of Democracy in India* (Delhi, 1996), pp. 220–221.

14 See C. Jaffrelot, *The Hindu Nationalist Movement in India* (Delhi, 1996); and K. W. Jones, 'Religious Identities and the Indian Census', in G. N. Barrier, ed., *The Census in British India* (Delhi, 1981), pp. 73–102.

15 See, for example, the missionary activities and the goals of the *Deendar Anjuman* movement in Nur Mohammad, *The Deendar Anjuman* (Bangalore, nd).

16 See D-S. Khan, 'The Mahdi of Panna: A Short History of the Prananamis', *Journal of Secular Studies*, Part I, 6:4 (2003), p. 63.

17 See N. Pyarelal, *Mahatma Gandhi*, Vol. I, Part I, *The Early Phase* (Ahmedabad, 1965), pp. 213–215. Curiously, Pyarelal, mentioning the Pranami temple of Porbandar on p. 213, does not seem to realize that this shrine is the same as the *haveli* he mentions on p. 173.

18 N. Pyarelal, *Mahatma Gandhi*, Vol. I, Part I, p. 68.

19 See S. Mangal Ram, *Swami Laldas krit Mahamati Prannath bitak ka nadhykalin itihas ka yogdan* (Delhi, 1996), p. 227.

20 For example, see a discussion of the sixteenth-century poet Eknath and his drama-poem *Hindu-Turk Samvad* in Narendra K. Wagle, 'Hindu-Muslim interactions in medieval Maharashtra', in Gunther D. Sontheimer and Hermann Kulke, eds., *Hinduism Reconsidered* (Delhi, 1991), pp. 55–56; see also the *ginan* attributed to the Nizari Ismaili missionary Pir Shams: '... the Hindu goes to the sixty-eight places of pilgrimage, while the Muslim goes to the mosque ...', quoted by A. Nanji in *The Nizari Ismaili Tradition in the Indo-Pakistan Subcontinent* (Delmar, 1978), pp. 121–122.

21 See A. Ahmad, *An Intellectual History of Islam in India* (Edinburgh, 1969).

22 Aghoris form a special category of Tantric yogis who challenge the Brahmanical values of purity; they live in cremation grounds and perform a range of rituals. On the Aghoris, see G. W. Briggs, *Gorakhnath and the Kanphata Jogís* (Delhi, [1938] 1990), pp. 71–72, no. 2.

23 The term 'Sarpvale' literally associates the *shaykh* with snakes. But according to Qur'anic tradition, a *shaykh* cannot manifest himself in the form of a snake. However, jinns are believed to assume the form of cobras, and thus it may be that, to his followers, Sarpvale Baba is perceived as a kind of jinn.

24 On the Guptis, see, for instance, Z. Moir, 'Historical and Religious Debates Amongst Indian Ismailis 1840–1920', in Mariola Offredi, ed., *The Banyan Tree* (Delhi, 2001), p. 133; and M. A. Tajddin Sadik, *Ismailis through History* (Karachi, 1997), p. 591.

25 See D-S. Khan, *Conversion and Shifting Identities: Ramdev Pir and the Ismailis in Rajasthan* (Delhi, 1997).

26 Z. Moir, 'Historical and Religious Debates', p. 135.

27 Shafique Virani has done some interesting research on these communities. His article on the subject is forthcoming. See also S. A. Mohamed's booklet, *Heroes of Surat* (Surat, 1968).

28 S. Mayaram is currently preparing a publication on this subject. I thank her for generously sharing with me her knowledge of this aspect of the VHP, which has largely remained unexplored to this day.

29 See D-S. Khan and Z. Moir, 'Coexistence and Communalism: The Shrine of Pirana in Gujarat', *South Asia*, 22 (1999), p. 147; and D-S. Khan, 'Karsan Das, *un heros vivant*', in V. Bouillier and C. Le Blanc, eds., *L'usage des heros. Traditions narratives et affirmations identitaires dans le monde indien* (Paris, 2006), pp. 95–120.

30 Selling vegetables is indeed the traditional occupation of this caste, which enjoys a rather low status in comparison with the contemporary Patidars, who also claim the title and surname of 'Patel'. The latter were formerly regarded as a low caste community and known as Kanbis. See J. M. Campbell, ed., *Hindu Tribes and Castes of Gujarat* (Guragaon, 1988–1990), Vol. I, pp. 153–154.

31 See, for example, A. R. Saiyed, 'Saints and Dargahs in the Indian Subcontinent: A Review', in Christian W. Troll, ed., *Muslim Shrines in India: Their Character, History and Significance* (Delhi, 1989), pp. 241–244.

32 *Ashraf* and *Ajlaf*, a traditional division of Muslim communities. The Ashraf are considered to be of 'noble' (foreign) origin and are divided into four castes (*jati*): the Sayyids who claim to be descendants of the Prophet family; the Shaykhs, who claim descent from a Muslim Sufi; the Mughals, who assert that their ancestors were the Mughal emperors of India; and the Pathan, of

noble Afghan origin. The Ajlaf include all the converted communities, mainly artisans, but there are also Rajputs who claim descent from the earlier Kshatrya warrior-kings. One should add a third category among the Ajlaf, the Arzals, generally identified with the ex-untouchable converted groups. See Y. Sikand, *The Origins and Development*, pp. 18–20, 21.

33　*Mali* means 'gardener', indicating that Prem belongs to this particular community, which is ranked rather low but not traditionally regarded as untouchable.

34　See S. Mayaram, 'Spirit Possession: Reframing Discourses of the Self and Other', in J. Assayag and G. Tarabout, eds., *La possession en Asie du Sud: parole, corps, territoire, Collections Purusartha*, 21 (1999), pp. 101–131. An interesting case is that of a Hindu temple priest, who was possessed by the *pir* of a neighbouring *dargah* as a punishment for having stolen the flowers in his garden. See also D-S. Khan, *Crossing the Threshold*.

35　I thank Yoginder Sikand for permitting me to quote his interview with Makhdoom Syed Chan Pir Qadri, where the existence of this community is mentioned.

36　H. J. Witteveen, *Universal Sufism* (Shaftesbury, 1997).

37　See D-S. Khan, *Conversion*, pp. 21–22; and D-S. Khan, *Crossing the Threshold*.

38　S. Mayaram, 'Spirit Possession', pp. 101–131.

39　This definition is taken from the glossary included in one of the printed versions of two poems, *Marfat Sagar* and *Kayamatnama*, composed, according to the Pranami tradition, by Prannath himself. See V. Mehta and R. Saha, eds., *Mahamati Prannath pranit marfat sagar kayamatnama (chhota aur bara)* (Delhi, 1990), p. 410.

40　A. Esmail, *The Poetics of Religious Experience*, p. 40.

4. Religious Pluralism in the Light of American Muslim Identities

1　See Council on American-Islamic Relations (CAIR), *Guilt by Association: The Status of Muslim Civil Rights in the United States 2003* (Washington, DC, 2003).

2　O. Riis, 'Modes of Religious Pluralism under Conditions of Globalisation', *International Journal on Multicultural Societies*, 1:1 (1999), p. 21.

3　E. Craig, 'Pluralism', in *Routledge Encyclopedia of Philosophy* (London, 1998), VCl. 7, p. 463. Also available online at: http://www.rep.routledge.com/article/N042 (accessed 28 August 2009).

4　S. Stich, 'Cognitive Pluralism', in *Routledge Encyclopedia of Philosophy* (London, 1998), Vol. 2, p. 396. Also available online at: http://www.rep.routledge.com/article/P008 (accessed 28 August 2009).

5   S. Stich, 'Cognitive Pluralism', p. 397.

6   S. Stich, 'Cognitive Pluralism', p. 397.

7   S. Stich, 'Cognitive Pluralism', p. 397.

8   S. Stich, 'Cognitive Pluralism', p. 397.

9   S. Stich, 'Cognitive Pluralism', p. 397.

10 M. Lynch, *The Nature of Truth: Classical and Contemporary Perspectives* (Cambridge, MA, 2001).

11 M. Lynch, *The Nature of Truth*, p. 618.

12 M. Lynch, *The Nature of Truth*, p. 619.

13 M. Lynch, *The Nature of Truth*, p. 619.

14 M. Lynch, *The Nature of Truth*, p. 620.

15 M. Lynch, *The Nature of Truth*, pp. 620–621.

16 E. Craig, 'Pluralism', p. 464.

17 D. Weinstock, 'Pluralism' in *Routledge Encyclopedia of Philosophy* (London, 1998), Vol. 6, p. 529. Also available online at: http://www.rep.routledge. com/article/L058 (accessed 28 August 2009).

18 D. Weinstock, 'Pluralism', p. 529.

19 D. Weinstock, 'Pluralism', p. 529.

20 D. Weinstock, 'Pluralism', p. 529.

21 D. Weinstock, 'Pluralism', p. 529.

22 M. Taylor, *The Moment of Complexity: Emerging Network Culture* (Chicago, 2001).

23 The Fundamentalisms Project proved beyond doubt the modern roots of religious fundamentalism, identifying them with specific developments in American Christianity dating back to the second decade of the twentieth century. See N. T. Ammerman, 'North American Protestant Fundamentalism', in M. Marty and S. Appleby, eds., *Fundamentalisms Observed* (Chicago, 1991), Vol. 1, p. 2.

24 P. Quinn, 'Religious Pluralism', in *Routledge Encyclopedia of Philosophy* (London, 1993), Vol. 8, p. 260. Also available online at: http://www.rep.routledge.com/article/K086 (accessed 28 August 2009).

25 P. Quinn, 'Religious Pluralism', p. 261.

26 P. Quinn, 'Religious Pluralism', p. 261.

27 For such guidelines, see P. Brodeur, 'Introduction to the Guidelines for an Inter-faith Celebration', *Journal of Ecumenical Studies*, 34:4 (Fall 1997), especially at p. 560.

28 D. Eck, *A New Religious America* (San Francisco, 2001), pp. 70–72.

29 There is a tendency to forget how influential Christian denominations have been in Western history up to the present, because of the prevalent stereotype about the division between church and state in so many Western nation-states. One recent example to counter this tendency is

P. Freston's book *Protestant Political Parties: A Global Survey* (Aldershot, 2004).

30 For a careful scholarly example of the use of '*convivencia*', see V. Cornell, '*Convivencia* Then and Now: Lessons and Limits for Contemporary Interfaith Relations', in a keynote address delivered at the Elijah Interfaith Academy Meeting of the Board of World Religious Leaders, Seville, Spain, on 14 December 2003.

31 E. Boehlert, 'The Muslim Population Riddle', available online at: http://dir.salon.com/story/news/feature/2001/10/31/american_muslims/ (accessed 28 August 2009). He refers to Tom Smith's report, released on 23 October 2001, entitled *Estimating the Muslim Population in the United States*. It was sponsored by the American Jewish Committee. The study suggested that there were slightly less than two million American Muslims or, at most, 1 per cent of the American population, i.e. slightly less than three million.

32 'The Mosque in America: A National Portrait' was conducted by the Council on American-Islamic Relations (CAIR), based in Washington, DC. The results were made public on 26 April 2001. It is now available in an eighty-page book format under the title *The Mosque in America: A National Portrait* (Washington, DC, 2001).

33 'The American Muslim Poll' (November/December 2001) was conducted by Zogby International, an independent research company specializing in polling, which was commissioned by the Project MAPS: Muslims in American Public Square, with partial funding from the Pew Charitable Trusts. The results were made public on 19 December 2001. The same title was kept for a second poll, made public on 19 October 2004. See http://www.zogby.com/News/readnews.cfm?ID=869 (accessed 28 August 2009).

34 The 'Islam and Muslims: A Poll of American Public Opinion' was conducted by Genesis Research Associates in June/July 2004, which was commissioned by the Council on American-Islamic Relations (CAIR). The results were made public on 4 October 2004. See http://www.cair.com/cairsurveyanalysis.pdf (accessed 28 August 2009).

35 O. Riis, 'Modes of Religious Pluralism', p. 21.

36 O. Riis, 'Modes of Religious Pluralism', p. 21.

37 The United States Internal Revenue Code lists types of non-profit organizations that are exempt from paying some federal income taxes. The code number for this provision is 501c3. For statistical tables on the rapid increase in mosque building, see the 2001 CAIR survey *The Mosque in America: A National Portrait* (Washington, DC, 2001), pp. 23–24. The 1980s and 1990s witnessed an incredible expansion of the number of mosques in the USA.

38 For a comparison of the drastic increase in political participation and change in political allegiance between the 2000 and 2004 national elections, see the 'Executive Summary' of the Project MAPS and Zogby International survey, *Muslims in the American Public Square: Shifting Political Winds and Fallout from 9/11, Afghanistan, and Iraq* (October 2004).

39 See the home page of the CAIR website, http://www.cair.com/Home.aspx (accessed 28 August 2009), where under the tab 'American Muslim' there is a list of recent interfaith activities. See http://www.cair.com/ AmericanMuslims/Interfaith.aspx (accessed 28 August 2009).

40 Statistical numbers on American Muslim interest to participate in interfaith activities are found on p. 40 of the 2001 CAIR survey, *The Mosque in America: A National Portrait*, available online. See http://www.cair.com/ Portals/0/pdf/The_Mosque_in_America_A_National_Portrait.pdf-2007-08-22 (accessed 28 August 2009). In mosques with smaller than 500 members, the percentage varies between 60 and 70 per cent interest. With larger mosques, the percentage goes up to 80 per cent. However, on the question of participation in an inter-faith social service project, the percentage drops significantly, ranging from 34 to 50 per cent. In both categories, when broken down by ethnicity, the positive response of African-Americans is almost double that of other groups (i.e. Arabs and South Asians).

41 These various changes are best reflected in the CAIR survey of April 2001 mentioned earlier.

42 The post-9/11 changes are best reflected in the comparison between the 2001 and 2004 *American Muslim Poll*.

43 For a list of the most prominent statements by Muslim organizations against terrorism, see http://www.cair.com/AmericanMuslims/ AntiTerrorism.aspx (accessed 28 August 2009).

44 See P. Brodeur, 'The Changing Nature of Islamic Studies and American Religious Studies (Part 2)', *The Muslim World*, 92:1&2 (Spring 2002), pp. 185–220.

45 Traditional Islamic law (*shari'a*) developed measures for Muslim minorities living in non-Muslim polities, but more often than not on the assumption that this situation is temporary. Because this assumption is no longer valid for a majority of Muslims living in the West today, the need to develop a new category of Islamic law emerged with the resulting new *fiqh al-aqalliyat* (jurisprudence of minorities). See W. Boender, 'Islamic Law and Muslim Minorities', *ISIM Newsletter*, 12 (June 2003), p. 13.

46 O. Riis, 'Modes of Religious Pluralism', p. 24 (italics are in the original).

47 D. Eck, *A New Religious America*, pp. 70–72.

48 For a critique of the strong US bias in political philosophy because of its limits on religious arguments in the public square, see V. Bader, 'Taking

Religious Pluralism Seriously: Arguing for an Institutional Turn', *Ethical Theory and Moral Practice*, 6:1 (March 2003), pp. 3–22.

49   S. Jackson, 'Muslims, Islamic Law and Public Policy in the United States', in A. S. Mazrui, S. M. Jackson and A. McCloud, *American Public Policy and American-Muslim Politics* (Chicago, 2000). Available online at http://www.ispi-usa.org/policy/policy4.html (accessed 28 August 2009).

50   D. Eck, *A New Religious America* (San Francisco, 2001), p. 71.

51   V. Bader, 'Taking Pluralism Seriously: Arguing for an Institutional Turn in Political Philosophy', in *Philosophy & Social Criticism*, 29:4 (2003), pp. 375–406.

5.   *Islamic Art and Doctrinal Pluralism: Seeking Out the Visual Boundaries*

1   C. Williams, 'The Cult of 'Alid Saints in the Fatimid Monuments of Cairo. Part 1: the Mosque of Aqmar', *Muqarnas* 1 (1983), pp. 37–52.

2   J. Allan, 'Some Mosques of the Jebel Nefusa', *Strato da Libya Antiqa*, 9–10 (Rome, 1972–1973), pp. 147–169; Ibadism is an offshoot of Kharijism, and is found today in Oman, East Africa, Libya and Southern Algeria.

3   These should be distinguished from *tekke* or *tekiyye*, an Ottoman dervish lodge.

4   M. V. Fontana, '*Iconografia dell'Ahl al-Bayt*', in *Immagini di arte persiana dal XII al XX secolo, Supplemento 78 de Annali del Istituto Universitario Orientale*, 5:1 (1994), p. 44, no. 67.

5   O. Watson, 'The Masjid-i 'Ali, Quhrud: An Architectural and Epigraphic Survey', *Iran* 12 (1975), p. 72.

6   R. Hillenbrand, 'Safavid Architecture', in P. Jackson, ed., *The Cambridge History of Iran*, Vol. 6: *The Timurid and Safavid Periods* (Cambridge, 1986), pp. 762–763.

7   See, for example, J. M. Rogers, *Empire of the Sultans: Ottoman Art from the Collection of Nasser D. Khalili* (London, 1995), no. 1.

8   W. Seipel, ed., *Schätze der Kalifen Islamische Kunst zur Fatimidzeit*, Kunsthistorisches Museum (Wien) (Milan and Vienna, 1998), nos. 120, 122.

9   N. Safwat, *Golden Pages: Qur'ans and Other Manuscripts from the Collection of Ghassan I. Shaker* (Oxford, 2000), nos. 52–54, 69.

10   K. Emami, ed., *Golestan Palace Library: A Portfolio of Miniature Paintings and Calligraphy* (Tehran, 2000), plates 36–37.

11   K. Emami, ed., *Golestan Palace Library*, plates 40–41.

12   K. Emami, ed., *Golestan Palace Library*, plates 32–33.

13 K. Emami, ed., *Golestan Palace Library*, plates 30–31.

14 A. J. Arberry, B. W. Robinson, E. Blochet and J. V. S. Wilkinson, *The Chester Beatty Library: A Catalogue of the Persian Manuscripts and Miniatures*, Vol. 3 (Dublin, 1962), no. 254, plate 23.

15 British Library MS Add. 19776; See N. Titley, *Miniatures from Persian Manuscripts: A Catalogue and Subject Index of Paintings from Persia, India and Turkey in the 1977 British Library and the British Museum* (London, 1977), no. 193.

16 A. J. Arberry, M. Minovi and E. Blochet, *The Chester Beatty Library*, Vol. 1 (Dublin, 1959), pp. 38–39; Eleanor Sims with B. I. Marshak and E. Grube, *Peerless Images: Persian Painting and its Sources* (New Haven and London, 2002), plate 52.

17 M. S. Simpson, *Persian Poetry, Painting and Patronage: Illustrations in a Sixteenth-century Masterpiece* (New Haven/London, 1998).

18 Metropolitan Museum of Art no. 63.210.18. See *The Language of the Birds*: *Special Issue of The Bulletin of the Metropolitan Museum of Art*, New York, May 1976; E. Sims, *Peerless Images*, plates 60, 98, 168, 250.

19 For *kashkuls,* dervish staffs and dervish axes, see J. Allan and B. Gilmour, *Persian Steel: The Tanavoli Collection* (Oxford, 2000), pp. 313–321.

20 P. Tanavoli, *Kings, Heroes and Lovers: Pictorial Rugs from the Tribes and Villages of Iran* (London, 1994), no. 54.

21 J. Allan, *Islamic Metalwork: The Nuhad Es-Said Collection* (London, 1982), no. 24.

22 Hayward Gallery (Arts Council), *The Arts of Islam* (London, 1976), no. 180.

23 *The Arts of Islam*, no. 178.

24 F. Bagherzadeh, 'Iconographie Iranienne', in L. de Meyer and E. Haerinck, eds., *Archaeologica Iranica et Orientalis, Miscellanea in honorem Louis Vanden Berghe* (Ghent, 1989), Vol. 2, pp. 1007–1028; O. Watson, 'The Masjid-i 'Ali, Quhrud', *Iran* 12 (1975), pp. 59–74.

25 M. Zebrowski, *Gold, Silver & Bronze from Mughal India* (London, 1997), plate 528.

26 M. Zebrowski, *Gold, Silver & Bronze*, chapter 20 and its plates.

27 J. Allan and B. Gilmour, *Persian Steel*, pp. 402–420.

28 J. Allan and B. Gilmour, *Persian Steel*, pp. 304–307.

29 See, for example, a divination bowl in the Victoria and Albert Museum (London, UK) which bears both prayers, in A. S. Melikian-Chirvani, *Islamic Metalwork from the Iranian World, 8th–18th Century* (London, 1982), no. 125.

30 See, for example, K. Folsach, T. Lundbaek and P. Mortensen, *Sultan, Shah and Great Mughal: The History and Culture of the Islamic World* (Copenhagen, 1996), no. 41.

31   D. Eustache, *Corpus des Dirhams Idrisites et contemporains* (Rabat, 1970–1971), p. 63.

32   S. M. Stern, 'The Coins of Amul', *Numismatic Chronicle*, seventh Series, 7 (1967), pp. 217, 219.

33   W. Kazan, *The Coinage of Islam (Collection of William Kazan)* (Beirut, 1983), no. 446.

34   H. L. Rabino di Borgomale, *Coins, Medals and Seals of the Shahs of Iran (1500–1941)* (Hertford, 1945), especially pp. 9–10, plates 1–2.

35   The Mosque of al-Hakim was, of course, originally known as 'Masjid al-Anwar' ('the Mosque of Lights'), see I. A. Bierman, *Writing Signs: The Fatimid Public Text* (Berkeley and Los Angeles, 1998), p. 76.

36   J. Bloom, 'The Mosque of al-Hakim in Cairo', *Muqarnas* 1 (1983), p. 18.

37   J. Bloom, 'The Mosque of al-Hakim in Cairo', p. 19.

38   C. Williams, 'The Cult of 'Alid Saints, Part I', p. 44 and plate 4.

39   K. A. Creswell, *The Muslim Architecture of Egypt* (Oxford, 1952–1959), Vol. I, plate 84d; C. Williams, 'The Cult of 'Alid Saints, Part I', plate 6.

40   C. Williams, 'The Cult of 'Alid Saints, Part I', plate 5.

41   I. Bierman, *Writing Signs*, pp. 62–70.

42   I. Bierman, *Writing Signs*, p. 68.

43   I. Bierman, *Writing Signs*, p. 74.

44   C. Williams, 'The Cult of 'Alid Saints, Part I', plate 4.

45   F. Barry Flood, 'Light in Stone: The Commemoration of the Prophet in Umayyad Architecture', in J. Raby and J. Johns, eds., *Bayt al-Maqdis: 'Abd al-Malik's Jerusalem/Jerusalem and Early Islam* (Oxford, 1992–1999), p. 321. It should be noted, however, that there are problems with the reading of the word translated here (and by Le Strange) as 'circle'.

46   J. D. Weill, *Catalogue Général du Musée Arabe du Caire. Les bois à épigraphes jusqu'à l'époque mamlouke* (Cairo, 1931), nos. 6852, 6854, plate I; E. Englade, *Musée du Louvre: Catalogue des boiseries de la section islamique* (Paris, 1988), no. 10, figures 10 and 10a.

47   A. N. Khan, *Al-Mansurah: A Forgotten Arab Metropolis in Pakistan* (Karachi, 1990), pp. 42–55.

48   F. Gabriel and U. Scerrato, *Gli Arabi in Italia* (Milan, 1979), pls. 337–340. The design of the inscription on the plate of the eleventh-century knocker in the David collection, thought to come from southern Italy, is exceptional, for it is the only early inscription known to me which is read on the outside.

49   C. Williams, 'The Cult of 'Alid Saints, Part I'; Caroline Williams, 'The Cult of 'Alid Saints, Part II', *Muqarnas*, 3 (1985), pp. 39–60; F. Barry Flood, 'Iconography of Light in the Monuments of Mamluk Cairo', *Cosmos, The Yearbook of the Traditional Cosmology Society*, Vol. 8 (1992), pp. 169–193.

50   C. Williams, 'The Cult of 'Alid Saints, Part I', p. 46.
51   Acc. No. 1984402, unpublished. For other textile fragments with similar inscriptions, see Louise W. Mackie, 'Toward an Understanding of Mamluk Silks: National and International Considerations', *Muqarnas*, 2 (1984), plate 7 and no. 46.
52   For the full significance of the lamp, and in particular the pearly star to which its glass is compared in the Qur'an, see F. Barry Flood, 'Light in Stone', pp. 334–339.
53   C. Williams, 'The Cult of 'Alid Saints, Part I', p. 45.
54   K. A. Creswell, *Muslim Architecture*, Vol. 1, plate 83c.
55   K. A. Creswell, *Muslim Architecture*, Vol. 1, plates 118b, 119, 120a–b, 121b–c.
56   K. A. Creswell, *Muslim Architecture*, Vol. 1, plates 26a, d, and p. 92, figure 35 (latter around five-petalled rosette).
57   Mosque of al-Hakim, north minaret; see K. A. Creswell, *Muslim Architecture*, Vol. 1, p. 92, figure 34.
58   K. A. Creswell, *Muslim Architecture*, Vol. 1, plate 31d, pp. 99–100, figures 41–42.
59   K. A. Creswell, *Muslim Architecture*, Vol. 1, plate 65a.
60   K. A. Creswell, *Muslim Architecture*, Vol. 1, plate 82c.
61   K. A. Creswell, *Muslim Architecture*, Vol. 1, plate 120a.
62   K. A. Creswell, *Muslim Architecture*, Vol. 1, plates 121b, c.
63   C. Williams, 'The Cult of 'Alid Saints, Part I', no. 62.
64   C. Williams, 'The Cult of 'Alid Saints, Part II', p. 44.
65   K. A. Creswell, *Muslim Architecture*, Vol. 1, plate 17.
66   K. A. Creswell, *Muslim Architecture*, Vol. 1, plate 83a.
67   C. Williams, 'The Cult of 'Alid Saints, Part I', pp. 46–47. Intriguingly, Williams is not able to make much sense of the pair of doors forming a comparable design at the right end of this area of façade, suggesting that they represent the doors of the room inside the mosque where the Qur'an was kept. Surely, the more likely interpretation is that they are a pictorial rendering of 'Ali as the *bab* (gate), following the well-known *hadith* in which Muhammad is quoted as saying: 'I am the city of knowledge, and 'Ali is the gate; will you enter the city other than by its gate?'; see D. M. MacEion, '*Bab*', in *Encyclopaedia Iranica*, Vol. 3 (1989), pp. 277–278.
68   It is also likely to symbolize the view held by some Ismaili *da'is* of the Fatimid period in cyclical history and concomitant interest in numbers. See, for example, F. Daftary, *A Short History of the Ismailis* (Edinburgh, 1998), pp. 53–54.
69   K. A. Creswell, *Muslim Architecture*, Vol. 1, figure 115; J. Allan, *Metalwork of the Islamic World: The Aron Collection* (London, 1986), no. 12; G. Fehérvári, *Islamic Metalwork of the Eighth to the Fifteenth Century in the*

Keir Collection (London, 1976), no. 125, colour plate F; J. Allan, *Islamic Metalwork*, no. 15; G. Wiet, *Catalogue général du Musée Arabe du Caire, Objets en cuivre* (Cairo, 1984), plate LI no. 4121.

70 J. Allan, *Islamic Metalwork*, no. 9, p. 66.

71 K. A. Creswell, *Muslim Architecture*, Vol. 1, plate 82b.

72 E. Akurgal, C. Mango and R. Ettinghausen, *Les Trésors de Turquie: L'Anatolie des premiers empires. Byzance. Les siècles de l'Islam* (Geneva, 1966), p. 147.

73 J. Allan, *Islamic Metalwork*, no. 15, p. 86.

74 M. Meinecke, *Fayencedekorationen Seldschukischer Sakralbauten in Kleinasien* (Tubingen, 1976), Vol. 1, plate 22, no. 4.

75 M. Meinecke, *Fayencedekorationen Seldschukischer Sakralbauten*, Vol. 1, plate 15, no. 3 and plate 35, no. 3.

76 Ashmolean Museum, Oxford, Newberry Collection Acc. No. 1984.44, unpublished.

77 K. A. Creswell, *Muslim Architecture*, Vol. 2, plate 73a. The inscription reads: *'izz li-mawlana al-sultan al-a'zam al-malik al-mansur said al-dunya wa'l-din Qalaun al-salihi*. I am grateful to Professor Bernard O'Kane for help with the architectural inscriptions on Mamluk buildings in Cairo.

78 K. A. Creswell, *Muslim Architecture*, Vol. 2, plate 84c. The inscription consists of Qur'an, 10:62.

79 *The Arts of Islam*, no. 214.

80 G. Wiet, *Catalogue général*, plates I–II.

81 E. Atil, *Renaissance of Islam. Art of the Mamluks* (Washington, 1981), pp. 86–87, no. 25.

82 *The Arts of Islam*, no. 225.

83 *The Arts of Islam*, no. 217; for the attribution to Sultan Hasan, see J. Allan, *Metalwork of the Islamic World*, p. 61.

84 J. Allan, *Islamic Metalwork*, pp. 25–26. The circular inscription read on the outside also appears on objects manufactured in Cairo for the Rasulid Sultans of Yemen, though here the changeover seems to be later, during the reign of al-Mujahid 'Ali (1321–1363); see V. Porter, 'Die Kunst der Rasuliden', in W. Daum, ed., *Jemen* (Innsbruck and Frankfurt/Main, 1978), pp. 225–236.

85 S. Blair, 'The Coins of the Later Ilkhanids: A Typological Analysis', *Journal of the Economic and Social History of the Orient*, 26:3, 1983, plate IX, nos. 1 and 3.

86 S. Blair, 'The Coins of the Later Ilkhanids', plate X, nos. 9–10 (Coinage Types C & D).

6. The Contestation and Resolution of Inter- and Intra-School Conflicts through Biography

1 It appears that, in the first three centuries of Islamic history, there were hundreds of 'personal schools' of law dedicated to the ideas of individual thinkers, most of which failed to survive long after the deaths of their founders. By the fifth and sixth Islamic centuries, five Sunni schools of law emerged that received widespread followings, these being the Shafi'i, Hanafi, Hanbali, Maliki and Zahiri schools (see Ibn Ishaq al-Shirazi's *Tabaqat al-fuqaha'* for a description of their rise to prominence). The Zahiri school, however, failed to last, leaving the remaining four Sunni schools that exist today.

2 Christopher Melchert, *The Formation of the Sunni Schools of Law* (New York, 1997), pp. 87–115.

3 Christopher Melchert, *The Formation*, pp. 116–136.

4 See Richard Martin, Mark Woodward and Dwi Atmaja, *Defenders of Reason in Islam: Mu'tazilism from Medieval School to Modern Symbol* (Oxford, 1997), pp. 28–29.

5 See Nurit Tsafrir, *The History of an Islamic School of Law: The Early Spread of Hanafism* (Cambridge, 2004), pp. 95–101. Lore about the first generation of Shafi'i jurists in Egypt developed as a manifestation of these tensions, especially in the biographies of Yusuf b. Yahya al-Buwayti (d. 845–846), who is said to have died in prison for his refusal to agree with the created Qur'an doctrine. See, for example, Ibn Qadi Shuhba, *Tabaqat al-fuqaha' al-shafi'iyah*, al-Hafiz 'Abd al-'Ali Khan, ed. (Beirut, 1987), Vol. 1, pp. 70–72.

6 Chase Robinson, *Islamic Historiography* (Cambridge, 2003), pp. 72–74.

7 S. al-Dhahabi, *Siyar a'lam al-nubala'* (Beirut, 1984).

8 See Ibrahim Hafsi, 'Recherches sur le genre Tabaqat dans la littérature arabe', *Arabica* 23 (September 1976), pp. 227–265; 24 (February 1977), pp. 1–41; 24 (June 1977), pp. 150–186.

9 See R. Kevin Jaques, *Authority, Conflict, and the Transmission of Diversity in Medieval Islamic Law* (Leiden, forthcoming).

10 See Devin Stewart, 'Capital, Accumulation, and the Islamic Academic Biography', *Edebiyat* 7 (1997), pp. 356–360.

11 There are a wide variety of scholars who had addressed the transmission of historical material in early Islam. Most of these studies deal with *hadith* transmission, which was decidedly more rigorously examined by traditionists than were historical (*akhbar*) accounts. See G. H. A. Juynboll, *The Authenticity of the Tradition Literature: Discussions in Modern Egypt* (Leiden, 1969), especially pp. 100–113; John Burton, *An Introduction to the*

Hadith (Edinburgh, 1994), pp. 106–118; and M. M. Azami, *Studies in Early Hadith Literature* (Indianapolis, 1978), pp. 28–182.

12   Although there have been interesting and detailed studies of Muslim biographical traditions, these have tended not to look at the dynamics of inter-textual structures and rhetorical strategies. The following represents a brief list of texts that are important examinations and applications of the genre: Michael Cooperson, *Classical Arabic Biography: The Heirs of the Prophet in the Age of al-Ma'mun* (Cambridge, 2000); Jonathan P. Berkey, *The Transmission of Knowledge in Medieval Cairo: A Social History of Islamic Education* (Princeton, 1992); Richard W. Bulliet, 'A Quantitative Approach to Medieval Muslim Biographical Dictionaries', *The Journal of Economic and Social History*, 13 (1970), pp. 195–211; also see his *Conversion to Islam in the Medieval Period: An Essay in Quantitative History* (Cambridge, 1979) and his *Islam: The View from the Edge* (New York, 1994); Claude Cahen, 'History and Historians', in M. J. L. Young et al., eds., *Cambridge History of Arabic Literature* (Cambridge, 1990), Vol. 3, pp. 188–233, and his 'Editing Arabic Chronicles: A Few Suggestions', *Islamic Studies*, 1:3 (1962), pp. 1–25; Michael Chamberlain, *Knowledge and Social Practice in Medieval Damascus, 1190–1350* (Cambridge, 1994); Hartmut Fähndrich, 'The *Wafayat al-a'yan* of Ibn Khallikan: A New Approach', *Journal of the American Oriental Society*, 93 (1973), pp. 432–445; H. A. R. Gibb, 'Islamic Biographical Literature', in B. Lewis and P. M. Holt, eds., *Historians of the Middle East* (London, 1962), pp. 54–58; Ibrahim Hafsi, 'Recherches sur le genre Tabaqat dans la littérature arabe', *Arabica*, 23 (September 1976), pp. 227–265; *Arabica*, 24 (February 1977), pp. 1–41; *Arabica*, 24 (June 1977), pp. 150–186; Tarif Khalidi, *Arabic Historical Thought in the Classical Period* (Cambridge, 1994); Donald P. Little, *An Introduction to Mamluk Historiography: An Analysis of Arabic Annalistic and Biographical Sources for the Reign of al-Malik an-Nasir Muhammad ibn Qala'un* (Wiesbaden, 1970), and see his *History and Historiography of the Mamluks* (London, 1986) and 'Historiography of the Ayyubid and Mamluk Epochs', in Carl F. Petry, ed., *The Cambridge History of Egypt* (Cambridge, 1998), Vol. 1, pp. 640–651; Otto Loth, 'Die Ursprung und Bedeutung der Tabaqat', *Zeitschrift der Deutschen Morgenländischen Gesellschaft* (1869), pp. 593–614; George Makdisi, '*Tabaqat*-Biography: Law and Orthodoxy in Classical Islam', *Islamic Studies*, 32 (1993), pp. 371–396; Carl F. Petry, *The Civilian Elite of Cairo in the Later Middle Ages* (Princeton, 1981); William Popper, trans. *History of Egypt: An Extract from Abu l-Mahasin Ibn Taghri Birdi's Chronicle* (New Haven, 1967); Wadad al-Qadi, 'Biographical Dictionaries: Inner Structure and Cultural Significance', in George N. Atiyeh, ed., *The Book in the Islamic World: The Written Word and Communication in the Middle East* (Albany, 1995), pp. 93–122; Ruth

Roded, *Women in Islamic Biographical Collections* (Boulder, 1994); Franz
Rosenthal, 'On Medieval Authorial Biographies: Al-Ya'qubi and Ibn Hajar',
in Mustansir Mir, ed., *Literary Heritage of Classical Islam: Arabic and
Islamic Studies in Honor of James A. Bellamy* (Princeton, 1993), pp. 255–
274, and especially his *A History of Muslim Historiography* (Leiden, [1952]
1968); Devin Stewart, 'Capital, Accumulation, and the Islamic Academic
Biography', *Edebiyat*, 7 (1997), pp. 346–362; Ferdinand Wüstenfeld,
Academien der Araber und ihre Lehrer (Göttingen, 1837); M. J. L. Young,
'Arabic Biographical Writing', in M. J. L. Young, J. D. Latham and R. B.
Serjeant, eds., *The Cambridge History of Arabic Literature: Religion,
Learning and Science in the 'Abbasid Period* (Cambridge, 1990), pp. 168–
187; and Chase Robinson, *Islamic Historiography* (Cambridge, 2003), pp.
72–74.

13   For a discussion of this theory, see N. Calder, *Studies in Early Muslim
     Jurisprudence*, pp. 86–104.

14   N. Calder, *Studies*, pp. 67–85; C. Melchert, *The Formation of the Sunni
     Schools of Law*, pp. 68–86, especially pp. 80–86, for a discussion of the
     school in Egypt.

15   The material for outline biographies for both al-Muzani and al-Tahawi is
     drawn from the earliest biographies for each scholar. See Ibn Abi Hatim,
     Kitab al-jarh wa'l-ta'dil (Hyderabad, 1952–1953; Reprint, Beirut, n.d.), Vol.
     2, p. 204; Ibn Yunus, *Tarikh al-Misriyin*, ed., 'Abd al-Fattah Fathi 'Abd al-
     Fattah (Beirut, 2000), Vol. 1, p. 44; and Khalil b. 'Abdallah al-Khalili, *Kitab
     al-irshad fi ma'rifat 'ulama' al-hadith*, ed., Muhammad Sa'id b. 'Umar
     (Riyad, 1989), Vol. 1, pp. 431–435.

16   Ibn Abi Hatim, *Kitab al-jarh*, Vol. 2, p. 204.

17   Ibn Qadi Shuhbah, *Tabaqat al-fuqaha' al-Shafi'iyah*, Vol. 1, pp. 72–73.

18   'Abdallah b. As'ad b. 'Ali al-Yafi'i, *Mir'at al-jinan* (Beirut, 1997), Vol. 2, p.
     257; also see S. al-Dhahabi, *Tarikh al-Islam wa wafayat al-mashahir wa'l-
     a'lam*, ed., 'Umar 'Abd al-Salam Tadmuri (Beirut, 1999), Vol. 25, pp.
     381–382.

19   al-Dhahabi, *Tarikh al-Islam*, Vol. 25, p. 378.

20   Ibn Yunus, *Tarikh al-Misriyin*, Vol. 1, p. 45.

21   Ibn Yunus, *Tarikh al-Misriyin*, Vol. 1, p. 44.

22   Ibn Yunus, *Tarikh al-Misriyin*, Vol. 1, p. 45.

23   Ibn Yunus, *Tarikh al-Misriyin*, Vol. 1, p. 21.

24   See Michael Cooperson, *Classical Arabic Biography*, pp. 22–23.

25   See Michael Cooperson, *Classical Arabic Biography*. References to dreams
     are another kind of common rhetorical technique found in biographies.
     Biographers frequently make recourse to 'special or secret' information that
     gives the biography a special air of veracity by providing insights into

situations and events that other kinds of historical writings could not employ. Dreams have a certain authority because they functioned in medieval Muslim culture as an alternative and powerful version of waking reality. What happened in dreams reflected the status of the individual dreamt of, and spoke to a certain truth that eluded people when they were awake. See Annemarie Schimmel, *Die Träume des Kalifen: Träume und ihre Deutung in der islamischen Kultur* (München, 1998); also see her *Mystical Dimensions of Islam* (Chapel Hill, 1978).

26 See E. Lane's *Arabic-English Lexicon*, s.v. *"asaba"*.
27 Abu 'Abdallah al-Husayn b. 'Ali al-Saymari, *Akhbar Abi Hanifa wa ashabihi* (Beirut, 1976), p. 162.
28 al-Saymari, *Akhbar Abi Hanifa*, p. 162.
29 See Calder, *Studies in Early Muslim Jurisprudence*, pp. 88–89.
30 Abu Ibrahim al-Muzani, *Mukhtasar*, ed., Muhammad 'Abd al-Qadir Shahin (Beirut, 1998), p. 7.
31 See al-Saymari's introduction to *Akhbar Abi Hanifa wa ashabihi*.
32 See Ibn al-'Imad al-Hanbali. *Shadharat al-dhahab fi akhbar min dhahab* (Beirut, 1998), Vol. 3, p. 447.
33 al-Khalili, *Kitab al-irshad*, Vol. 1, p. 431.
34 al-Khalili, *Kitab al-irshad*, Vol. 1, p. 431.
35 al-Khalili, *Kitab al-irshad*, Vol. 1, p. 432.
36 See especially, in this regard, al-Khalili, *Kitab al-irshad*, Vol. 1, pp. 432–435.
37 al-Khalili, *Kitab al-irshad*, Vol. 1, p. 432.
38 Ibn Qadi Shuhbah, *Tabaqat al-fuqaha'* (Beirut, 1980), p. 142.
39 Ibn Qadi Shuhbah, *Tabaqat al-fuqaha'*, p. 142.
40 Ibn Qadi Shuhbah, *Tabaqat al-fuqaha'*, p. 97.
41 See al-Tahawi, *Ahkam al-Qur'an*, ed., Sa'id al-Din Awnal (Istanbul, 1995).
42 al-Saymari, *Akhbar Abi Hanifa wa ashabihi*, p. 162.
43 Ibn 'Asakir, *Tarikh madinat Dimashq*, ed., Muhibb al-Din Abi Sa'id 'Umar b. Gharamah al-'Amrawi (Beirut, 1995), Vol. 5, p. 369.
44 Ibn 'Asakir, *Tarikh madinat Dimashq*, Vol. 5, p. 369.
45 Ibn Khallikan, *Wafayat al-a'yan wa-abna' abna' al-zaman*, ed., Ihsan 'Abbas (Beirut, 1977).
46 See Abu al-Qasim al-Rafi'i, *al-'Aziz fi sharh al-wajiz*, ed., 'Ali Muhammad Mu'awwad and 'Adil Ahmad 'Abd al-Mawjud (Beirut, 1997), and Muhyi al-Din al-Nawawi, *Rawdat al-talibin*, ed., 'Adil Ahmad 'Abd al-Mawjud and 'Ali Muhammad Mu'awwad (Beirut, 1991).
47 R. Kevin Jaques, *Authority, Conflict and the Transmission*.
48 See, for instance, Abu al-Hasan al-Marwardi, *al-Hawi al-kabir fi fiqh madhhab al-Shafi'i wa huwa sharh mukhtasar al-Muzani*, ed., 'Ali Muhammad al-Mu'awwad et al. (Beirut, 1994).

49 S. al-Dhahabi, *Tarikh al-Islam*, Vol. 20, pp. 65–68; *Siyar aʻlam al-nubala'*, Vol. 12, pp. 492–497.

50 Ibn Hajar al-ʻAsqalani, *Lisan al-mizan*, ed., ʻAdil Ahmad ʻAbd al-Mawjud and ʻAli Muhammad Muʻawwad (Beirut, 1996), Vol. 1, pp. 380–386. Although this passage refers to the biography of al-Tahawi, he uses sections of the biography found in al-Shirazi for the same effect.

51 Ibn Khallikan, *Wafayat al-aʻyan*, Vol. 1, p. 217.

52 Ibn Khallikan, *Wafayat al-aʻyan*, Vol. 1, p. 217.

53 Abu Bakr al-Bayhaqi, *al-Manaqib al-Shafiʻi*, ed., Ahmad Saqr (Cairo, 1971), Vol. 1, pp. 347–348; Vol. 2, pp. 22–23.

54 Ibn Khallikan, *Wafayat al-aʻyan*, Vol. 1, p. 89.

55 Muhyi al-Din al-Nawawi, *Tahdhib al-asma' wa'l-lughat* (Cairo, 1927), Vol. 2, p. 258; Abd al-Rahim al-Isnawi, *Tabaqat al-Shafiʻiyah*, ed., Kamal Yusuf al-Hut (Beirut, 1987), Vol. 1, p. 32.

56 al-Khalili, *Kitab al-irshad*, Vol. 1, p. 432.

57 Ibn Khallikan, *Wafayat al-aʻyan*, Vol. 1, pp. 71–72.

58 Ibn Khallikan, *Wafayat al-aʻyan*, Vol. 1, pp. 217–218.

59 See Ibn Khallikan, *Wafayat al-aʻyan*, Vol. 1, pp. 271–272. Also see S. al-Dhahabi, *Tarikh al-Islam*, Vol. 20, pp. 70–73.

60 Ibn Khallikan, *Wafayat al-aʻyan*, Vol. 1, p. 71.

61 See al-Khalili, *Kitab al-irshad*, Vol. 1, p. 432.

62 See Noel Coulson, 'Doctrine and Practice in Islamic Law: One Aspect of the Problem', *Bulletin of the School of Oriental and African Studies*, 18:2 (1956), pp. 211–226.

63 See E. Tyan, "ʻAdl', *Encyclopaedia of Islam* (second edition), Vol. 1, pp. 209–210.

64 Ibn Khallikan, *Wafayat al-aʻyan*, Vol. 1, p. 72.

65 Al-Dhahabi, *Tarikh al-Islam*, Vol. 20, pp. 65–68, Vol. 24, pp. 77–79; S. al-Dhahabi, *Siyar aʻlam al-nubala'*, Vol. 12, pp. 492–497.

66 Salah al-Din Khalil b. Aybak al-Safadi, *Kitab al-wafi al-wafayat*, ed., Muhammad Yusuf Najm et al. (Wiesbaden, 1971), Vol. 8, pp. 9–10.

67 ʻAbdallah b. Asʻad b. ʻAli al-Yafiʻi, *Mirat al-jinan*, Vol. 2, p. 132, Vol. 2, p. 211.

68 Ismaʻil Ibn Kathir, *al-Bidayah wa 'l-nihayah*, ed., ʻAli Muhammad Muʻawwad et al. (Beirut, 1994), Vol. 11, pp. 207–208.

69 Muhammad b. Qasim al-Nuwayri, *Kitab al-ilman*, ed., ʻAziz Suryl Atiya (Hyderabad, 1979), Vol. 3, pp. 273, 283, 287–88.

70 ʻAbd al-Qadir b. Abi al-Wafa' al-Qurashi, *al-Jawahir al-mudiʻah fi tabaqat al-Hanafiyah* (Cairo, 1978), Vol. 1, pp. 271–277.

71 Ibn Hajar al-ʻAsqalani, *Lisan al-mizan*, Vol. 1, pp. 380–386.

72 Al-Qurashi, *al-Jawahir al-madiʻah fi tabaqat al-hanafiyah*, Vol. 1, pp. 271–277.

73 Ibn Tulun, *Mut'at al-adhhan min al-tamattu' bi'l-iqran bayna tarajim al-shuyukh wa'l-aqran* (Beirut, 1999), Vol. 1, p. 267; Vol. 2, pp. 614, 748; Shams al-Din Muhammad Abd al-Rahman al-Sakhawi, *al-Daw' al-lami' li-ahl al-qarn al-tasi'* (Beirut, 1966), Vol. 10, pp. 39–40; 'Abd al-Qadir b. Muhammad al-Nu'aymi, *al-Daris fi tarikh al-madaris* (n.p., 1988), Vol. 2, pp. 59, 105.

7. Traditions of Reform, Reformers of Tradition: Case Studies from Senegal and Zanzibar/Tanzania

1 I. Tahir, *Scholars, Sufis, Saints and Capitalists in Kano, 1904–1974* (PhD Dissertation, Cambridge, 1975), p. 515.

2 For an extensive discussion of the dynamics and dialectics of 'reform' in African Muslim contexts, see R. Loimeier, 'Patterns and Peculiarities of Islamic Reform in Africa', *Journal of Religion in Africa*, 33:3 (2003), pp. 237–263; and R. Loimeier, 'Is there something like "Protestant Islam"?', *Die Welt des Islams*, 45:2 (2005), pp. 216–254.

3 Such a modernizing orientation may, for instance, be expressed in specific features of organization. For an extensive discussion of different notions of reform, modernization and tradition, see M. Q. Zaman, *The Ulama in Contemporary Islam: Custodians of Change* (Princeton, 2002), pp. 3ff.

4 See J. O. Voll, 'Afrikanischer *localism* und das islamische Weltsystem', in R. Loimeier, D. Neubert and C. Weissköppel, eds., *Globalisierung im Lokalen Kontext. Perspektiven und Konzepte von Handeln in Afrika* (Hamburg, 2005), pp. 277–310.

5 The term 'episteme' is not only understood here in its literal sense, as 'knowledge' ('*Wissen, Erkenntnis*', in contrast to a 'doxa', an opinion, a dogma), but, in a wider sense, to include those aspects of the ritual and the religious sphere which are associated with a respective epistemic tradition, such as, in the case of the esoteric episteme, the veneration of the Prophet, the celebration of the *mawlid al-nabi* (birthday of the Prophet), the faith in saints and both their *baraka* and power to intercede, the allegoric interpretation of the Qur'an and a multitude of Sufi rituals, in particular the *dhikr*. For a discussion of the different notions of the term 'episteme' in the Malian context, see Louis Brenner, *Controlling Knowledge: Religion, Power and Schooling in a West African Muslim Society* (Bloomington, 2001), pp. 17ff.

6 Such understandings of 'reform' which advocate a renewed understanding of the faith translate particularly well into Arabo-Muslim contexts, where reform is often presented as *tajdid* (renewal) or *islah* (improvement). The Wahhabiyya of the eighteenth and twentieth centuries, the Tablighi Jama'at, the Ahl-i Hadith as well as the Nadwat al-'Ulama', could be regarded as

such movements of reform. See, for example, Muhammad Khalid Masud, ed., *Travellers in Faith. Studies of the Tablighi Jama'at as a Transnational Islamic Movement for Faith Renewal* (Leiden, 2000), and Zaman, *The Ulama*. Even a number of Sufi-oriented movements of reform did have such an orientation as, for instance, those linked with the teaching of Ahmad b. Idris and the Sanusiyya. See, for example, Sean Rex O'Fahey, *Enigmatic Saint: Ahmad ibn Idris and the Idrisi Tradition* (Evanston, 1990).

7   I am using the term 'paradigm' here to make a clear distinction between the underlying religious and/or ideological message (and its rootedness in a esoteric, literalist or rationalistic episteme) of a movement of reform, i.e. the religio-ideological 'superstructure' of a movement of reform, and its factual social, political or economic direction and impact, which may be modernizing, traditionalist, conservative or activist. A movement of reform may be committed to an esoteric, a literalist or a rationalistic episteme, while advocating, at the same time, programmes of social reform which would enhance processes of modernization, even if such a movement of reform would claim to fight against 'modernity' (or, at least, a 'Western' definition of modernity).

8   E. E. Rosander, 'Introduction: The Islamization of "Tradition" and "Modernity"', in E. E. Rosander and D. Westerlund, eds., *African Islam and Islam in Africa. Encounters between Sufis and Islamists* (London, 1997), pp. 1, 4.

9   A term coined by Robert Redfield in R. Redfield, *Peasant Society and Culture* (Chicago, 1956).

10 T. Asad, *The Idea of an Anthropology of Islam* (Georgetown, 1986), p. 14.

11 I am going to focus on Senegal and Zanzibar/Tanzania as I have had the chance to live and to undertake research in both of these countries (as well as Northern Nigeria) since 1981. Both countries may point to a long tradition of Islamic learning, yet, while Muslims constitute a majority of 95 per cent of the population in Senegal, their share in Tanzania's population is only 35 per cent, even if Muslims constitute a majority in the coastal areas and in Zanzibar. The Maliki school of law has always been predominant in Senegal, as well as all other parts of sub-Saharan West Africa, while East Africa has had a historical experience of a number of different Muslim scholastic traditions, in particular, Ibadi and Shi'i traditions, even if the Shafi'i school of law has been predominant.

12 Most recently in M. Gomez-Perez, 'Généalogies de l'islam réformiste au Sénégal: figures, savoirs et réseaux', in L. Fourchard, A. Mary and R. Otayek, eds., *Entreprises religieuses transnationales en Afrique de l'Ouest* (Paris, 2005), p. 194.

13 See G. Johnson, *Naissance du Sénégal contemporain: Aux origines de la vie politiques modernes (1900–1920)* (Paris, 1991).

14 R. Loimeier, *Säkularer Staat und islamische Gesellschaft. Die Beziehungen zwischen Staat, Sufi-Bruderschaften und islamischer Reformbewegung in Senegal im 20. Jahrhundert* (Hamburg, 2001), p. 90.

15 The sociologist Dieter Neubert has described these associations as '*Schatzmeister-Vereinigungen*', 'treasurer-associations', as these groups tend to duplicate organizational structures which are defined by a 'President-Secretary General-Treasurer' set-up of chartered associations ('*Vereine*'). Today, these associations are often organized as 'Islamic NGOs'.

16 R. Loimeier, *Säkularer Staat und Islamische Gesellschaft*, p. 168.

17 R. Loimeier, *Säkularer Staat und Islamische Gesellschaft*, p. 168.

18 For the expansion of the UCM into neighbouring countries, see M. Miran, 'Le wahhabisme à Abidjan: dynamisme urbain d'un islam réformiste en Côte d'Ivoire contemporaine (1960–1996)', *Islam et Sociétés au Sud du Sahara*, 12 (1998), pp. 5–74.

19 See A. Merad, *Le réformisme musulman en Algérie de 1925 à 1940* (Paris, 1967).

20 In North and West Africa, the term '*marabout*' (from the Arabic root '*murabit*', i.e. somebody who lives in a '*ribat*', to teach and/or to defend Islam) has come to be understood as describing a religious scholar and mystic. In Senegal, *marabout*s, in a much narrower sense, are the religious leaders of the *tariqas*.

21 This turn against the 'esoteric episteme' could be seen as being part and parcel of a process of 'secularization', a process which was characterized by Max Weber as a process of 'disenchantment of the world' and a process of gradual rationalization of religion and society, in which 'all forms of magic are rejected as superstition'. See M. Weber, *Gesammelte Aufsätze zur Religionssoziologie I.* (Tübingen, [1920] 1988), Vol. I, pp. 94–95.

22 For a discussion of this term, see R. Launay and B. F. Soares, 'The formation of an "Islamic sphere" in French Colonial West Africa', *Economy and Society*, 28:4 (1999), pp. 497–519; B. Soares, *Islam and the Prayer Economy: History and Authority in a Malian Town* (Edinburgh, 2005).

23 Personal Communication of Cheikh Touré (13 April 1992); for his biography, see R. Loimeier, 'Religiös-Ökonomische Netzwerke in Senegal: Das Beispiel der muridischen Expansion in Dakar', *Afrika Spectrum*, 1 (1994), pp. 99–112.

24 See M. Dia, *Mémoires d'un militant du tiers-monde* (Paris, 1985).

25 Abd al-Aziz Sy, Khalifa Général of the Tijaniyya in Senegal, in Wal Fadjri, No. 258, 25 April 1991.

26 For this term, see R. Launay, *Beyond the Stream. Islam and Society in a West African Town* (Berkeley, 1992), p. 92.

27 This is particularly true for the Muridiyya, which is often presented as a 'true Senegalese' *tariqa*. However, the different branches of the Tijaniyya have also stressed their Senegalese identity by cultivating *ziyarat* to the different places of Tijani history such as Tivavouane or Kaolack.

28 These 'cross-overs' have been diagnosed, with respect to Senegal, by Leonardo Villalon, as 'mutualities of position' in L. A. Villalon, 'The Moustarchidine of Senegal: The Family Politics of a Contemporary Tijan Movement', in J-L. Triaud and D. Robinson, eds., *La Tijaniyya: Une confrérie musulmane à la conquête de l'Afrique* (Paris, 2004), p. 69; and 'hybrid' features of organization in L. A. Villalon, 'Generational Changes, Political Stagnation, and the Evolving Dynamics of Religion and Politics in Senegal', *Africa Today*, 46:3–4 (1999), p. 142; as well as Monika Salzbrunn as a 'hybridization of religion and political practices', see M. Salzbrunn, 'Hybridization of Religious and Political Practices amongst West African Migrants in Europe', in D. Bryceson and U. Vuorela, eds., *The Transnational Family: New European Frontiers and Global Networks* (Oxford, 2002), pp. 217–229.

29 It has to be stressed that the term 'generation' is not understood here in its purely biological dimension. A generation of reform may comprise in fact two or even more biological generations of reformers, if the issues of reform and the orientation of a movement of reform are not modified substantially. A shift to an epistemological new generation of reformers implies a significant break with an established episteme.

30 An expression coined by David Robinson in D. Robinson, *Paths of Accommodation: Muslim Societies and French Colonial Authorities in Senegal and Mauritania 1880–1920* (Oxford, 2000).

31 L. A. Villalon, 'The Moustarchidine of Senegal', p. 134.

32 See F. Samson, *Les marabouts de l'islam politique. Le Dahiratoul Moustarchidina Wal Moustarchidaty un movement néo-confrérique sénégalais* (Paris, 2005), pp. 146–154.

33 See D. B. Cruise O'Brien, *The Mourides of Senegal: The Political and Economic Organization of an Islamic Brotherhood* (Oxford, 1971), and L. C. Behrman, *Muslim Brotherhoods and Politics in Senegal* (Cambridge, Mass., 1970). Some of these *marabout*s were also willing to cooperate with the ITI, for a number of reasons: internal rivalries, the quest for political allies, dislike of L. S. Senghor, or support for Senegal's struggle for independence.

34 For Cheikh Tidiane Sy's political career, see, extensively, L. C. Behrman, *Muslim Brotherhoods*; L. A. Villalon, 'The Moustarchidine of Senegal'; R. Loimeier, *Säkularer Staat und Islamische Gesellschaft*; and F. Samson, *Les marabouts de l'islam politique*.

35 C. Coulon, *Le Marabout et le Prince* (Paris, 1981), p. 280.

36 C. Gueye, *Touba: La capitale des mourides* (Paris, 2002), p. 200, as well as L. A. Villalon, 'Generational Changes', and L. A. Villalon, 'The Moustarchidine of Senegal', pp. 477ff.

37 The term '*marabouts mondains*' was coined by A. Diaw, M. C. Diop and M. Diouf. See X. Audrain, '*Du "Ndiggël" avorté au Parti de la Vérité: Évolution du rapport religion/politique à travers le parcours de Cheikh Modou Kara (1999–2004)*', *Politique Africaine* 96 (2004), p. 99.

38 For the MMUD, see X. Audrain, '*Du "Ndiggël" avorté au Parti de la Vérité*', pp. 100ff.

39 For an analysis of his speeches and public appearance, see Ousmane Kane and L. A. Villalon, 'Les Moustarshidin du Senegal', *Islam et Sociétés au Sud du Sahara*, 9 (2004), pp. 119–202.

40 Literally, 'the quest for both kinds of accomplishment', refers to success and accomplishment (*fawz*) in this world as well as the hereafter. The Matlaboul Fawzaïni was established as an initiative of Mourides in the European diaspora by Dame Ndiaye, in 1990, and has been recognized, in Senegal, as an 'NGO'. The organization is often seen as a '*dahira* of the émigrés', but has considerable support among intellectuals and academics of Mouride inclination; see C. Gueye, *Touba*, pp. 249ff.

41 See R. Loimeier, *Säkularer Staat und Islamische Gesellschaft*, pp. 315ff. The musician Youssou Ndour's most recent Compact Disc recording is 'Allah' (New York, 2004) (interestingly, the English title is 'Egypt', while in Senegal the recording is marketed under the label 'Sant', meaning praise; see L. A. Villalon, 'Senegal', *African Studies Review*, 47:2 (2004), p. 70), and features four songs in praise for the Muridiyya (Shukran Bamba, Bamba the poet, Cheikh Ibra Fall and Touba-Darou Salaam), two in praise of the Tijaniyya (Tijaniyya, Baay Niass) and one for the small brotherhood of the Layènes (Mahdiyu Laye).

42 D. B. Cruise O'Brien, 'Le contract social sénégalais à l'épreuve', *Politique Africaine* 45 (1992), p. 18.

43 See R. Loimeier, *Säkularer Staat und Islamische Gesellschaft*, pp. 328–329.

44 C. Gueye claims that the *ndiggël* has probably been overemphasized in the political analysis of the past as a spectacularly visible symbol of religious authority in the political domain. Still, the failure of the '*ndiggël politique*' since the late 1980s supports the argument of the fragmentation of the Muridiyya as a religio-political movement. For an analysis of the '*ndiggël électoral*', see X. Audrain '*Du "Ndiggël" avorté au Parti de la Vérité*', pp. 104ff, as well as C. Gueye, *Touba*, pp. 280ff.

45 See F. Samson, *Les marabouts de l'islam politique*, p. 38. According to Mustapha Sy, the DMM has about 500,000 members (Samson, *Les*

marabouts de l'islam politique, p. 48), a claim that seems to be frequently made by a number of religio-political movements in Senegal. See, for instance, corresponding claims of the *Hizbut Tarqiyya* and the MMUD.

46 Khalifa Diouf's father had been a secretary of Abubakar Sy, Cheikh Ahmad Tidiane Sy's father, and had also worked with Cheikh Ahmed Tidiane Sy in the 1960s (F. Samson, *Les marabouts de l'islam politique*, p. 120). In the electoral campaign, Mustafa Sy quickly withdrew his candidature for the office of the President, and PUR, as well as all other 'religious' candidates, failed to score a significant number of votes (see F. Samson, *Les marabouts de l'islam politique*). The elections of February and March 2000 brought about the victory of Abdoulaye Wade and a coalition of the opposition (L. A. Villalon, 'Generational Changes', pp. 142ff; and F. Samson, 'Une nouvelle conception des rapports entre religion et politique au Sénégal', in C. Coulon, ed., *L'Afrique Politique: Islams d'Afrique, entre le local et le global* (Paris, 2002), pp. 164ff); for an extensive presentation of the development of the DMM, see F. Samson, *Les marabouts de l'islam politique*.

47 The acronym DEM means 'to go' ('dem') in Wolof.

48 More recently, it has also become important for the Mouride diaspora.

49 C. Gueye, *Touba*, p. 245; also see C. Gueye, *Touba*, pp. 239ff, extensively for the development of the HT.

50 C. Gueye, *Touba*, p. 248.

51 L. A. Villalon, 'Generational Changes', pp. 138ff; and C. Gueye, *Touba*, pp. 239ff. The HT had actually eclipsed Moustapha Saliou's leading role in the *tariqa* in the context of the organization of the *magal* of 1996. Until then, Moustapha Saliou Mbakke had effectively led the *tariqa*, represented it in the context of international conferences, and had been in charge, due to his managerial qualities, of the major projects of development in Touba; see C. Gueye, *Touba*, p. 233.

52 L. A. Villalon, 'Generational Changes', p. 139.

53 In particular, Muhammad Abduh (d. 1905), whose articles in the journal *Al-Manar* were widely read.

54 The differentiation between 'marketable' and 'social' skills reflects to a certain degree an emic, Muslim, differentiation between the 'traditionally transmitted' (*manqulat*) disciplines such as Qur'an, *hadith*, *fiqh* and *kalam*, and the 'rational sciences' such as philosophy, arithmetic and medicine, and a respective debate about 'useful knowledge' (*al-'ilm an-nafi'*). In the nineteenth century, this debate acquired a new connotation in the course of the emergence of new Islamic schools in British India and the question as to which disciplines should be taught in these *madrasas*; see M. Q. Zaman, *The Ulama*, pp. 64–65.

55 For a discussion of the different styles and types of education, see M. Q. Zaman, *The Ulama*, pp. 64ff. Islamic education in sub-Saharan Africa is discussed in a number of recent studies; see, for instance, L. Brenner, *Controlling Knowledge*, and R. Loimeier, 'Je veux étudier sans mendier': The Campaign against the Qur'anic Schools in Senegal', in H. Weiss, ed., *Social Welfare in Muslim Societies in Africa* (Uppsala, 2002), pp. 118–137.

56 *Ujamaa* was linked, in particular, with President Julius Nyerere's concept of an 'African socialism'.

57 See A. Nimtz, *Islam and Politics in East Africa, The Sufi Order in Tanzania* (Minneapolis, 1980). In particular, a younger generation of Qadiri *shaykhs* from Bagamoyo and Dar es Salaam, representing the 'school' of Shaykh Ramiya, were prepared to rebel against established authorities such as Shaykh Hassan b. Ameir.

58 See, extensively, M. Said, *The Life and Times of Abdulwahid Sykes (1924–1968): The Untold Story of the Muslim Struggle against British Colonialism in Tanganyika* (London, 1998).

59 Communication Sören Gilsaa, 21 April 2005; for Shaykh Nur ud-Din's biography, see C. Ahmed, 'Networks of the Shadhiliyya-Yashrutiyya Sufi Order in East Africa', in R. Loimeier and R. Seesemann, eds., *The Global Worlds of the Swahili: Interfaces of Islam, Identity and Space in the 19th and 20th Century East Africa* (Hamburg, 2006).

60 For disputes over the issue of the *dhikr*, see below. Similar disputes have focused on the celebration of the *mawlid al-nabi*, the birthday of the Prophet, which has come to be celebrated in many parts of East Africa in many different forms, from the 'sober' and solemn recitation in Arabic of the *mawlid barzanji* to some rather ecstatic forms of the *mawlidi ya kiswahili*, which has come to be celebrated not only on the actual date of the Prophet's birthday (12 Rabi' al-awwal), but in the context of many societal occasions. As a consequence, *mawlid* celebrations have been attacked by both Muslim reformers, as well as the British colonial administration in Zanzibar, as 'un-Islamic' and a feature of 'conspicuous consumption' which should be stopped. Disputes over *mawlid* celebrations started in East Africa in the late nineteenth century, and continue until today. For the fight against '*mawlidi*' in Zanzibar, see R. Loimeier, 'Fighting Popular Culture: The "Ulama" and the State in Zanzibar', in R. Loimeier and R. Seesemann, eds., *The Global Worlds of the Swahili: Interfaces of Islam, Identity and Space in the 19th and 20th Century East Africa* (Hamburg, 2006).

61 An interesting case of a trans-religious 'cross-over' between activist Muslims and activist Christians, in particular, when looking at the modes in which both groups use and organize the public space, as, for instance, in

the context of *mihadhara* sermon meetings. Muslim *mihadhara* preaching in Tanzania actually started in 1981 after a visit of the South African Muslim preacher Ahmad Deedat, who had been invited by the Muslim Students' Association of the University of Dar es Salaam University (MSAUD) in order to support Muslim struggles against an increasingly encroaching Christian missionary presence on the Dar es Salaam University campus. Ahmad Deedat had again developed his style and strategy of preaching in the confrontation with South African Pentecostal churches, in particular Reinhard Bonnkes's 'Christ for all Nations' (CFAN) movement. For Ahmad Deedat, see D. Westerlund, 'Ahmed Deedat's Theology of Religion: Apologetics through Polemics', *Journal of Religion in Africa* 33:3 (2003), pp. 263ff, and S. Sadouni, 'Le minoritaire sud-africain Ahmed Deedat, une figure originale de la da'wa', *Islam et sociétés au Sud du Sahara* 12 (1998), pp. 149ff; for the development of *mihadhara* preaching in Tanzania and Ahmad Deedat's first visit to Tanzania, see H. Njozi, *Mwembechai Killings and the Political Future of Tanzania* (Ottawa, 2000), pp. 10ff.

62 *Tajwid* is the art of reciting the Qur'an according to a set of rules.

63 For Tanzania, see F. Ludwig, 'After Ujamaa: Is Religious Rivalism a Threat to Tanzania's Stability', in D. Westerlund, ed., *Questioning the Secular State. The Worldwide Resurgence of Religion in Politics* (London, 1996), pp. 216–236; for South Africa, see D. Westerlund, 'Ahmed Deedat's Theology of Religion: Apologetics through Polemics', *Journal of Religion in Africa*, 33:3 (2003), pp. 263–278; for Nigeria, see K. Hock, *Der Islam-Komplex. Zur christlichen Wahrnehmung des Islams und der christlich-muslimischen Beziehungen in Nordnigeria während der Militärherrschaft Babangidas* (Hamburg, 1996).

64 For a discussion of the term 'trans-local', see DAVO-Rundbrief, 'Translocality in the Modern History of the Middle East, Asia and Africa'. Presentation of the current research programme at the Zentrum Moderner Orient, Berlin (Mainz, 2003).

65 For an extensive presentation of trans-local legitimizing references, see R. Loimeier, 'Translocal Networks of Saints and the Negotiation of Religious Disputes in Local Contexts', *Archives de Sciences Sociales des Religions*, 133 (Paris, March 2006).

66 Activist and associationist groups in Northern Nigeria, such as the 'Muslim Brothers' of Shaykh Ibrahim al-Zakzaki or the 'Daawa' group of Shaykh Aminud-Din Abubakar, have become famous for having switched, since the late 1970s, from Iranian to Saudi Arabian, to Kuwait-Emirate, to Libyan, and back to Iranian or Saudi Arabian sources of inspiration and funding, while cultivating, at the same time, a plethora of less conspicuous

links with Sudan, Egypt, Malaysia and Pakistan, as well as the activist
diaspora in Great Britain; see R. Loimeier, *Islamic Reform and Political
Change in Northern Nigeria* (Evanston, 1997).

67 An example of a virtual, imagined link is the case of Abd al-Muhyi, a Javan
scholar of the seventeenth century, who in his dreams established a trans-
historical connection with the eleventh-century founder of the Qadiriyya,
Abd al-Qadir al-Jilani; see W. Kraus, *Imaginierte und reale Netzwerke in
Südostasien*, in *Die islamische Welt als Netzwerk*, Roman Loimeier, ed.,
Möglichkeiten und Grenzen des Nertzwerkansatzes im islamischen Kontext
(Würzburg, 2000), pp. 298ff.

68 For his biography, see Scott Reese, 'Urban Woes and Pious Remedies:
Sufism in Nineteenth-Century Benaadir (Somalia)', in *Africa Today*, 46:3–4
(1999), pp. 169–194.

69 Quoted in Abdallah Salih al-Farsi, *Baadhi ya Wanavyuoni wa Kishafi wa
Mashariki ya Afrika* (Mombasa, [1944] 1972), pp. 14–15.

70 A *dhikr* with '*dufu*' (*bandiri*) drums. *Dufu* or *bandiri* drums are half-open
drums, often lined with little bells. *Dufu* drums are usually not presented
by the proponents of the respective *dhikr* traditions as musical instruments,
but as rhythmic aids.

71 See T. Asad, *The Idea of an Anthropology of Islam*.

72 A. S. al-Farsi, *Baadhi ya Wanavyuoni*, pp. 14–15.

73 The dispute between Shaykh al-Amawi and Shaykh Uways not only had a
trans-traditional notion in a historical perspective when their dispute was
quoted, in the 1940s, by Shaykh Abdallah Salih al-Farsi in the context of his
own struggle against Shaykh Mahmud b. Kombo, but also and beyond
Shaykh Uways's legitimizing reference to Baghdad, a second trans-local
notion within the same tradition of reform, the Qadiriyya, in the same
period of time, the 1890s. This second trans-local notion of the dispute
between Shaykh Uways and Shaykh al-Amawi invoked different local
settings, Zanzibar and Brawa, and even allows for an open-ended reading
of their dispute, depending on a Zanzibar or Brawa perspective of
interpretation. Shaykh Uways seems to have claimed in Brawa that Shaykh
al-Amawi became one of his *muqaddamun* (local representatives) in
Zanzibar and that Shaykh al-Amawi eventually recognized Shaykh Uways's
spiritual leadership. This claim, as expressed in a list of 150 *muqaddamun*
of Shaykh Uways mentioned in a hagiographic account of Shaykh Uways's
life titled '*al-Jawhar al-nafis*' (The Perfect Jewel), may be interpreted in a
number of ways: first, Shaykh al-Amawi, while having initially opposed
Shaykh Uways, may indeed have come to accept the latter's leading role
within the Qadiriyya; second, Shaykh al-Amawi might have denounced, in
his poem, another form and practice of the *dhikr* that was not linked with

the forms of the *dhikr* as introduced by Shaykh Uways; or, third, the dispute between Shaykh al-Amawi and Shaykh Uways may reflect a Zanzibari perspective only: in Brawa, both *shaykhs* were accepted as well-learned scholars, even if Shaykh Uways originally had encountered problems due to his servile background. At the same time, the Qadiriyya had to face, in Brawa, staunch opposition from the Ahmadiyya movement of reform led by Sayyid Muhammad Abdille Hassan in Northern Somalia, who pursued a vicious war against the Qadiriyya. In this struggle, Shaykh Uways was killed by local allies of Sayyid Muhammad Abdulle Hassan in 1909. In Zanzibar, by contrast, the Qadiriyya did not face comparable opposition. Internal disputes may thus have been discussed in a more prominent way than in Brawa, where a common enemy had possibly brought about an alliance of convenience among otherwise competing scholars. I am grateful to Scott Reese for pointing out these different notions of interpretation of the Uways-Amawi conflict (communication Scott Reese, 8 August 2005). It has to be stressed that the Ahmadiyya movement of reform, as led by Sayyid Muhammad Abdulle Hassan, has also emerged from a Sufi background, namely the tradition of reform established by Ahmad b. Idris (d. 1837). On the Idrisi tradition of reform and the Ahmadiyya movement in Somalia, see B. G. Martin, *Muslim Brotherhoods in 19th Century Africa* (Cambridge, 1976); S. R. O'Fahey, *Enigmatic Saint*; and A. Sheikh-Abdi, *Divine Madness: Mohammed Abdulle Hassan (1856–1920)* (London, 1993).

74 *Was instrumentalisiert wird, kann nicht gleichzeitig 'essentialisiert' werden, oder, anders gesagt: der angeblich 'essentialistische' (und a-historische) Charakter von 'Islam' wird durch faktische Instrumentalisierungen von Texten, Traditionen etc. widerlegt.* I am grateful to Réné Otayek for this remark. At the same time, it has to be stressed that strategic instrumentalizations, manipulations or interpretations of traditions, texts, links or the canon as such are mostly confined to contexts of dispute. The strategic instrumentalization or manipulation of trans-local, trans-historical, trans-traditional or trans-generational legitimizing references is, at least, less visible in seemingly banal contexts such as constructions of identities through genealogies for family histories or the quest to collect rare books.

75 I am grateful to Zulfikar Hirji for this expression.

8. *Justifying Islamic Pluralism: Reflections from Indonesia and France*

1 The four *madhhab*s in the Sunni tradition were developed by Abu Hanifa (d. 767), Malik ibn Abbas (d. 795), Muhammad ibn Idris al-Shafi'i (d. 820)

and Ahmad ibn Hanbal (d. 855), and are known as the Hanafi, Maliki, Shafiʻi and Hanbali schools. Shiʻi groups developed additional traditions. On the development of jurisprudential reasoning, see the classic work by N. Coulson, *A History of Islamic Law* (Edinburgh, 1964); and the recent analysis by W. Hallaq, *A History of Islamic Legal Theories* (Cambridge, 1997). For a background in practical jurisprudence, see B. Johansen, *Contingency in a Sacred Law: Legal and Ethical Norms in the Muslim Fiqh* (Leiden, 1999), and D. S. Powers, *Law, Society and Culture in the Maghrib, 1300–1500* (Cambridge, 2002).

2   Some scholars (e.g. Ira Lapidus) distinguish between 'modernist' thinkers concerned with creating an Islam that would fit with the modern world, and 'reformist' scholars who urged a return to scriptures, but these lines are not so neat, as one possible argument for 'modernism' is that scripture can be interpreted in such a way as to accommodate modern norms, for example of gender equality, once one jettisons the baggage of medieval jurisprudence. See I. Lapidus, *A History of Islamic Societies* (Cambridge, 2002). On modernism, see A. Hourani, *Arabic Thought in the Liberal Age, 1798–1939* (Cambridge, 1983); and on the legal theoretical problems it engenders and encounters, see W. Hallaq, *A History*, pp. 207–262.

3   I use the phrase 'Muslim public intellectual' to refer to Muslims taking part in public debates concerning Islam, regardless of their education or training. Some of these intellectuals might also consider themselves to be scholars or jurists, and they might also be so referred to by others, but such designations vary greatly by region. In Indonesia, the term *'ulama'* is used to designate persons learned in Islam, whether they hold office or not. In France, such titles are rarely used, and many of the leading figures in debates about norms and law do not have traditional training in *fiqh*.

4   For an extended analysis of legal pluralism in Indonesia, see J. R. Bowen, *Islam, Law, and Equality in Indonesia: An Anthropology of Public Reasoning* (Cambridge, 2003). For the relationship of Islam and politics in recent decades, see R. W. Hefner, *Civil Islam: Muslims and Democratization in Indonesia* (Princeton, 2000). A broader historical overview of Indonesian history is offered by M. C. Ricklefs, *A History of Modern Indonesia since c. 1200* (Stanford, 2002).

5   On the history of *adat* and the term '*adat*', see J. Bowen, *Islam*, pp. 22–63.

6   Hazairin, *Hukum Baru di Indonesia* (Jakarta, 1950), pp. 13–15. See also the extended analysis of Islamic jurisprudential thought in Indonesia in R. M. Feener, *Developments of Muslim Jurisprudence in twentieth century Indonesia* (Boston University, 1999).

7   M. D. Ali, '*Asas-asas hukum kewarisan dalam Kompilasi Hukum Islam*', *Mimbar Hukum*, 9 (1993), pp. 1–17.

8 For overviews of Islam in France, see the sociological study by G. Kepel, *Les banlieues de l'Islam: Naissance d'une religion en France* (Paris, 1991), the recent account by *Le Monde* journalist X. Ternisien, *La France des mosquées* (Paris, 2002), and J. Cesari, *Être Musulman en France: Associations, militants et mosques* (Paris, 1994). On French, and contrasting British, ideas of nationhood and citizenship, see Adrian Favell, *Philosophies of Integration: Immigration and the Idea of Citizenship in France and Britain* (Houndmills, 2002). On contrasting ideas of *laïcité* and Islamic reform among French Muslims, see J. R. Bowen, 'Two Approaches to Rights and Religion in Contemporary France', in R. A. Wilson and J. P. Mitchell, eds., *Human Rights in Global Perspective* (London, 2003), pp. 33–53.

9 Elsewhere I explore the conflicts between differing ideas of *laïcité* and its implications for French Muslim religious and social practices. See J. R. Bowen, 'Does French Islam Have Borders? Dilemmas of Domestication in a Global Religious Field', *American Anthropologist*, 106:1 (2004), pp. 43–55; and J. R. Bowen, *Can Islam be French: Pluralism and Pragmatism in a Secularist State* (Princeton, 2009).

10 On the finer points of these debates, see the study by K. Abou El Fadl, 'Islamic law and Muslim Minorities: The Juristic Discourse on Muslim Minorities from the Second/Eighth to the Eleventh/Seventeenth Centuries', *Islamic Law and Society*, 1:2 (1994), pp. 143–187, which shows that similar debates occupied early jurists as well. Of particular interest in the context of the contemporary debates is the argument advanced by the eleventh-century Shafi'i jurist al-Mawardi that a land where Muslims could freely practise their religion was also part of *dar al-Islam*.

11 T. Ramadan, *Dar ash-shahada: L'Occident, espace du témoignage* (Lyon, 2002).

12 A French-language collection of the Council's *fatwas* was recently published: Conseil Européen des Fatwas et de la Recherché, *Receuil de fatwas* (Lyon, 2002). The *fatwa* discussed here appears on the Council's website in the list of resolutions taken at the 1999 session: see www.e-cfr.org/en/: 'Decisions: Final Statement of the Fourth Ordinary Session of the European Council for Fatwa and Research 1-2-3' (October 1999) (accessed 10 December 2006). See also the study by Alexandre Caeiro, *La normativité islamique à l'épreuve de l'Occident: le cas du Conseil européen de la fatwa et de la recherche* (Paris, 2003). On the traditional approach to interest, see J. Schacht, 'Riba', in *The Shorter Encyclopedia of Islam* (Ithaca, 1953), pp. 471–473.

13 On the early modern Hanafi position, see K. Abou El Fadl, 'Islamic law', pp. 173–174.

14 Interview, Paris, April 2001.

15 See A. Rashid, *Jihad: The Rise of Militant Islam in Central Asia* (New York, 2003).

16 Interview, Paris, May 2001.

17 T. Oubrou, 'Le "minimum islamique" pour l'abbatage ritual en France', *La Médina* 5 (2000), pp. 42–43.

18 T. Oubrou, 'Le "minimum islamique" ', p. 43.

19 See the same argument made in his extended debate with Leïla Babès, in L. Babès and T. Oubrou, *Loi d'Allah, loi des hommes: Liberté, égalité et femmes en Islam* (Paris, 2002), p. 328.

20 See M. K. Masud, *Islamic Legal Philosophy: A Study of Abu Ishaq al-Shatibi's Life and Thought* (Islamabad, 1977).

21 For further development of these ideas, see J. R. Bowen, 'Pluralism and Normativity in French Islamic Reasoning', in R. Hefner, ed., *Remaking Muslim Politics: Pluralism, Contestation, Democratization* (Princeton, 2005), pp. 326–346; and J. R. Bowen, *Can Islam be French: Pluralism and Pragmatism in a Secularist State* (Princeton, 2009). On the problems associated with the *maqasid* tradition, see W. Hallaq, *A History*, pp. 162–206.

22 More difficult are the bilateral conventions made between France and former colonies, and protectorates that guarantee the legal recognition in France of marriages and divorces made in Morocco or Algeria, even if the marriage is polygamous and the divorce made by unilateral repudiation. These conventions are likely to be abrogated in the next few years.

Glossary

Ahl al-Kitab	Lit. 'people of the book'; monotheists, adherents to a revealed religion
Ahl al-Bayt	The household of the Prophet
baraka	Grace or a blessing or beneficence bestowed by God on humankind; a quality associated with the Prophet, imams (in the Shi'i tradition) and pious individuals; a quality inherent in religious sites and in objects associated with pious persons.
bid'a, bidat	modified or unprecedented religious practice
chilla	Muslim shrine
dargah	Sufi shrine
dharm	religion
dhikr	Lit. remembrance; devotions
fiqh	Islamic jurisprudence
firqa	Sect; religious division
fitra	innate human nature
furu'	Division of Islamic jurisprudence; substantive law; practices
hadith	Report, tradition
imam	Spiritual guide; leader of prayer
jama'a, jama'at	Meeting; congregation; community of believers
jilbab	Coat or mantle; a women's garment
kafir	Infidel, non-believer, atheist
khanaqa	A building where Sufis congregate, live or are taught

khimar	headscarf
madhhab	School of Islamic jurisprudence
madrasa	School; a school that teaches religious subjects
marabout	a religious leader or teacher
milla	religion
mihna	inquisition
mujavar *mujawir,*	caretaker; a person who resides in the proximity of a mosque of religious site
murid	disciple
murshid	master
mushrikun	A person accused of shirk – association with God; polytheism
ndiggël	Power of command
pir	Spiritual guide
qalandar	Wandering dervish
shari'a	Religious law
shahada	Affirmation of faith
shahid	martyr
shaykh	Lit. elder; head of group; spiritual guide
shirk	Association of others with God; polytheism
Sufi	Muslim mystic
sura	Chapter of the Qur'an
tajwid	Art of Qur'anic recitation
takiya	Arena or theatre used for performance of *ta'ziya*
tariqa	Path; Sufi order
taqiyya	Religious dissimulation
ta'ziya	Passion play commemorating the martyrdom of Imam al-Husayn b. 'Ali, the grandson of the Prophet
umma, ummat	The community of Muslims

Bibliography

1. Debating Islam from Within: Muslim Constructions of the Internal Other

Abu-Lughod, Lila. 'Zones of Theory in the Anthropology of the Arab World', *Annual Review of Anthropology*, Vol. 18 (1989), pp. 267–306.

Adang, C. 'Belief and Unbelief', in J. D. McAuliffe, ed., *Encyclopaedia of the Qur'an*. Leiden, 2001, Vol. 1, pp. 218–226.

____ 'Hypocrites and Hypocrisy', in J. D. McAuliffe, ed., *Encyclopaedia of the Qur'an*. Leiden, 2001, Vol. 2, pp. 468–472.

Arkoun, M. 'Rethinking Islam Today', *Annals of the American Academy of Political and Social Sciences*, 588 ([1987] July 2003), pp. 18–39.

Asad, T. *Formations of the Secular: Christianity, Islam, Modernity*. Stanford, 2003.

____ *The Idea of an Anthropology of Islam*. Georgetown, 1986.

Aslan, A. *Religious Pluralism in Christian and Islamic Philosophy: The Thought of John Hick and Seyyed Hossein Nasr*. Curzon, 1998.

Bosworth, C. E. *The New Islamic Dynasties*. Edinburgh, 1996.

Crone, P. 'The Rise of Islam in the World', in F. Robinson, ed., *Cambridge Illustrated History of the Islamic World*. Cambridge, 1996, pp. 2–31.

Dallal, A. S. '*Ummah*', in J. Esposito et al., eds., *Oxford Encyclopaedia of Islam in the Modern World*. New York, 1995, Vol. 4, pp. 267–270.

Denny, F. M. 'Community and Society', in J. D. McAuliffe, ed., *Encyclopaedia of the Qur'an.* Leiden, 2001, Vol. 2, pp. 367–386.

Derrida, J. '*Différance*', *Bulletin de la Société française de philosophie*, 62:3 (July–September 1968), pp. 73–101.

Eickelman, D. *The Middle East and Central Asia: An Anthropological Approach.* New Jersey, 2001.

_____ and J. Piscatori, eds. *Muslim Travellers.* London, 1990.

El-Zein, A. H. 'Beyond Ideology and Theology: The Search for the Anthropology of Islam', *Annual Review of Anthropology*, 6 (1977), pp. 227–254.

Esack, F. *Qur'an, Liberation & Pluralism: An Islamic Perspective of Interreligious Solidarity against Oppression.* Oxford, 1997.

Fischer, M. and M. Abedi. *Debating Muslims.* Madison, 1990.

Foucault, M. *Discipline and Punishment: The Birth of the Prison*, tr. A. Sheridan. London, 1977.

Furnivall, J. *A Comparative Study of Burma and Netherlands India.* Cambridge, 1948.

_____ *Netherlands India: A Study of Plural Economy.* Cambridge, 1939.

Geertz, C. 'The Uses of Diversity', *Michigan Quarterly Review*, 25:1 (Winter 1986), pp. 105–123.

_____ *Islam Observed: Religious Development in Morocco and Indonesia.* New Haven and London, 1968.

Gellner, E. *Muslim Society.* Cambridge, 1981.

Gilsenan, M. *Recognising Islam: Religion and Society.* London and Sydney, 1982.

Grillo, R. *Pluralism and the Politics of Difference: State, Culture and Ethnicity in Comparative Perspective.* Oxford, 1998.

Hashmi, S., ed., *Islamic Political Ethics: Civil Society, Pluralism, and Conflict.* Princeton, 2002.

Headley, S. and D. Parkin, eds., *Islamic Prayer across the Indian Ocean.* Richmond, 2000.

Holy, L., ed., *Comparative Anthropology.* London, 1987.

Huntington, S. P. *The Clash of Civilizations and the Remaking of World Order.* New York, 1996.

_____ 'The Clash of Civilizations?', *Foreign Affairs*, 72:3 (Summer 1993), pp. 22–49.

Ingold, T., ed., *Key Debates in Anthropology*. London, 1996.

Kymlicka, W. *Multicultural Citizenship: A Liberal Theory of Minority Rights*. Oxford, 1995.

Legenhausen, M. *Islam and Religious Pluralism*. London, 1999.

Lukens-Bull, R. A. 'Between Text and Practice: Considerations in the Anthropological Study of Islam', *Marburg Journal of Religion*, 4:2 (1999), pp. 10–20.

Mamdani, M. *Good Muslim, Bad Muslim: America, The Cold War, and the Roots of Terror*. New York, 2004.

Manger, L., ed., *Muslim Diversity*. Richmond, 1999.

Marranci, G. *The Anthropology of Islam*. London and New York, 2008.

Merleau-Ponty, M. *The Phenomenology of Perception*, tr. C. Smith. London and New York, [1945] 1962.

Metcalf, B. D., ed., *Making Muslim Space in North America and Europe*. Berkeley, 1996.

Mir-Hosseini, Z. 'Debating Women: Gender and the Public Sphere in Post-Revolutionary Iran', in A. B. Sajoo, ed., *Civil Society in the Muslim World: Contemporary Perspectives*. London, 2002, pp. 95–122.

Nanji, A., ed., *The Muslim Almanac*. New York, 1995.

Nasr, V. *The Shia Revival*. New York, 2006.

Parekh, B. *Rethinking Multiculturalism: Cultural Diversity and Political Theory*. New York, 2000.

Parkin, D. 'Comparison as Search for Continuity', in L. Holy, ed., *Comparative Anthropology*. London, 1987, pp. 52–69.

Pearl, J. 'Islam Struggles to Stake out its Position', *International Herald Tribune*, 20 July 2005, posted on http://www.iht.com/articles/2005/07/19/opinion/edpearl.php (accessed 28 August 2009).

Purpura, A. 'Portrait of Seyyid Silima from Zanzibar: Piety and Subversion in Islamic Prayer', in D. Parkin and S. Headley, eds., *Islamic Prayer across the Indian Ocean*. Curzon, 2000, pp. 117–136.

Rahman, F. *Islam*. Chicago, [1966] 1979.

Sachedina, A. A. *The Islamic Roots of Democratic Pluralism*. Oxford, 2001.

Said, E. W. *Covering Islam*. London, 1981.

____ *Orientalism*. New York, 1979.

Sajoo, A. B. *Civil Society in the Muslim World: Contemporary Perspectives*. London, 2002.

____ *Pluralism in Old and New States: Emerging ASEAN contexts*. Singapore, 1994.

Sartre, J. P. *Being and Nothingness: An Essay on Phenomenological Ontology*, tr. H. E. Barnes. London and New York, [1943] 2003.

Sen, A. *Identity and Violence*. New York, 2006.

Shatzmiller, M., ed., *Nationalism and Minority Identities in Islamic Societies*. Montreal, 2005.

Smith, J. Z. 'Differential Equations: On Constructing the "Other"', in J. Z. Smith, *Relating Religion: Essays in the Study of Religion*. Chicago, 2004, pp. 230–250.

____ 'What a Difference A Difference Makes', in J. Neusner and E. S. Freichs, eds., *'To See Ourselves as Others See Us': Christians, Jews, 'Others' in Late Antiquity*. Chico, 1985, pp. 3–48.

Spivak, G. 'Can the Subaltern Speak?', in C. Nelson and L. Grossberg, eds., *Marxism and the Interpretation of Culture*. Urbana, 1988, pp. 271–313.

Tapper, R. 'Islamic Anthropology and the Anthropology of Islam', *Anthropological Quarterly*, 68:3 (1995), pp. 185–193.

Tibi, B. *Islam between Culture and Politics*. New York, 2001.

Varisco, D. M. *Islam Obscured*. New York, 2005.

Weekes. R., ed., *Muslim Peoples: A World Ethnographic Survey*. London, 1978.

2.   Pluralism and Islamic Traditions of Sectarian Divisions

al-Ghazali, Abu Hamid Muhammad. *Fada'il al-'anam min rasa'il hujjat al-Islam*, ed. Mo'ayyad Thabeti. Tehran 1333/1914.

al-Baghdadi. *al-Farq bayn al-firaq*, ed. M. Badr, trans. K. C. Seelye as *Moslem Schisms and Sects*. New York, 1920.

al-Kulayni, Abu Ja'far Muhammad. *al-Kafi*. Tehran, 1982.

al-Razi, Fakhr al-Din. *Tafsir al-Fakhr al-Razi*. Cairo, 1985.

al-Zamakhshari, Abu'l-Qasim Mahmud b. 'Umar. *al-Kashshaf*. Riyadh, 1998.

Bell, G. L. *Poems from the Divan of Hafiz*. London, 1928.

Gaiser, A. R. 'Satan's Seven Specious Arguments: al-Shahrastani's *Kitab al-milal wa'l-nihal* in an Isma'ili Context', *Journal of Islamic Studies*, 19:2 (2008), pp. 178–195.

Goldziher, I. 'Le dénombrement des sectes mahométanes', in I. Goldziher, *Gesammelte Schriften* (Volume 4). Hildesheim, 1968. Reprinted in *Revue de l'histoire des religions* 26 (1892), pp. 129–137.

Hafiz. *Divan*, ed. S. Naysari. Tehran, 1993.

Khayyam, Omar. *Rubaiyat*, E. Fitzgerald (translator). London, 1859. Reprinted in Arberry, A. S. *The Romance of the Rubaiyat*. London, 1959, pp. 149–174.

Lewinstein, K. 'Studies in Islamic Heresiography: The Khawarij in Two *Firaq* Traditions'. Princeton University, 1989 (PhD Dissertation).

Mahdavi-Damghani, A. *Hasil-i awqat*. Tehran, 2002.

Mashkur, M. J. *Haftad-o do millat*. Tehran, 1962.

Muslim, A. H. *Sahih*, ed. M. F. Abd al-Baqi. Cairo: n.d.

Nicholson, R. A. *Masnavi*. Text, Translation and Commentary. London, 1925–1960.

Schimmel, A. *The Mystery of Numbers*. New York, 1993.

3. Being One and Many Among the Others: Muslim Diversity in the Context of South Asian Religious Pluralism

Ahmad, A. *An Intellectual History of Islam in India*. Edinburgh, 1969.

Briggs, G. W. *Gorakhnath and the Kanphata Jogis*. Delhi, [1938] 1990.

Campbell, J. M., ed., *Hindu Tribes and Castes of Gujarat* (Volume 1). Guragaon, 1988–1990.

Esmail, A. *The Poetics of Religious Experience: The Islamic Context*. London and New York, 1998.

Freitag, S. B. 'Contesting in Public: Colonial Legacies and Contemporary Communalism', in D. Ludden, ed., *Making India Hindu: Religion, Community and the Politics of Democracy in India*. Delhi, 1996, pp. 211–234.

_____ 'The Roots of Muslim Separatism in South Asia: Personal Practice and Public Structures in Kanpur and Bombay', in E. Burke III and Ira M. Lapidus, eds., *Islam, Politics and Social Movements*. Berkeley, 1988, pp. 115–145.

Gottschalk, P. *Beyond Hindu and Muslim: Multiple Identity in Narratives from Village India*. Oxford, 2000.

Jaffrelot, C. *The Hindu Nationalist Movement in India*. Delhi, 1996.

Jones, K. W. *Arya Dharm: Hindu Consciousness in 19th-century Punjab*. Berkeley, 1976.

_____ 'Religious Identities and the Indian Census', in G. N. Barrier, ed., *The Census in British India*. Delhi, 1981, pp. 73–102.

Khan, D. S. *Crossing The Threshold: Understanding Religious Identities in South Asia*. London, 2004.

_____ *Conversion and Shifting Identities: Ramdev Pir and the Ismailis in Rajasthan*. Delhi, 1997.

_____ 'Karsan Das, *un heros vivant*', in V. Bouillier and C. Le Blanc, eds., *L'usage des heros. Traditions narratives et affirmations identitaires dans le monde indien*. Paris, 2006, pp. 95–119.

_____ 'The Mahdi of Panna: A Short History of the Prananamis', *Journal of Secular Studies*, Part I, 6:4 (2003), pp. 61–93; Part II, 7:1, pp. 46–66.

_____ and Z. Moir. 'Coexistence and Communalism: The Shrine of Pirana in Gujarat', *South Asia*, 22 (1999), pp. 133–154.

Mehta, V. and R. Saha, eds., *Mahamati Prannath pranit marfat sagar-kayamatnama (chhota aur bara)*. Delhi, 1990.

Mohamed, S. A. *Heroes of Surat*. Surat, 1968.

Mohammad, N. *The Deendar Anjuman*. Bangalore, n.d.

Moir, Z. 'Historical and Religious Debates Amongst Indian Ismailis 1840–1920', in M. Offredi, ed., *The Banyan Tree*. Delhi, 2001, pp. 131–153.

Nanji, A. *The Nizari Ismaili Tradition in the Indo-Pakistan Subcontinent*. Delmar, NY 1978.

Oberoi, H. *The Construction of Religious Boundaries: Culture, Identity and Diversity in the Sikh Tradition*. Delhi, 1994.

Pyarelal, N. *Mahatma Gandhi*. Ahmedabad, 1965.

Ram, S. M. *Swami Laldas krit Mahamati Prannath bitak ka nadhykalin itihas ka yogdan*. Delhi, 1996.

Sadik, M. A. T. *Ismailis through History*. Karachi, 1997.

Saiyed, A. R. 'Saints and *Dargah*s in the Indian Subcontinent: A Review', in C. W. Troll, ed., *Muslim Shrines in India: Their Character, History and Significance*. Delhi, 1989, pp. 240–256.

Shail, M. 'Spirit Possession: Reframing Discourses of the Self and Other', in J. Assayag and G. Tarabout, eds., *La possession en Asie du Sud: parole, corps, territoire, Collections Purusartha* 21, Paris, 1999, pp. 101–131.

Shodhan, A. 'Legal Formulation of the Question of Community: Defining the Khoja Collective', *Indian Social Science Review*, 1 (1999), pp. 137–151.

Sikand, Y. *The Origins and Development of the Tablighi Jama'at (1920–2000): A Cross-country Comparative Study*. Delhi, 2002.

Vasudha, D. and H. Von Stietencron, eds. *Representing Hinduism: The Construction of Religious Traditions and National Identity*. Delhi, 1995.

Wagle, N. K. 'Hindu-Muslim Interactions in Medieval Maharashtra', in G. D. Sontheimer and H. Kulke, eds., *Hinduism Reconsidered*. Delhi, 1991, pp. 51–66.

Witteveen, H. J. *Universal Sufism*. Shaftesbury, 1997.

4. Religious Pluralism in the Light of American Muslim Identities

Ammerman, N. T. 'North American Protestant Fundamentalism', in M. Marty and S. Appleby, eds., *Fundamentalisms Observed* (Volume 1). Chicago, 1991, pp. 1–15.

Bader, V. 'Taking Pluralism Seriously: Arguing for an Institutional Turn in Political Philosophy', *Philosophy & Social Criticism*, 29:4 (2003), pp. 375–406.

_____ 'Taking Religious Pluralism Seriously: Arguing for an Institutional Turn: Introduction', *Ethical Theory and Moral Practice*, 6:1 (March 2003), pp. 3–22.

Boehlert, E. 'The Muslim Population Riddle' (31 October 2001), available online at: http://dir.salon.com/story/news/feature/2001/10/31/american_muslims/ (accessed 28 August 2009).

Boender, W. 'Islamic Law and Muslim Minorities', *ISIM Newsletter*, 12 (Leiden, June 2003), p. 13.

Brodeur, P. 'Introduction to the Guidelines for an Inter-faith Celebration', *Journal of Ecumenical Studies*, 34:4 (1997), pp. 551–572.

_____ 'The Changing Nature of Islamic Studies and American Religious Studies (Part 2)', *The Muslim World*, 92:1 and 2 (Spring 2002), pp. 185–220.

Cornell, V. '*Convivencia* Then and Now: Lessons and Limits for Contemporary Interfaith Relations', in a keynote address delivered at the Elijah Interfaith Academy Meeting of the Board of World Religious Leaders, Seville, Spain, 14 December 2003.

Council on American-Islamic Relations. *Guilt by Association: The Status of Muslim Civil Rights in the United States 2003*. Washington, DC, 2003.

_____ *The Mosque in America: A National Portrait*. Washington, DC, 26 April 2001. See www.cair.com/Portals/0/pdf/The_Mosque_in_America_A_National_Portrait.pdf – 2007-08-22 (accessed 28 August 2009).

Craig, E. 'Pluralism', in E. Craig, ed., *Routledge Encyclopedia of Philosophy* (Volume 7), London, 1998. Also available online at: http://www.rep.routledge.com/article/N042 (accessed 28 August 2009).

Dudley, C. S. and D. A. Roozen. *Faith Communities Today: A Report on Religion in the United States Today*. Hartford, CT, 2001.

Eck, D. *A New Religious America*. San Francisco, 2001.

Freston, P. *Protestant Political Parties: A Global Survey*. Aldershot, 2004.

Lynch, M., ed., *The Nature of Truth: Classic and Contemporary Perspectives*. Cambridge, MA, 2001.

Jackson, S. 'Muslims, Islamic Law and Public Policy in the United States', in A. S. Mazrui, S. M. Jackson and A. McCloud, eds., *American Public Policy and American-Muslim Politics*. Chicago, 2000. Available online at http://www.ispi-usa.org/policy/policy4.html (accessed 28 August 2009).

Project Maps and Zogby International. *Muslims in the American Public Square: Shifting Political Winds and Fallout from 9/11, Afghanistan and Iraq* (October 2004).

Quinn, P. 'Religious Pluralism', in E. Craig, ed., *Routledge Encyclopedia of Philosophy* (Volume 8). London, 1998. Also available online at http://www.rep.routledge.com/article/K086 (accessed 28 August 2009).

Riis, O. 'Modes of Religious Pluralism under Conditions of Globalisation', *International Journal on Multicultural Societies*, 1:1 (1999), pp. 20–34.

Stich, S. 'Cognitive Pluralism', in E. Craig, ed., *Routledge Encyclopedia of Philosophy* (Volume 2). London, 1998. Also available online at http://www.rep.routledge.com/article/P008 (accessed 28 August 2009).

Taylor, M. *The Moment of Complexity: Emerging Network Culture*. Chicago, 2001.

Weinstock, D. M. 'Pluralism', in E. Craig, ed., *Routledge Encyclopedia of Philosophy* (Volume 6). London, 1998. Also available online at http://www.rep.routledge.com/article/L058 (accessed 28 August 2009).

5.   Islamic Art and Doctrinal Pluralism: Seeking Out the Visual Boundaries

Akurgal, E., C. Mango and R. Ettinghausen. *Les Trésors de Turquie. L'Anatolie des premiers empires. Byzance. Les siècles de l'Islam*. Geneva, 1966.

Allan, J. *Metalwork of the Islamic World: The Aron Collection*. London, 1986.

_____ *Islamic Metalwork: The Nuhad Es-Said Collection*. London, 1982.

_____ 'My Father is a Sun, and I am a Star: Fatimid Symbols in Ayyubid and Mamluk Metalwork', *Journal of the David Collection* 1 (2003), pp. 25–48.

_____ 'Some Mosques of the Jebel Nefusa', *Strato da Libya Antiqa*, 9–10 (Rome, 1972–1973), pp. 147–169.

_____ and B. Gilmour. *Persian Steel: The Tanavoli Collection.* Oxford, 2000.

Arberry, A. J., B. W. Robinson, E. Blochet and J. V. S. Wilkinson, *The Chester Beatty Library: A Catalogue of the Persian Manuscripts and Miniatures* (Volume 3). Dublin, 1962.

_____, M. Minovi, and E. Blochet, *The Chester Beatty Library: A Catalogue of the Persian Manuscripts and Miniatures* (Volume 1). Dublin, 1959.

Arnold, T. *Painting in Islam*. Oxford, 1928.

Atil, E. *Renaissance of Islam: Art of the Mamluks*. Washington, 1981.

Bagherzadeh, F. 'Iconographie Iranienne', in L. de Meyer and E. Haerinck, eds., *Archaeologica Iranica et Orientalis, Miscellanea in honorem Louis Vanden Berghe*. Ghent, 1989, Vol. 2, pp. 1007–1028.

Baker, P. L. *Islam and the Religious Arts*. London, 2003.

Bierman, I. A. *Writing Signs: The Fatimid Public Text*. Berkeley and Los Angeles, 1998.

Blair, S. 'The Coins of the Later Ilkhanids: A Typological Analysis', *Journal of the Economic and Social History of the Orient*, 26:3 (1983), pp. 295–317.

Bloom, J. 'The Mosque of al-Hakim in Cairo', *Muqarnas*, 1 (1983), pp. 15–36.

Creswell, K. A. C. *The Muslim Architecture of Egypt*. Oxford, 1952–1959.

Daftary, F. *A Short History of the Ismailis*. Edinburgh, 1998.

Emami, K., ed., *Golestan Palace Library: A Portfolio of Miniature Paintings and Calligraphy*. Tehran, 2000.

Englade, E. *Musée du Louvre: Catalogue des boiseries de la section islamique*. Paris, 1988.

Eustache, D. *Corpus des Dirhams Idrisites et contemporains*. Rabat, 1970–1971.

Fehérvári, G. *Islamic Metalwork of the Eighth to the Fifteenth Century in the Keir Collection.* London, 1976.

Flood, F. B. 'Iconography of Light in the Monuments of Mamluk Cairo', *Cosmos: The Yearbook of the Traditional Cosmology Society*, 8 (1992), pp. 169–193.

____ 'Light in Stone. The Commemoration of the Prophet in Umayyad Architecture', in J. Raby and J. Johns, eds., *Bayt al Maqdis: 'Abd al-Malik's Jerusalem/Jerusalem and Early Islam.* Oxford, 1992–1999, pp. 311–360.

Folsach, K., T. Lundbaek and P. Mortensen. *Sultan, Shah and Great Mughal: The History and Culture of the Islamic World.* Copenhagen, 1996.

Fontana, M. V. 'Iconografia dell'Ahl al-Bayt', in *Immagini di arte persiana dal XII al XX secolo, Supplemento 78 de Annali del Istituto Universitario Orientale*, 5:1 (1994), pp. 47–55, 51–61.

Gabriel, F. and U. Scerrato. *Gli Arabi in Italia.* Milan, 1979.

Hayward Gallery (Arts Council), *The Arts of Islam.* London, 1976.

Hillenbrand, R. 'Safavid Architecture', in P. Jackson, ed., *The Cambridge History of Iran (Volume 6: The Timurid and Safavid Periods).* Cambridge, 1986, pp. 759–842.

Kazan, W. *The Coinage of Islam (Collection of William Kazan).* Beirut, 1983.

Khan, A. N. *Al-Mansurah: A Forgotten Arab Metropolis in Pakistan.* Karachi, 1990.

MacEion, D. M. '*Bab*', in E. Yarshater, ed., *Encyclopaedia Iranica.* London, 1989, Vol. 3, pp. 277–278.

Mackie, L. W. 'Toward an Understanding of Mamluk Silks: National and International Considerations', *Muqarnas*, 2 (1984), pp. 127–146.

Meinecke, M. *Fayencedekorationen Seldschukischer Sakralbauten in Kleinasien*, Tubingen, 1976.

Melikian-Chirvani, A. S. *Islamic Metalwork from the Iranian World, 8th–18th Century*, London, 1982.

Metropolitan Museum of Art, *The Language of the Birds: Special Issue of The Bulletin of the Metropolitan Museum of Art.* New York, May 1976.

Porter, V. 'Die Kunst der Rasuliden', in W. Daum, ed., *Jemen: 3000 Jahre Kunst und Kultur des glucklichen Arabien*. Innsbruk and Frankfurt/Main, 1987, pp. 225–236.

Rabino di Borgomale, H. L. *Coins, Medals and Seals of the Shahs of Iran (1500–1941)*. Hertford, 1945.

Rogers, J. M. *Empire of the Sultans: Ottoman Art from the Collection of Nasser D. Khalili*. London, 1995.

Safwat, N. *Golden Pages: Qur'ans and Other Manuscripts from the Collection of Ghassan I. Shaker*. Oxford, 2000.

Seipel, W., ed., *Schätze der Kalifen Islamische Kunst zur Fatimidzeit*, Kunsthistorisches Museum (Wien). Milan and Vienna, 1998.

Simpson, M. S. *Persian Poetry, Painting and Patronage: Illustrations in a Sixteenth-century Masterpiece*. New Haven and London, 1998.

Sims, E. with B. I. Marhsak and E. Grube. *Peerless Images: Persian Painting and its Sources*. New Haven and London, 2002.

Smith, J. M. *The History of the Sarbadarid Dynasty 1336–1381 A.D. and its Sources*. The Hague & Paris, 1970.

Stern, S. M. 'The Coins of Amul', *The Numismatic Chronicle*, 7th Series, 7 (1967), pp. 205–278.

Tanavoli, P. *Kings, Heroes and Lovers: Pictorial Rugs from the Tribes and Villages of Iran*. London, 1994.

Titley, N. *Miniatures from Persian Manuscripts: A Catalogue and Subject Index of Paintings from Persia, India and Turkey in the 1977 British Library and the British Museum*. London, 1977.

Vernoit, S. *Occidentalism: Islamic Art in the 19th Century: The Nassar D. Khalili Collection of Islamic Art*, Volume 23. New York, 1997.

Watson, O. 'The Masjid-i 'Ali, Quhrud: An Architectural and Epigraphic Survey', *Iran*, 12 (1975), pp. 59–74.

_____ *Persian Lustre Ware*. London, 1985.

Weill, J. D. *Catalogue Général du Musée Arabe du Caire. Les bois à épigraphes jusqu'à l'époque mamlouke*. Cairo, 1931.

Wiet, G. *Catalogue général du Musée Arabe du Caire, Objets en cuivre*. Cairo, 1984.

Williams, C. 'The Cult of 'Alid Saints in the Fatimid Monuments of Cairo. Part II: The Mausolea', *Muqarnas*, 3 (1985), pp. 39–60.

_____ 'The Cult of ʿAlid Saints in the Fatimid Monuments of Cairo. Part I: The Mosque of Aqmar', *Muqarnas*, 1 (1983), pp. 37–52.

Zebrowski, M. *Gold, Silver & Bronze from Mughal India*. London, 1997.

6. The Contestation and Resolution of Inter- and Intra-School Conflicts through Biography

Azami, M. M. *Studies in Early Hadith Literature*. Indianapolis, 1978.

al-Bayhaqi, Abu Bakr. *al-Manaqib al-Shafiʿi*, ed. A. Saqr. Cairo, 1971.

Berkey, J. P. *The Transmission of Knowledge in Medieval Cairo: A Social History of Islamic Education*. Princeton, 1992.

Bulliet, R. W. *Islam: The View from the Edge*. New York, 1994.

_____ *Conversion to Islam in the Medieval Period: An Essay in Quantitative History*. Cambridge, 1979.

_____ 'A Quantitative Approach to Medieval Muslim Biographical Dictionaries', *The Journal of Economic and Social History*, 13 (1970), pp. 195–211.

Burton, J. *An Introduction to the Hadith*. Edinburgh, 1994.

Cahen, C. 'Editing Arabic Chronicles: A Few Suggestions', *Islamic Studies*, 1:3 (1962), pp. 1–25.

_____ 'History and Historians', in M. J. L. Young et al. eds., *Cambridge History of Arabic Literature*. Cambridge, 1990, Vol. 3, pp. 188–233.

Calder, N. *Studies in Early Muslim Jurisprudence*. Oxford, 1993.

Chamberlain, M. *Knowledge and Social Practice in Medieval Damascus, 1190–1350*. Cambridge, 1994.

Cooperson, M. *Classical Arabic Biography: The Heirs of the Prophet in the Age of al-Maʾmun*. Cambridge, 2000.

Coulson, N. 'Doctrine and Practice in Islamic Law: One Aspect of the Problem', *Bulletin of the School of Oriental and African Studies*, 18:2 (1956), pp. 211–226.

al-Dhahabi, S. *Tarikh al-Islam wa wafayat al-mashahir waʾl-aʿlam*, ed. ʿUmar ʿAbd al-Salam Tadmuri. Beirut, 1999.

_____ *Siyar aʿlam al-nubala*. Beirut, 1984.

Fähndrich, H. 'The Wafayat al-A'yan of Ibn Khallikan: A New Approach', *Journal of the American Oriental Society*, 93 (1973), pp. 432–445.

Gibb, H. A. R. 'Islamic Biographical Literature', in B. Lewis and P. M. Holt, eds., *Historians of the Middle East*. London, 1962, pp. 54–58.

Hafsi, I. 'Recherches sur le genre Tabaqat dans la littérature arabe', *Arabica*, 23 (September 1976), pp. 227–265; 24 (February 1977), pp. 1–41; 24 (June 1977), pp. 150–186.

Ibn Abi Hatim. *Kitab al-jarh wa'l-ta'dil*. Hyderabad, 1952–1953. (Reprint, Beirut, n.d.)

Ibn 'Asakir. *Tarikh madinat Dimashq*, ed. Muhibb al-Din Abi Sa'id 'Umar b. Gharamah al-'Amrawi. Beirut, 1995.

Ibn Hajar al-'Asqalani. *Lisan al-mizan*, ed. 'Adil Ahmad 'Abd al-Mawjud and 'Ali Muhammad Mu'awwad. Beirut, 1996.

Ibn al-'Imad al-Hanbali. *Shadharat al-dhahab fi akhbar min dhahab*. Beirut, 1998.

Ibn Kathir, Isma'il. *al-Bidayah wa'l-nihayah*, ed. 'Ali Muhammad Mu'awwad et al. Beirut, 1994.

Ibn Khallikan, Abu'l-'Abbas Ahmad b. Muhammad. *Wafayat al-a'yan wa anba' al-zaman*, ed. Ihsan 'Abbas. Beirut, 1977.

Ibn Qadi Shuhbah. *Tabaqat al-fuqaha' al-Shafi'iyah*, ed. al-Hafiz 'Abd al-'Ali Khan. Beirut, 1987.

Ibn Tulun. *Mut'at al-adhhan min al-tamattu' bi'l-iqran bayna tarajim al-shuyukh wa'l-aqran*. Beirut, 1999.

Ibn Yunus. *Tarikh al-Misriyin*, 'Abd al-Fattah Fathi 'Abd al-Fattah (editor). Beirut, 2000.

al-Isnawi, Abd al-Rahim. *Tabaqat al-shafi'iyah*. Kamal Yusuf al-Hut (editor). Beirut, 1987.

Jaques, R. K. *Authority, Conflict, and the Transmission of Diversity in Medieval Islamic Law*. Lieden, 2006.

Juynboll, G. H. A. *The Authenticity of the Tradition Literature: Discussions in Modern Egypt*. Leiden, 1969.

Khalidi, T. *Arabic Historical Thought in the Classical Period*. Cambridge, 1994.

al-Khalili, Khalil b. 'Abdallah. *Kitab al-irshad fi ma'rifat 'ulama' al-hadith*. Muhammad Sa'id b. 'Umar (editor). Riyad, 1989.

Lane, E. "*asaba*', *Arabic-English Lexicon*. Cambridge, 1984.

Little, D. P. 'Historiography of the Ayyubid and Mamluk Epochs', in C. F. Petry, ed., *The Cambridge History of Egypt*. Cambridge, 1998, Vol. 1, pp. 412–444, 640–1051.

_____ *An Introduction to Mamluk Historiography: An Analysis of Arabic Annalistic and Biographical Sources for the Reign of an-Malik al-Nasir Muhammad ibn Qala'un*. Wiesbaden, 1970.

_____ *History and Historiography of the Mamluks*. London, 1986.

Loth, O. 'Die Ursprung und Bedeutung der Tabaqat', *Zeitschrift der Deutschen Morgenländischen Gesellschaft*, 23 (1869), pp. 593–614.

Makdisi, G. '*Tabaqat*-Biography: Law and Orthodoxy in Classical Islam', *Islamic Studies*, 32 (1993), pp. 371–396.

Martin, R., M. Woodward and D. Atmaja. *Defenders of Reason in Islam: Mu'tazilism from Medieval School to Modern Symbol*. Oxford, 1997.

al-Marwardi, Abu'l-Hasan. *al-Hawi al-kabir fi fiqh madhhab al-shafi'i wa huwa sharh mukhtasar al-muzani*, ed. 'Ali Muhammad al-Mu'awwad. Beirut, 1994.

Melchert, C. *The Formation of the Sunni Schools of Law*. New York, 1997.

al-Muzani, Abu Ibrahim. *Mukhtasar*, ed. Muhammad 'Abd al-Qadir Shahin. Beirut, 1998.

al-Nawawi, Muhyi al-Din. *Rawdat al-talibin*, ed. 'Adil Ahmad 'Abd al-Mawjud and 'Ali Muhammad Mu'awwad. Beirut, 1991.

_____ *Tahdhib al-asma' wa'l-lughat*. Cairo, 1927.

al-Nu'aymi, 'Abd al-Qadir b. Muhammad. *al-Daris fi tarikh al-madaris*. n.p., 1988.

al-Nuwayri, Muhammad b. Qasim. *Kitab al-ilman*, ed. 'Aziz Suryl Atiya. Hyderabad, 1979.

Petry, C. F. *The Civilian Elite of Cairo in the Later Middle Ages*. Princeton, 1981.

Popper, W., tr. *History of Egypt: An Extract from Abu l-Mahasin Ibn Taghri Birdi's Chronicle*. New Haven, 1967.

al-Qadi, W. 'Biographical Dictionaries: Inner Structure and Cultural Significance', in G. N. Atiyeh, ed., *The Book in the Islamic World: The Written Word and Communication in the Middle East.* Albany, 1995, pp. 93–122.

al-Qurashi, 'Abd al-Qadir b. Abi al-Wafa'. *al-Jawahir al-mudi'ah fi tabaqat al-Hanafiya.* Cairo, 1978.

al-Rafi'i, Abu al-Qasim. *'Aziz fi sharh al-wajiz*, ed., 'Ali Muhammad Mu'awwad and 'Adil Ahmad 'Abd al-Mawjud. Beirut, 1997.

Robinson, C. *Islamic Historiography.* Cambridge, 2003.

Roded, R. *Women in Islamic Biographical Collections.* Boulder, 1994.

Rosenthal, F. 'On Medieval Authorial Biographies: Al-Ya'qubi and Ibn Hajar', in Mustansir Mir, ed., *Literary Heritage of Classical Islam: Arabic and Islamic Studies in Honor of James A. Bellamy.* Princeton, 1993, pp. 255–274.

____ *A History of Muslim Historiography.* Leiden, [1952] 1968.

al-Safadi, Salah al-Din Khalil b. Aybak. *Kitab al-wafi al-wafayat*, ed. Muhammad Yusuf Najm et al. Wiesbaden, 1971.

al-Sakhawi, Shams al-Din Muhammad Abd al-Rahman. *al-Daw' al-lami' li-ahl al-qarn al-tasi'.* Beirut, 1966.

al-Saymari, Abu 'Abdallah al-Husayn b. 'Ali. *Akhbar Abi Hanifah wa ashabihi.* Beirut, 1976.

Schimmel, A. *Die Träume des Kalifen: Träume und ihre Deutung in der Islamischen Kultur.* München, 1998.

____ *Mystical Dimensions of Islam.* Chapel Hill, 1978.

al-Shirazi, Abu Ishaq. *Tabaqat al-fuqaha'.* Beirut, 1980.

Stewart, D. 'Capital, Accumulation, and the Islamic Academic Biography', *Edebiyat*, 7 (1997), pp. 345–362.

al-Tahawi, Abu Ja'far. *Ahkam al-qur'an*, Sa'id al-Din Awnal (editor). Istanbul, 1995.

Tsafrir, N. *The History of an Islamic School of Law: The Early Spread of Hanafism.* Cambridge, 2004.

Tyan, E. "Adl', *Encyclopaedia of Islam* (second edition), Vol. 1, pp. 209–210.

Wüstenfeld, F. *Academien der Araber und ihre Lehrer.* Göttingen, 1837.

al-Yafi'i, 'Abdallah b. As'ad b. 'Ali. *Mir'at al-jinan.* Beirut, 1997.

Young, M. J. L. 'Arabic Biographical Writing', in M. J. L. Young, J. D. Latham and R. B. Serjeant, eds., *The Cambridge History of Arabic Literature: Religion, Learning and Science in the 'Abbasid Period*. Cambridge, 1990, pp. 168–187.

7. Traditions of Reform, Reformers of Tradition: Case Studies from Senegal and Zanzibar/Tanzania

Ahmed, C. 'Networks of the Shadhiliyya-Yashrutiyya Sufi Order in East Africa', in R. Loimeier and R. Seesemann, eds., *The Global Worlds of the Swahili: Interfaces of Islam, Identity and Space in 19th and 20th-Century East Africa*. Hamburg, 2006, pp. 325–350.

Asad, T. *The Idea of an Anthropology of Islam*. Georgetown, 1986.

Audrain, X. 'Du "Ndiggël" avorté au Parti de la Vérité. Évolution du rapport religion/politique à travers le parcours de Cheikh Modou Kara (1999–2004)', *Politique Africaine* 96 (2004), pp. 99–118.

Behrman, L. C. *Muslim Brotherhoods and Politics in Senegal*. Cambridge (Mass), 1970.

Brenner, L. *Controlling Knowledge: Religion, Power and Schooling in a West African Muslim Society*. Bloomington, 2001.

Cruise O'Brien, D. B. *The Mourides of Senegal: The Political and Economic Organization of an Islamic Brotherhood*. Oxford, 1971.

____ 'A Lost Generation? Youth Identity and State Decay in West Africa', in R. Werbner and T. Ranger, eds., *Postcolonial Identities in Africa*. London, 1996, pp. 55–74.

____ 'Le contrat social sénégalais à l'épreuve', *Politique Africaine*, 45 (1992), pp. 9–20.

Coulon, C. *Le Marabout et le Prince*. Paris, 1981.

DAVO-Rundbrief. *Translocality in the Modern History of the Middle East, Asia and Africa*. Presentation of the current research programme at the Zentrum Moderner Orient, Berlin. Mainz, 2003.

Dia, M. *Mémoires d'un militant du tiers-monde*. Paris, 1985.

al-Farsi, A. S. *Baadhi ya wanavyuoni wa kishafi wa mashariki ya Afrika*. Mombasa, [1944] 1972.

Gomez-Perez, M. 'Généalogies de l'islam réformiste au Sénégal: figures, savoirs et réseaux', in L. Fourchard, A. Mary and R. Otayek, eds., *Entreprises religieuses transnationales en Afrique de l'Ouest*. Paris, 2005, pp. 193–222.

Gueye, C. *Touba. La capitale des mourides*. Paris, 2002.

Hock, K. *Der Islam-Komplex. Zur christlichen Wahrnehmung des Islams und der christlich-muslimischen Beziehungen in Nordnigeria während der Militärherrschaft Babangidas.* Hamburg, 1996.

Johnson, G. *Naissance du Sénégal contemporain: Aux origines de la vie politique moderne (1900–1920).* Paris, 1991.

Kane, O. and L. Villalon. 'Les Moustarshidin du Senegal', *Islam et Sociétés au Sud du Sahara*, 9 (1995), pp. 119–202.

Kraus, W. 'Imaginierte und reale Netzwerke in Südostasien', in R. Loimeier, ed., *Die islamische Welt als Netzwerk. Möglichkeiten und Grenzen des Nertzwerkansatzes im islamischen Kontext*. Würzburg, 2000, pp. 289–310.

Launay, R. *Beyond the Stream: Islam and Society in a West African town.* Berkeley, 1992.

_____ and B. F. Soares. 'The Formation of an "Islamic Sphere" in French Colonial West Africa', *Economy and Society*, 28:4 (1999), pp. 497–519.

Loimeier, R. 'Fighting Popular Culture: The "*Ulama*" and the State in Zanzibar', in R. Loimeier and R. Seesemann, eds., *The Global Worlds of the Swahili: Interfaces of Islam, Identity and Space in 19th and 20th-Century East Africa*. Hamburg, 2006, pp. 113–132.

_____ 'Translocal Networks of Saints and the Negotiation of Religious Disputes in Local Contexts', *Archives de Sciences Sociales des Religions* (ASSR, Paris), 133 (March 2006).

_____ 'Is There Something Like "Protestant Islam"?', *Die Welt des Islams*, 45:2 (2005), pp. 216–254.

_____ 'Patterns and Peculiarities of Islamic Reform in Africa', *Journal of Religion in Africa*, 33:3 (2003), pp. 237–263.

_____ 'Je veux étudier sans mendier: The Campaign against the Qur'anic Schools in Senegal', in H. Weiss, ed., *Social

Welfare in Muslim Societies in Africa. Uppsala, 2002, pp. 118–137.

____ *Säkularer Staat und Islamische Gesellschaft. Die Beziehungen zwischen Staat, Sufi-Bruderschaften und islamischer Reformbewegung in Senegal im 20. Jahrhundert.* Hamburg, 2001.

____ *Islamic Reform and Political Change in Northern Nigeria.* Evanston, 1997.

____ 'Religiös-Ökonomische Netzwerke in Senegal: Das Beispiel der muridischen Expansion in Dakar', *Afrika Spectrum*, 1 (1994), pp. 99–112.

Ludwig, F. 'After Ujamaa: Is Religious Rivalism a Threat to Tanzania's Stability', in D. Westerlund, ed., *Questioning the Secular State: The Worldwide Resurgence of Religion in Politics.* London, 1996, pp. 216–236.

Martin, B. G. *Muslim Brotherhoods in 19th Century Africa.* Cambridge, 1976.

Masud, M. K., ed., *Travellers in Faith: Studies of the Tablighi Jama'at as a Transnational Islamic Movement for Faith Renewal.* Leiden, 2000.

Merad, A. *Le réformisme musulman en Algérie de 1925 à 1940.* Paris, 1967.

Miran, M. 'Le wahhabisme à Abidjan: dynamisme urbain d'un islam réformiste en Côte d'Ivoire contemporaine (1960–1996)', *Islam et Sociétés au Sud du Sahara* 12 (1998), pp. 5–74.

Nimtz, A. *Islam and Politics in East Africa: The Sufi Order in Tanzania.* Minneapolis, 1980.

Njozi, H. *Mwembechai Killings and the Political Future of Tanzania.* Ottawa, 2000.

O'Fahey, S. R. *Enigmatic Saint: Ahmad ibn Idris and the Idrisi Tradition.* Evanston, 1990.

Redfield, R. *Peasant Society and Culture.* Chicago, 1956.

Reese, S. 'Urban Woes and Pious Remedies: Sufism in Nineteenth-Century Benaadir (Somalia)', *Africa Today*, 46:3–4 (1999), pp. 169–194.

Robinson, D. *Paths of Accommodation. Muslim Societies and French Colonial Authorities in Senegal and Mauritania 1880–1920.* Oxford, 2000.

Rosander, E. E. 'Introduction: The Islamization of "Tradition" and "Modernity"', in E. E. Rosander and D. Westerlund, eds., *African Islam and Islam in Africa: Encounters between Sufis and Islamists*. London, 1997, pp. 1–27.

Sadouni, S. 'Le minoritaire sud-africain Ahmed Deedat, une figure originale de la da'wa', *Islam et Sociétés au Sud du Sahara*, 12 (1998), pp. 149–172.

Said, M. *The Life and Times of Abdulwahid Sykes (1924–1968): The Untold Story of the Muslim Struggle against British Colonialism in Tanganyika*. London, 1998.

Salzbrunn, M. 'Hybridization of Religious and Political Practices amongst West African Migrants in Europe', in D. Bryceson and U. Vuorela, eds., *The Transnational Family: New European Frontiers and Global Networks*. Oxford, 2002, pp. 217–229.

Samson, F. *Les marabouts de l'islam politique. Le Dahiratoul Moustarchidina Wal Moustarchidaty un mouvement néo-confrérique sénégalais*. Paris, 2005.

_____ 'Une nouvelle conception des rapports entre religion et politique au Sénégal', in C. Coulon, ed., *L'Afrique Politique: Islams d'Afrique, entre le local et le global*. Paris, 2002, pp. 161–171.

Sheikh-Abdi, A. *Divine Madness. Mohammed Abdulle Hassan (1856–1920)*. London, 1993.

Soares, B. *Islam and the Prayer Economy: History and Authority in a Malian Town*. Edinburgh, 2005.

Tahir, I. *Scholars, Sufis, Saints and Capitalists in Kano, 1904–1974*. Cambridge, 1975 (PhD Dissertation).

Villalon, L. A. 'The Moustarchidine of Senegal: The Family Politics of a Contemporary Tijan Movement', in J-L. Triaud and D. Robinson, eds., *La Tijaniyya. Une confrérie musulmane à la conquête de l'Afrique,*. Paris, 2000, pp. 469–498.

_____ 'Senegal', *African Studies Review*, 47:2 (2004), pp. 61–72.

_____ 'Generational Changes, Political Stagnation, and the Evolving Dynamics of Religion and Politics in Senegal', *Africa Today*, 46:3–4 (1999), pp. 129–148.

Voll, J. O. 'Afrikanischer *localism* und das islamische Weltsystem', in R. Loimeier, D. Neubert and C. Weissköppel, eds.,

Globalisierung im lokalen Kontext. Perspektiven und Konzepte von Handeln in Afrika. Hamburg, 2005, pp. 277–310.

Weber, M. *Gesammelte Aufsätze zur Religionssoziologie I.* Tübingen, [1920] 1988.

Westerlund, D. 'Ahmed Deedat's Theology of Religion: Apologetics through Polemics', *Journal of Religion in Africa*, 33:3 (2003), pp. 263–278.

Zaman, M. Q. *The Ulama in Contemporary Islam: Custodians of Change.* Princeton, 2002.

8. Justifying Islamic Pluralism: Reflections from Indonesia and France

Abou El Fadl, K. 'Islamic Law and Muslim Minorities: The Juristic Discourse on Muslim Minorities from the Second/Eighth to the Eleventh/Seventeenth Centuries', *Islamic Law and Society*, 1:2 (1994), pp. 143–187.

Babès, L. and T. Oubrou. *Loi d'Allah, loi des hommes: Liberté, égalité et femmes en Islam.* Paris, 2002.

Bowen, J. R. *Can Islam be French? Pluralism and Pragmatism in a Secularist State.* Princeton, 2009.

_____ *Islam, Law, and Equality in Indonesia: An Anthropology of Public Reasoning.* Cambridge, 2003.

_____ *Shari'ah, State, and Social Norms in France and Indonesia.* Leiden, 2001.

_____ 'Pluralism and Normativity in French Islamic Reasoning', in R. Hefner, ed., *Remaking Muslim politics: pluralism, contestation, democratization.* Princeton, 2005, pp. 326–346.

_____ 'Two Approaches to Rights and Religion in Contemporary France', in R. A. Wilson and J. P. Mitchell, eds., *Human Rights in Global Perspective.* London, 2003, pp. 33–53.

_____ 'Does French Islam Have Borders? Dilemmas of Domestication in a Global Religious Field', *American Anthropologist*, 106:1 (2004), pp. 43–55.

Caeiro, A. *La normativité islamique à l'épreuve de l'Occident: le cas du Conseil européen de la fatwa et de la recherche.* Paris, 2003.

Cesari, J. *Être Musulman en France: Associations, militants et mosques*. Paris, 1994.

Conseil européen de la fatwa et de la recherche. *Recueil de fatwas*. Lyon, 2002.

Coulson, N. *A History of Islamic Law*. Edinburgh, 1964.

Daud Ali, M. 'Asas-asas hukum kewarisan dalam Kompilasi Hukum Islam', *Mimbar Hukum*, 9 (1993), pp. 1–17.

Favell, A. *Philosophies of Integration: Immigration and the Idea of Citizenship in France and Britain*. Houndmills, 2002.

Feener, R. M. *Developments of Muslim Jurisprudence in twentieth century Indonesia*. Boston University, 1999 (PhD Dissertation).

Hallaq, W. *A History of Islamic Legal Theories*. Cambridge, 1997.

Hazairin. *Hukum Baru di Indonesia*. Jakarta, 1950.

Hefner, R. W. *Civil Islam: Muslims and Democratization in Indonesia*. Princeton, 2000.

Hourani, A. *Arabic Thought in the Liberal Age, 1798–1939*. Cambridge, 1983.

Johansen, B. *Contingency in a Sacred Law: Legal and Ethical Norms in the Muslim Fiqh*. Leiden, 1999.

Kepel, G. *Les banlieues de l'Islam: Naissance d'une religion en France*. Paris, 1991.

Lapidus, I. *A History of Islamic Societies*. Cambridge, 2002.

Lewis, P. *Islamic Britain: Religion, Politics and Identity among British Muslims*. London, 2002.

Masud, M. K. *Islamic Legal Philosophy: A Study of Abu Ishaq al-Shatibi's Life and Thought*. Islamabad, 1977.

Nielsen, J. S. *Towards a European Islam*. London, 1999.

Oubrou, T. 'Le "minimum islamique" pour l'abbatage ritual en France', *La Médina*, 5 (2000), pp. 42–43.

Powers, D. S. *Law, Society and Culture in the Maghrib, 1300–1500*. Cambridge, 2002.

Ramadan, T. *Dar ash-shahada: L'Occident, espace du témoignage*. Lyon, 2002.

Rashid, A. *Jihad: The Rise of Militant Islam in Central Asia*. New York, 2003.

Ricklefs, M. C. *A History of Modern Indonesia since c. 1200*. Stanford, 2002.

Schacht, J. 'Riba', in *The Shorter Encyclopedia of Islam*. Ithaca, 1953.

Ternisien, X. *La France des mosquées*. Paris, 2002.

Werbner, P. S. *Pilgrims of Love: The Anthropology of a Global Sufi Cult*. Indianapolis, 2003.

Index

9/11 incidence 3, 19, 61, 69,
    72–73

Abbasid policies 107
Abdul Sattar's personal story
    52–53
Abubakar Sy 144
'adat law' *(hukum adat)* 166–167
Adda'wa Mosque 176
Aga Khan III, Sultan Muhammad
    Shah 54
Ahl al-Kitab 6
Ajlaf 53
Ali, Muhammad Daud 168–170
Ali Mansab, Sayyid Ahmad b.
    150
American Muslims and pluralism
    66–67
  post-9/11 world 74–80
Andalusian *convivencia* 72–73
Arnold, Matthew 31
Asad, Talal 13
Ayyubids 23
al-Aziz Sy, Abd 148

Baba, Sarpvale 52–53
Bamba, Ahmad 144
Bamba, Amadou 144

Baraza Kuu la Jumuiya na Taasisi
    za Kiislamu 153
Baraza Kuu la Waislamu Tanzania
    (BAKWATA) 151–154, 157
Bell, Gertrude 37
bid'a (bidat) 18, 27, 47, 140, 142,
    157–159
biography
  Abu Ishaq's retelling of events
    123
  al-Muzani 115–120
    al-Khalili's biography of
        120–121
    biographical tradition
        114–115
    Ibn Khallikan's biography of
        126–130
    Ibn Yunus's account of
        116–117
    *Jawahir al-mudi'ah fi tabaqat
        al-Hanafiyah* (al-Qurashi)
        133
    Tarikh al-Misriyin text 116
  al-Qurashi's text 133
  al-Shafi'i
    responses to early Hanafi
        presentations 120–126
    statements of 122–123

biography (*contd*)
  al-Tahawi 115–120
    commentary on al-Muzani's
      Mukhtasar 119–120, 126
    Ibn 'Asakir's biography of
      124–125
    Ibn Khallikan's biography of
      130–133
    Ibn Yunus's account of dream
      of 117–118
    texts and transmission of
      annotations in 117
      brief biographical entries
        109–110
      formation of 108–115
      hypertextual relationships in
        clusters 110–112
      inter-school conflicts
        126–133
      Mu'jam text 108–109
      Mukhtasar text 114
      'parallel' information in
        109–110
      role in creating identity 108
      tabaqat texts 108–109
      transmission of materials
        112–114
al-Bouti, Mohamed Tawfik 176
Bush, George W. 78

Christians 5, 6, 9, 11, 15, 32, 33,
    43, 62, 66, 68, 69, 72
civil war between Muslims
    (656–661) 14–15
Clinton, Bill 78
coinage and circular inscriptions
    92–93, 95–97, 103
colonial period and religious
    categories 43–44
Compilation of Islamic Law 168

cultural pluralism, in Indonesia
    165–170

Dahira des Étudiants Mourides de
    Dakar (DEM) 148
*Da'irat al-Mustarshidin
    wa-l-Mustarshidat* (DMM)
    146–8
dar al-da'wa 173
dar al-harb 28, 172
dar al-'ilm 84
dar al-Islam 28, 172
dar al-shahada 173
*dargah*s 56
Das, Kaka Karsan 54–55
Dawlat, Takiya 85
Derrida, Jacques 9
descriptive cognitive pluralism
    62
dharm paravartan (conversion)
    campaign 54
dhikr 140, 158–159
discourses, themes of differences
    in
    counter-discourses of debating
      Muslims 27–30
    paradigmatic *umma* 14–20
    social construction of the
      internal other 20–27
diversity
    amongst Muslims 8
    Dominique-Sila Khan (quote)
      18
    hadith 15
    human 12
    making sense of 30
    Muslim voices, perspectives 11
    of Muslims 3
    social and cultural 12
Divine as Love 40

Dutch East Indies and Islamic
    laws 166

El Ghisassi, Hakim 181
El Halfaoui, Abdelfattah 175–176
evaluative cognitive pluralism
    63–64

Fatimids
    architectural inscriptions and
        motifs 94–95
    candlestick art 101
    cusped roundel patterns 102
    decorative motifs 97–98
    geometry and numbers 98–
        100
    inscriptions 95–97, 102–103
    use of strapwork interlace 101
    visual symbols 101
Fatimid 23, 84, 86
Feast of Sacrifice (*'Id al-Adha*)
    179–181
Fédération des Associations
        Islamiques du Sénégal
        (FAIS) 141
fiqh 169–70, 173, 176–178
Foucault, Michel 9

Geertz, Clifford 30
al-Ghazali 34
glorification of God 39–40
Goldziher, Ignaz 34–35
gri-gris 140
Gulf War (1991) 77
Gupti 53, 54, 55

hadith 15, 32, 175
hadith al-tafriqa 15, 17
Hafiz 37
al-Hajj Malik Sy 144

Hanafi *madhhab* 107
Harakat al-Falah (HF) 142
Harun-e Velayat 87
Hatim, Ibn Abi 115–116
Hazairin 28–29, 167–168
Hindu personal law 44
Hizb ut-Tahrir 177
Hizbut Tarqiya (HT) 146–148
Huntington, Samuel 1
Husayniyyas 85
Hussein, Shaykh Nur ud-Din 152

Ibn Surayj 119
'Id al-Fitr 78
identity 3–7
Imamshahi Guptis 54–55, 58
*imamzada*s 92
imamzadeh 84
Indian constitution and religious
        categories 43–44
Indian Muslims
    colonial classification 46–48
    Shi'a 45–46
    Sunni 45–46
    unity of Islam (among
        Muslims) 48–51
intracommunal plurality 7
intra-Muslim differences
    amongst *madhhab*s 24–25
    artistic products 20–23
    associated with Shi'ism 22–23
    boundaries and definitions of
        'Sufi' and 'Islamist' 20
    on matters of existential
        concern 29–30
    'self' *vs* 'other' 27–30
Islam, in South Asian context
    58–60
Islam and the Religious Arts
        (Patricia L. Baker) 83–84

Islamic art
  in *Ahsan al-kibar fi ma'rifat
    al-a'imma al-athar* 89
  books on 83–84
  coinage and circular
    inscriptions 92–93,
    95–97, 103
  Fatimid 93–104
  Fatimid buildings in Egypt
    86–87
  in Ghassan I. Shaker collection
    88–89
  in the *Golestan* 90
  inlaid bronze object 91
  in Iran 91–92
  in *Khavaran-nama* 90
  locksmith industry 92
  in *madrasa*s 84–85
  mosques constructed by
    Ottomans 87
  objects made of
    metal, ceramic and wood
      90–93
    steel or copper alloy 92
  in Qur'an manuscripts 88
  relating to 'Ali *(Sad kalimeh)*
    89
  in Shi'i shrine building
    tradition 84–87
islamologues fonctionnariés 148
Islamophobia 76
'Islam's compatibility with
    Western democracy', issue
    of 1–2
Ismailis
  Fatimid 93–100, 104
  in India 54
  Nizari 45
al-Ittihad al-Thaqafi al-Islami
    (ITI) 140–141

JabFallah, Ahmed 174
Jam'iyyat al-'Ulama' al-Muslimin
    al-Jaza'iriyyin 140
Jama'at 'Ibad ar-Rahman (JIR) 142
Jews 5, 6, 9, 15, 32, 33, 66, 72

Kant, Emmanuel 62
al-Karkhi, Abu al-Hasan 107
Khan, Inayat 58, 59
*khanaqa*s 86
Kitab al-irshad (al-Khalili) 121

La Médina 175, 179, 181
Liwa' Ta'akhi al-Muslimas-Salih
    140
Love of the Divine 40

*madhhab*s 21, 24, 107–108,
    126–127, 133, 163, 167,
    177
Mahdavi-Damghani 34
Mali, Prem 56–7
Mama-Bhanje, shrine of 56
Mamluks 23
maqasid 28
marabouts-fils 145–146
marabouts-petit-fils 146, 148
Matlaboul Fawzaini (MF) 146
mawlid al-nabi 150
Mbakke, Saliou 149
Metcalf, Barbara 14
mihna 107
moral pluralism 67–68
Mosque
  of al-Aqmar 94
  of al-Hakim 94
Mouvement Mondial pour
    l'Unicité de Dieu
    (MMUD) 146
mu'minun 5

al-Muqaddasi 33
Musa, Shaykh Saidi 154
The Muslim Painter and the Divine (Sarwat Okasha) 83
Muslim Peoples: A World Ethnographic Survey (R. Weekes) 12
Muslim personal law 44
Muslims' views, of other Muslims 8
anthropological bias 12–14
issue of 'pluralism' 10–11
'otherness' concept 8–11
self-identification 10
Mustafa Sy, Sérigne 145
al-Muzani, Abu Ibrahim Isma'il b. Yahya 24, 108

N'Diaye, Rokhaya 144
ndiggël 147
Niang, Safiétou 145
Niass, Abdallah 144
Niass, Abdoulaye Khalifa 145
Niass, Ibrahim 135
Niass, Muhammad 144
Niass, Sidi Lamine 145
Nicholson, R. A. 38, 39
Ni'matallahi Sufi order 86
Nizari Ismaili communities, in South Asia 53–54
normative cognitive pluralism 63
Nyerere, Julius 151

Orientalism (Edward Said) 8
Oubrou, Tareq 179–182

Pahlavi, Reza Shah 85
Painting in Islam (Thomas Arnold) 83

People of the Book concept 72
pirs 56
pluralism of Islamic norms, justifications
amongst Muslims 28
in Europe 170–178
in Indonesia 165–170
Islamic principles *vs* jurisprudence (*fiqh*) 179–182
'political' 11
'religious' 11
pluralism, theories of
American notions of religious pluralism 69
case of American Muslims 66–67
Western interpretation 71–73
Pranami glossaries 60
present-day world population of Muslims 2–3

Qadiriyya *tariqas* 135
qalandars 53
Qur'an 3, 7, 13, 23
Abdul Sattar 53
commentary on 34, 36
differences in interpretation 175–178, 180
inscriptions 94–97, 103
literal understanding of 136
motif 98
People of the Book 72
Professor Hazairin approach to 167–169
recited seventy times 35–36
and religious texts 87–90
Rumi and 42
Qur'anic vocabulary 5–6

Ramadan, Tariq 179
Rashad, Ali 154
Rawdat al-safa 90
al-Razi, Fakhr al-Din 34
reflexivity 12
reform movements, Muslim
    societies
  in coastal East Africa
    150–154
  dialectical interactions between
    different generations
    within 154–160
reform movements, Muslim
    societies (*contd*)
  examination of 135–139
  forms of learning 151
  markers of reform 155
  pluralistic character 156–157
  Senegalese tradition 139–150
  Sufi-oriented reformers 150–
    151
  traditions 161–162
Riis, Ole 74–75, 77
Rubaiyat (Omar Khayyam) 31
Rumi, Jalal al-Dini, *Masnavi* of
    37–42

Sahifa-ye sajjadiyyeh 89
al-Sarraf, Shiyma 176
Satpanth, Satpanthi 55
Schimmel, Annemarie 35
sectarian divisions
  family of division traditions
    34–35
  in heresies 34
  Islamic tradition and Biblical
    'seventies' 35–36, 38,
    40–42
  Sufi mystical tradition 37–42
  traditional 32–33

secular democratic state,
    characteristics 43–44
Sen, Amartya 4, 12
Senegal
  trans-generational disputation
    in 25
  Islamic state reformism in
    141
Senegalese 'écoles franco-arabes'
    151
al-Shafi'i 107
al-Shahrastani 33
Shah, Mushtaq 'Ali 90
Shah, Nasir al-Din 85
Shah, Nur 'Ali 90
Shahada 55, 57–58, 79, 93
Shi'i inscriptions, on coins 92
Shi'i metalwork 92
Sikh Muslims 58
Smith, Jonathan Z. 8–9
Surat al-Ma'ida 42
Surat al-Tawbah 36
syncretism, religious 59

al-Tahawi, Abu Ja'far Ahmad b.
    Muhammad 24, 108
takiyas 85–86
Tanzania, trans-generational
    disputation in 26
Tanzanian 'islamologues
    fonctionnariés' 151
taqiyya 53, 54, 55
tariqas 25, 26, 135, 140, 141, 142,
    143, 146, 147, 149–152
ta'ziya performances 85
Tidiane Sy, Cheikh 144, 146,
    148
Tijaniyya *tariqas* 135
Touré, Cheikh 139–141, 149
truth, theory of 64–65

umma 6, 74, 76, 80
  paradigmatic
    in American context 19–20
    competing representations of
    Islam in pre- and post-
    independence India
    17–19
    differences within *umma*
    16–18
Union fraternelle des Pelèrins
  Musulmans de l'A.O.F.
  139

Union Progressiste Sénégalaise
  (UPS) 142
Universal Sufism movement 59

watu wa bid'a 27

al-Zamakhshari, Abu'l-Qasim
  Mahmud b. 'Umar 36
zikri ya dufu 158–159
zikri ya kukohoa 158–159
ziyarat-nama 92
Zoroastrians 33